Ways of the Spirit,

And Other Essays.

BY

FREDERIC HENRY HEDGE,

AUTHOR OF "REASON IN RELIGION," "PRIMEVAL WORLD OF HEBREW TRADITION," ETC.

BOSTON:
ROBERTS BROTHERS.
1877.

Copyright,
BY ROBERTS BROTHERS,
1877.

Cambridge:
Press of John Wilson and Son.

CONTENTS.

I.

THE WAY OF HISTORY.

HISTORY, in the sense of a systematic survey of the progress of society, based on the principle of a necessary order of human development, is emphatically a modern science. The ancients had no history in this sense of the term, no "universal" history as distinguished from the history of single nations. They recounted the acts or described the fortunes of tribes and states, but had nothing to say of the human family. They knew no human family. They knew only Greeks and Barbarians, Romans and Outsiders (*exteri*), Jews and Gentiles. Polybius, indeed, called his history *Καθολική* — universal — but only as comprehending in its survey of Roman affairs some account of the nations with which Rome came in contact. His starting point is Rome, not man. No classic historiographer, from Herodotus to Herodian, has attempted a history of man.

In one remarkable instance, however, the idea of such a history, and with it, of a human family, is distinctly recognized. In the Biblical Book of Genesis we have the beginning of a history of man, but one which stops short with the mythic age of the world. Biblical history brings man to the building of Babel, or the period of greatest concentration, succeeded by disruption and dispersion; and then, dismissing the theme, confines itself to the single Hebrew line. Brief and fragmentary as the narrative is, these first chapters of the Bible contain more important contributions to the science of history than all the classics.

Christianity, by intoning the brotherhood of man, awakened a new interest in human destiny. The Christian Fathers manifest a truer appreciation of the unity of the race. Bunsen calls Clement of Alexandria "the first Christian philosopher of the history of mankind." St. Augustine's "City of God" embraces in its scope the whole human race as the subject of divine education, and distributes the ages of man in six days of a thousand years each, to end with the millennium.

Of the historiographers of the Middle Age the Western are simply chroniclers; [1] and the Byzan-

---

[1] Such are Eginhard, Paulus Diaconus, William of Malmesbury, Gregory of Tours, Albert of Aix, William of Tyre, Geoffroy de Villehardouin, Froissart, and Matthew Paris.

tines — immensely important in their line — confine themselves, with one or two exceptions,[1] to the Lower Empire.

With the impulse given to the human mind by the stirring events of the fifteenth and sixteenth centuries, this branch of science blossoms into new significance. The astounding discoveries of the great navigators who solved the "ocean secret," and lifted the veil from what till then had been considered the night-side of the globe; the enlarged geographic and ethnographic views, and the wider survey of human kind resulting from these discoveries, combining with the recent "Revival of Letters" and the Saxon Reformation of the Church, — gave to history not only a new impulse but a new direction. No longer partial, local, it becomes encyclopædic, cosmopolitan. The writers of history task themselves with new and higher aims, evincing a new-born consciousness of unity and integrity pervading all the epochs and all the races and generations of man. The study of history becomes academic, and Torsellino's "Epitome Historiarum" is used as a text-book in the universities of Europe.

---

[1] Zonaras wrote a "History of the World;" Glycas, a "History of the World from the Creation to the Death of Alexius Comnenus;" Zosimus, a "History of the Roman Empire from Augustus to Honorius."

It was not, however, until after the lapse of another century, that the fundamental principle of all history was adequately stated. It was not till then that the discovery was made of a science of history. For this science we are indebted to Italy. The country which unlocked the New World was the first to suggest the true interpretation of the annals of the Old. John Baptist Vico, a native of Naples, published in 1725 his "Scienza Nuova," or "Principles of a New Science relative to the Common Nature of Nations." This work contains the germ of many of the speculations of subsequent philosophies of history; but its principal merit consists in its clear and emphatic assertion of the principle of divine necessity, — that is, of a natural law in historic processes and revolutions. Vico was the first to point out distinctly the analogies and parallelisms in the history of nations, and to show that the progress of society follows a given order; that nations have their necessary, preappointed course of evolution and revolution; that human history, in short, no less than the material universe, is governed by fixed laws: consequently that history is a science, or that a science of history is possible. "It is found," says Michelet, in his essay on the New Science, "that nations the most remote in time and space follow in their political revolutions and in those of their languages a strikingly analogous course." "To disengage the regular from the accidental; to trace the universal, eternal history which develops itself in time in the form of particular histories; to describe the ideal circle within which the real world revolves, — this is the aim of the new science. It is at once the philosophy and the history of humanity."

From an examination of the languages, laws, and religions of different peoples, and a survey of the course of events in the principal nations, Vico deduces these positions: I. Human society is based on three fundamental conditions, — worship, or the belief in Divine Providence; marriage, or the restraint of the passions; sepultural rites, or the belief in immortality. These are what Tacitus calls *fœdera generis humani.* II. Society has three great periods, — the theocratic, the heroic, and the humane. III. The civil and political life of nations, so long as they preserve their independence, assumes successively four different forms of government. The theocratic age produces domestic monarchy (patriarchism). The heroic produces aristocracy, or the government of the city, limiting the abuse of power. Then comes democracy, founded on the idea of natural equality. And lastly despotism, or imperial rule, establishes itself on the ruins of democracy, and puts an end to the anarchy and public corruption to which popular governments give rise. Or, if that remedy fails, the degenerate nation, given over to anarchy and corruption, becomes the prey of the spoiler, and succumbs to a foreign yoke. IV. When a nation or when society has passed through these stages, and unreclaimed by the revolutions it has experienced still continues to decline and degenerate, it passes at last into a second barbarism. Faith expires, religion languishes, men grow brutal, cities decay, society becomes effete and lies supine until regenerated by some providential impulse from without. Then the cycle of history begins anew, and humanity repeats with new auspices its appointed course. V. From the facts thus observed, from the indications of law and a regular succession in human events, Vico derives the idea of a great city of nations, whose founder and governor is God, — a republic of the universe, the miracle of whose constitution is, that through all its revolutions it finds in the very corruptions of each preceding state the elements of a new and better birth.

Since the publication of the "Scienza Nuova," the philosophy of history has found no end of expositors. Among the numerous works in this department, Montesquieu's "Esprit des Loix," Ferguson's "Civil Society," Lessing's little treatise, "The Education of the Human Race," Herder's "Ideen zur Philosophie der Geschichte der Menschheit," Kant's "Zur Philosophie der Geschichte," Fichte's "Grundzüge des gegenwärtigen Zeitalters," the chapters relating to the progress of human society in Comte's "Cours de Philosophie Positive," Krause's and Hegel's "Philosophie der Geschichte," deserve especial mention. I am speaking of the philosophy of history in the narrowest sense, not of historic criticism or historic art; else would a host of names of equal and even graver note demand to be noticed in this connection.

It is now understood that history has its laws, as well as astronomy; that the course of events is a necessary, not a fortuitous, succession, and the march of humanity through the nations and through the ages a series of progressive developments. The supposition is fundamental to the study of history as a science. If the course of events and the destiny of nations were governed by no law and subject to no method, there could be no science of history, but only chronicles, registries of facts unreferred to any principle or ruling idea, incapable of classification. The study of history in that case wonld be useless, because it would lead to nothing. The end of all study is the discovery of law; that is, of spirit, that is, of Deity in the facts studied. If in any class of facts no law were discoverable, the knowledge of those facts would be hardly worth the labor spent in acquiring it. We read history to little purpose, if we read it only as a record of facts, and see in it no demonstration of Divine method. The facts themselves are not truly apprehended, unless we see them in the light of some principle or law which they illustrate. Take the battle of Actium, in Roman history. I read that the forces of Octavius met those of Antonius in the Ambracian Gulf, and obtained a signal victory over them. What signifies that fact to me? What do I know of Roman history, if all I gather from it is that Octavius was the better general or the luckier man of the two? The real fact has escaped me, if I fail to perceive its historic import. It was not valor nor luck, but historic necessity that triumphed in that encounter. It was necessary that democracy should replace an aristocratic oligarchy, like that of republican Rome. It was necessary that democratic anarchy should be replaced by an imperial head. Octavius represents in that conflict the Latin or popular element in Roman history. Antonius represents the Sabine or patrician. The internal history of the Roman Republic, and especially that of the previous century, had been a conflict of these two elements, the former seeking to disengage itself from the latter. The battle of Actium was the consummation of that struggle. With the triumph of Octavius, — *qui cuncta discordiis civilibus fessa nomine principis sub imperium accepit*,[1] — democracy came to a head, Latin civility came to maturity, and in its turn became the matrix of its successor in empire, — the Christian Church.

An objection may be raised against the doctrine of historic necessity, on the score of human free will. The conduct of history lies in the hands of human free agents. A glance at the course of events shows us that those revolutions which have furnished the materials and given the direction to history have been the work of individuals following the impulse of their own wills. How, then, can we affirm them to be the operation of a law, or how can history conducted by free will be a necessary process? If one looks at the matter *a priori*, it seems *a priori* improbable that the destinies of humanity should be committed to individual caprice, or that able and designing men should shape the world according to their whim. But what is the fact? Free agency acts under given conditions, and those conditions are contained in the natural order of things. There is no more escape from that order in the moral world than in the physical. All the motions on the earth's surface,

---

[1] Tacitus.

however arbitrary and contrary one to another, obey the parent motion of the earth, and are swept along in the spheral march. So all possible movements of the human will are comprehended in the providential sweep of the parent will which works in each. The contradiction between freedom and necessity, so perplexing in the sphere of private life, disappears in the large dynamic of history. There, freedom and necessity are seen to be different factors of one movement, — freedom the human, necessity the divine. The highest freedom is the strongest necessity, as in chemistry those affinities which are termed elective are precisely the most determined. Says Kant: "Whatever notion, in a metaphysical point of view, we may form to ourselves of the freedom of the will, its manifestation, — *i. e.* human actions, — like every other natural event, is determined by general laws of Nature."[1]

To the eye of sense "the river windeth at its own sweet will," but reflection knows that the valley through which it winds has been scooped by the action of unchangeable laws; and in human life all freedom that succeeds is free occupation of appointed paths. The course of destiny is the providential channel in which human freedom

[1] Zur Philosophie der Geschichte; Idee zu einer Allgemeinen Geschichte in Weltbürgerlichen Absicht.

elects to run. Accordingly, the great men of history — the history-makers — are the "providential men;" they are those, in the language of Hegel,[1] "whose private purposes contain the substance of that which is willed by the spirit of the world." They may not be aware of their providential function; they may not contemplate all the results they are used to effect; the ulterior consequences of their free action may not come within the scope of their design; — the consequences follow none the less. Leo the Isaurian issues an edict prohibiting the use of images and pictures in the churches; Pope Gregory repudiates the edict, and resists its execution in the West. What follows? While Emperor and Pontiff quarrel among themselves, the empire splits between them; a goodly fraction comes off in Gregory's hands. Following the bent of his own will in his own ecclesiastical affairs, that prelate becomes the providential means of sundering East and West, never to be united again. Rolf, from the coast of Norway, bent on plunder, lands his pirates on the soil of France, and extorts from Charles the Simple a slice of his kingdom. Rolf has no prevision of a Norman landing on the coast of Sussex, and an Anglo-Norman kingdom, and an English House of Lords, all which the future drew from that raid of his, whose

[1] Philosophie der Geschichte.

providential import was to give to the finest of the Gothic races a worthy field for their development.

Sometimes, however, the providential men — like Julius Cæsar, Mohammed, Cromwell — have shown themselves conscious of that Divinity which shapes our ends, and subsidizes our free will in accomplishing its designs. It was no affectation or puerile vanity which prompted the first Napoleon to call himself the "Child of Destiny," but an irresistible conviction of a power behind him, whose minister he was in spite of himself.

Assuming, then, as a settled truth, that the course of history is governed by natural laws, the question arises, How far are those laws discoverable and demonstrable by scientific investigation? This is a question which only the future of scientific investigation can answer. The application of logic to history is yet too recent, history itself is too recent, to furnish a complete solution. All that we can thus far assert with any degree of confidence is, that enough of law is discoverable to constitute history a science; or that a science of history is possible.

The subject of this science is Man. To distinguish it from anthropology, let us say Man in Society. To distinguish it from ethnology, let us say Man the subject of progressive development. We have then three distinct topics: Man, Society or the State, and Social Progress.

I. Man. To the catholic eye of history he is one. The science presupposes what all its discoveries tend to demonstrate, — the unity of the human race. We need not trouble ourselves with the question whether all men actually originated from one pair, or whether different portions of the globe have given birth to independent varieties of the animal man. Enough that man, as the subject of history, is one. The historic nations have descended from one original. If any of the races that inhabit the earth have a different origin, those races are not historic; they have no part in human destiny, and will finally disappear from the earth, or be absorbed by historic man. Man, as the subject of history, is one. The nations that compose him have one geographical, probably one genealogical, origin.

Historic man, according to tradition, was born in Western Asia, precisely where speculative ethnology would place his origin. If we glance at a map of the world on Mercator's projection, we shall find that the portion of the earth's surface which lies between the thirtieth and fortieth degrees of north latitude, and between the fortieth and sixtieth of east longitude, is about the centre of the habitable globe. Here it is, or hereabout, that tradition first discovers man, on the banks of the Tigris and the Euphrates. From this natal centre we find him radiating eastward and south-eastward to the borders of the Pacific and the Indian Ocean, westward and north-westward to the Mediterranean and the Atlantic. In later ages his course has been prevailingly westward, across the Atlantic into South and North America. And now having crossed the American continent, and reached the uttermost verge of the west, on the borders of that Pacific which long since bounded his eastern migration, he has "come full circle" around the globe.

The where being settled, the next question is, How did man begin his race? Civilized or savage, in rude ignorance or furnished with science and art? This has long been a point in debate between ethnologists and theologians. The latter have taught that man's first estate was superior, not only in moral purity but also in intellectual illumination, to every subsequent age. Philosophy, on the contrary, maintains that the original state was a savage state, — such as we find it to this day in South Africa and New Zealand, — and that ages went by before the race attained to the knowledge and arts of civilized life. Happily, our subject is not burdened with the responsibility of this question. We have nothing to do with man prior to the period when history finds him; that is, the earliest period marked by contemporary or nearly contemporary records. The existence of records implies civilization. The word "history," it will be observed, has a twofold sense. We use it to denote the course of events, and we also use it to denote the record of those events. This double meaning, says Hegel, is not accidental. It shows that actual history and written history are nearly related and cannot exist independently the one of the other. History does not begin to be until it is written. A people has no history until it is sufficiently mature to record its life; until it arrives at that degree of self-consciousness which makes the recording of it inevitable. The intellectual life of the individual does not begin with the animal birth; it begins with the birth of consciousness. It dates from the period of reflection, from the time when the individual begins to act knowingly, accounting to himself for his action. History is the record of the intellectual life of society; it begins with the self-consciousness of society. It dates from the time when man associates in civil bonds under fixed and accepted laws; from the time when society becomes organized, with settled functions and mutual responsibilities. Whatever, then, may have been man's primal state, when history first finds him he is civilized, skilled in arts, governed by laws, living in cities, worshipping in temples. Of the times antecedent to that state, with their confused struggles, history knows nothing. The exploration of those unrecorded ages belongs to another province than that of the historian: it belongs to the province of archæology or fore-history. History is coeval with civility; that is, with the formation of States.

II. Accordingly, our next topic is the State. It is not with man absolute or man as such, but with man conditioned by social organizations, that the science of history is concerned. These organizations — monarchical, republican, democratic, or despotic — are the stated conditions of man's development, the ordained method by which he accomplishes his moral destiny, by which especially he satisfies two pressing demands of his nature, — liberty and right. Liberty and right are both the product of civil organization; *i. e.* of the State.

Of liberty the contrary opinion prevails. It is thought that liberty belongs to man in his "natural state" as it is called, that is, in a savage state, and is lost or impaired by civilization; that liberty is older than civil society; that, being originally unlimited, when States were formed it was surrendered for the sake of the State. It has been affirmed, as a self-evident proposition, that man is "born free." That means, man is born with a natural capacity for freedom, and, co-ordinate with the development of that capacity, has a natural right to freedom. It can mean nothing more.

Rousseau, unconscious of self-contradiction, declares that man "is born free, but is everywhere found in bonds." He should have said, Man was made to be free, but has nowhere realized that destination. But Rousseau meant something more. He meant that man possessed originally a freedom which he has lost by civilization. He and others have imagined a condition of humanity, a so-called "state of nature," in which man was freer, and in many respects more fortunate, than we find him in civil society. Since none of these theorists have informed us where in the present this state is to be found, nor furnished any proofs of its existence in time past, we are warranted in treating the notion as a fancy or a fiction. The term "natural," applied to any primitive condition of man, imaginary or real, to distinguish it from subsequent conditions, is a foolish limitation of nature, — equivalent to saying that the root of a plant is natural and the blossom not natural. Civilization is the product of human nature; it contains nothing that human nature does not contain, and cannot therefore in any rational sense be considered as less a state of nature than that of the Camanches or New Zealanders. "If we are asked," says Ferguson, "where the state of nature is to be found, we may answer, it is here. And it matters not whether we are understood to speak in the island of Great

Britain, or at the Cape of Good Hope, or the Straits of Magellan." "If we admit that man is susceptible of improvement, and has in himself a principle of progression and a desire of perfection, it is improper to say that he has quitted the state of nature when he has begun to proceed, or that he finds a station for which he was not intended, while, like other animals, he only follows the disposition and employs the powers that Nature has given." "If Nature is opposed to art, in what situation of the human race are the footsteps of art unknown?"[1]

The notion that primitive man is freer than civilized man is an error which springs from not distinguishing between liberty and caprice. We may dream of a state which combines what is best in civilization with all that is charming in aboriginal nature; but reality knows nothing of the kind. Reality knows only the civilized man and the savage; and the question is, Which is the freer of the two? Superficial observation may decide in favor of the savage, but closer inspection will change that decision. The savage is less bound by conventions, but is bound in other ways. He is more the slave of his passions, more dependent on occasion, more fettered by necessity, less master of

[1] Essay on the History of Civil Society.

himself and the world, and therefore less free than the civilized. With less of law, he experiences greater limitation. The nearer we come to savage life, the more we find in it of tyranny and violence, of the bondage of passion and caprice. The nearer we come to it, the more we find the condition of the savage to be one of thraldom and restraint; the more we find him bounded and bound. Ferguson, with one word, refutes Rousseau's fancy of savage liberty, when he says, "No person is free where any person is suffered to do wrong with impunity;" and Hegel, who defines liberty to be "the spirit's realization of its own nature," insists that, so far from being an accident of primitive man, it is something which must be wrought out, achieved, by a perpetual "mediation between knowledge and will." Right and morality are its indispensable constituents. It is true, society as such imposes restraints, but the necessary restraints imposed by society are merely limitations of individual caprice which hampers liberty: they promote that emancipation of the will in which true freedom consists.[1] The notion of an antecedent natural liberty surrendered to society, and of social contracts requiring such surrender, is a pure fiction. Liberty is not an original but an

---

[1] See Hegel's "Philosophie der Geschichte."

acquired possession ; not an accident but a product, — the product of reflection, of legislation, of scientific adjustment ; in a word, the product of the State.

Likewise, the State is the parent and condition of morality. Morality as sentiment, disposition, faculty, is innate. Morality as fact is the product of law. Its earliest form — respect for others' rights — originates with the institution of property. But property in its first beginnings provokes the worst passions of the human breast, occasions strife and shedding of blood. It has therefore been deemed unfriendly to morality, one of the evils which civilization has inflicted on mankind. "The first man," says Rousseau, "who, having enclosed a piece of ground, took it into his head to say, 'This is mine,' and found people foolish enough to believe him, was the true founder of civil society. How many crimes, wars, murders, miseries, and horrors might have been spared to the human race, if some one at that juncture had pulled up the stakes or filled up the trenches, and had called to his fellow-men, 'Beware how you listen to this impostor ; you are lost if you forget that the fruits of the ground belong to all, and that the earth is no man's property !'"[1]

---

1 Rousseau, "Sur l'origine de l'inegalité parmi les Hommes."

But if property has been the occasion of strife and deeds of violence, it has also served to develop the idea of *right* in which all morality is founded; and though some of the virtues — such as courage, fortitude, and patience — might certainly exist without it, most of the duties and most of the topics and occasions of moral discipline which society now furnishes would be wanting. Most of the duties of social life, as now constituted, are directly or indirectly connected with property. Rousseau himself confesses that the first rules of justice are derived thence. "For in order to render to each one his own," he remarks, "it is necessary that each should own something."

Property begins with agriculture. To till the land it was necessary to enclose it. From tillage for the use of the tribe of land belonging to the tribe, — such as we still find at certain stages of savage life, — the transition was easy and natural to tillage for private use; the fruits and the land being both the property of the tiller.

The relation of agriculture to civil law and the moral well-being of society was represented by the Greeks in the fable of Demeter, the mythical goddess of agriculture; who was called Θεσμοφόρος, law-bringer. An ancient cameo represents her as accompanying Triptolemus, the planter, in his tour around the earth. She exhibits a scroll containing a code of laws, while Triptolemus scatters wheat-seed. Hebrew tradition has embodied the same idea in the story of Cain, the first tiller of the ground; who is also the first city-builder and civilizer.

And not only by the institution of property which it authorizes and protects, and around which cluster so many motives and obligations to virtue, but also by establishing stricter relations between man and man; by civil jurisprudence making the moral sense of the wisest the rule for all; and more especially by maintaining the sanctity of wedded life, — parent and nurse of domestic virtues, — the State develops the moral life of society. If then, and so far as, man has a moral calling to fulfil in this world, he belongs to the State and the State to him. States are at once the theme and the organ of history.

III. Our next and last topic is Social Progress. Man is the subject of progressive development. The world's history is not an aimless succession of events, — a heap of facts fanned together by the flight of time, as the wind piles sand-drifts in the desert, — but a process and a growth. The ages are genetically as well as chronologically related. The succession of events is rational; they follow each other by a necessary order, in such wise that one is the exponent of another, and all are moments of one process. We say, then, that as civil society is the topic, so progress is the method, of history. In saying this we pronounce no judgment on the question of man's perfectibility and final perfection. We assert nothing as to the ultimate destiny of the race, — whether the consummation of history is to be the perfection of society, according to the visions of the millennarians, or whether it is to be the utter dissolution of society by the action of some remediless evil. These are questions as to which history may aid us in forming an opinion, but which history thus far is incompetent to decide. But, surveying the past and present of society, we see such evidence of progress hitherto as warrants us in assuming — since some aim and purpose must be assumed to make history intelligible — that progress is that aim and purpose. We postulate progress as the key to history; as the mathematician uses an hypothetical number in determining an unknown quantity.

Progress in what and whitherward? Progress in liberty, answers Hegel, — progress first in the idea and then in the thing. This progress, according to him, has three stages, dividing the world's history into three epochs, — the period of the Oriental nations, when only one was allowed to be free; the period of Greek and Roman civilization, when freedom was accorded to many; and lastly, the period of the Germanic nations, when freedom is seen to be the rightful property of all. Instead of liberty, let us say progress in social organization, — a more comprehensive interest of which liberty is one element among many: progress in social union and toward a state in which that union shall be complete, in which nationalities shall no longer divide mankind, when the human family shall consciously unite in one organic whole, — a state combining the greatest freedom of the individual with the greatest compactness of social union, and securing to all the members of the common-weal the greatest possible advantage in their connection with each other. This destination is at present strictly hypothetical: the immeasurable future alone can verify it. It is rendered probable, however, by the course of events thus far, of which it furnishes the most satisfactory solution. According to this view, every epoch of human history is a new stage of social development; every state a fresh experiment in social organization; and every historic revolution, exposing the inadequacy of each former state, inaugurates a new.

The condition of all development is antagonism. Nothing grows without resistance, without opposition of contrary elements. Society is no exception to the universal law. There, too, is a perpetual conflict of opposing forces, bursting often into open war.

War is a normal crisis in human affairs, and must therefore occupy a large share in the world's annals. Judged from the point-of-view of Christian ethics, it presents solely the aspect of a moral evil, and incurs unreserved condemnation. So far as war is the product of individual volition and design, so far as it originates in or enkindles conscious malevolent passion, it bears this character so distinctly and so appallingly, that the moral view becomes paramount and excludes every other. But war is not always, seldom indeed, on both sides the product of malevolent passions; and the moral aspect of war is not the only one to be considered. It has its objective, providential side, which demands the attention of the philosophic historian. The same divine Teacher who inculcated peace in his precepts, acknowledges the historic necessity of war, when he says, "I am not come to send peace on earth, but a sword." Wars differ widely in their moral character, according to the purposes of those who engage in them. There are wicked wars of vengeance and ambition, and there are also righteous wars of self-defence. There are idle wars of passion and caprice, and there are necessary wars of antagonist races, and conflicting ideas, principles, religions. The Persian war to the Greeks was a holy war, — a war of liberty, which decided the destiny of Hellenic civilization. On the other hand, the Peloponnesian war was an idle war of rivalry, which decided nothing, but proved finally ruinous to all the States engaged in it, and prepared the way for the downfall of Greece. The Thirty Years' War, in the seventeenth century, was a necessary war of principles, which decided for the most intellectual portion of Europe the momentous question of the right of private judgment. But the Seven Years' War of the eighteenth century was a foolish war of princely ambition and princely spleen, which cost Europe over a million of lives, and secured to Austria, the aggressor in that conflict, none of the prizes for which she had contended.

Besides this antagonism of contrary elements, the progress of society is further conditioned by a principle of alternation within itself which causes it to swing between opposite attractions, or to gyrate around them as around the foci of an ellipse, and which makes the development of humanity a series of revolutions instead of a uniform movement in one direction. Humanity gains something with each revolution; each lands society on a higher plane: and so the course of history becomes a *spiral* movement, at once revolutionary and progressive. There is a periodicity in the alternations of society, a regular recurrence of the same phases, — which indicates a law whose action is calculable.

An instance of this periodicity is the regular recurrence of periods of migration, which succeed each other at stated intervals in the world's history in conformity with a law of development inherent in society. There never was an age when migration entirely ceased, but we may distinguish certain epochs in which it has proceeded with special activity; and these epochs we shall find to be the natural product of the social developments which preceded them. The dispersion of the builders of Babel, in Biblical history, indicates the commencement of one of these periods of migration, which seems to have been a necessary reaction on a period of immature concentration, when, in Biblical phrase, "the whole earth was of one speech and one language," and when a city intended to be a centre of consolidation for the human race was projected on the plain of Shinar. This migration may be supposed to have covered a period of five hundred years. The next occurs after an interval of five centuries, about two thousand years before the Christian era, and continues with intermissions and fluctuations, and different degrees of activity, for a thousand years. This great evolution, or series of evolutions, which colonized Asia Minor, Phœnicia, Palestine, Greece, Italy, and the Grecian Archipelago, appears to have been a reaction against the excessive spiritualism of the old Asiatic polities. It was followed by a thousand years in which the concentrative tendency again predominates, and migration, with occasional exceptions, ceases. Then, again, the excess of sensualism in Greek and Roman civilization encountered a reaction in Christianity, and Christianity required new races and new regions in and through which to develop its ideas. And now begins a new exodus from the North, by which Europe is flooded with the German and Scandinavian races, and which, with brief interruptions, occupies another term of nearly a thousand years. The next five centuries are consumed in consolidating the European monarchies, sometimes in antagonism, sometimes in harmony, but always within the bands of the Church of Rome. Then Church and State become oppressive; the human mind, new-quickened by the recently invented art of printing, reacts on ecclesiastical tradition, reacts on civil oppression, reacts on feudal privilege; a new-found continent invites adventure, and simultaneously with the Protestant Reformation inaugurates the last of the migratory epochs now in progress.

In accordance with this outline, instead of the

usual division of history into ancient, mediæval, and modern, a more philosophic arrangement will distinguish four great periods, — the Asiatic (including the early African), the Greco-Roman, the Germanic, and the American. Of these, the first and the third may be subdivided into an earlier and later Asiatic and Germanic.

Another example of periodicity in history is the alternation of the positive and negative forces of the mind, — imagination and reflection. The old Asiatic civilization discovers in every province of social life, and in all the action of the human mind, the predominance of imagination. Life is overshadowed by huge superstitions; all is prodigious, titanic, — colossal temples, colossal idols, in which the monstrous predominates over the beautiful and humane: everywhere mountainous theocracies piled upon poor humanity, absorbing and crystallizing its best juices. The institutions of society rise frowning and pitiless like stranded icebergs, while society itself, a scarcely perceptible stream, creeps lazily out from beneath. In secular or Japhetic history, the Persian war with the Greeks marks the boundary line of this era. When Themistocles, by tampering with the priests at Delphi, could bend the oracle in accordance with his plans, the despotism of faith and fate had ceased for Greece. The secular element thenceforth asserts itself in civil life. Reflection encounters Imagination in the Gulf of Salamis, and puts a limit to his sway. There is no excess as yet of the former faculty, but a happy equilibrium between the two. Then appeared that miracle of Greek and Roman culture which history is never weary of portraying. Then the world's genius awoke, and lifted up the hands which had hung down, and opened the long silent lips. Then was the blossom time of art and song and philosophy and science; the age of the Parthenon, of the Apollo-Belvedere, of Sophocles and Plato; followed, before its light had utterly gone out, by the age of Cicero and the first Cæsar, and the great Augustan age of Latin civility and letters.

But now the negative power acquires a disproportionate ascendancy; imagination grows torpid, art and religion decline, materialism becomes rampant, all truth and reverence depart out of life. The poets of Alexandria employ themselves with shaping verses into eggs and axes. Lucian of Samosata has turned the Pantheon into a cenotaph. Plutarch inquires "why the oracles cease to give answers," and a voice from the island of Paxos proclaims, "Great Pan is dead!"

"Apollo from his shrine
Can no more divine,
With hollow shriek the steep of Delphos leaving,
No nightly trance or breathèd spell
Inspires the pale-eyed priest from the prophetic cell."

The fire is gone out on the altar, the marble sleeps in the quarry. Come, Longobards and Franks, from the depths of the Odenwald and the Black Forest! — come, pour your fresh life into withered humanity; revive the perished world or bury it!

The age of reflection ends, and a new era of despotic imagination begins: another long cycle wherein the huge and grotesque prevail over the beautiful and just. Again the portentous misgrowths of time. Farewell to letters and science and beautiful works of art!

> "Now entertain conjecture of a time
> When creeping murmur and the poring dark
> Fill the wide vessel of the universe."

The world's stage is cleared for a new act of the great drama. The actors are harnessed warriors with closed visors, and scarlet priests. The old decorations — the storied friezes and Corinthian capitals — are replaced by the feudal castle, that, perched on a cliff at the angle of the river, seems a continuation of the rock itself, wrought by some freak of Nature into pinnacles and parapets. In the valley below, the symbol of penal torture is displayed in the cruciform church. The age of the Argonauts reappears in the crusades. Europe hurls herself upon Asia. The East and the West contend for the prize of the Holy Land.

Such was life in those centuries, — wild, monstrous, extreme in devotion and in arms.

> "Der Mönch und die Nonne zergeisselten sich,
> Der eiserne Ritter turnierte."

Again there was a day when the empire of imagination received a check, and impassable limits were set to its sway. And this time the change was effected by the pen instead of the sword; and the agent was a German Professor of Philosophy. The birthday of the new era was the 31st October, 1517, when Martin Luther nailed to the church at Wittenberg his ninety-five propositions, which reinstated reason and conscience in their long-suppressed rights, opened an irreparable breach between the Roman and the Saxon mind, and initiated the second age of reflection; which has not yet expired, and which comprises the great names of modern literature and science, from Galileo to Humboldt, from Shakspeare to Goethe.

Such is the method of history. Progress by alternation, by conflict, by revolution, — always progress. These are the steps by which Humanity moves in its fore-ordained path, advancing, not simultaneously in all its faculties and members, but in one or another part for ever advancing. To what result and final consummation of its course it is not in the Muse of History to predict, until, perhaps, some thousands of years have been added to her age, —

> "And old Experience do attain
> To something of prophetic strain."

II.

THE WAY OF RELIGION.

RELIGION, in the broadest sense, is the life of the sentiments as contra-distinguished from that of the understanding, — of the sentiments turned from self, and directed to objects sought and cherished for their own sake, with no reflex view to private advantage. It is losing oneself in ideas, persons, things, which attract or command by their own intrinsic, or supposed intrinsic, worth. It is the heart's response to the claims of beauty, duty, honor, man. All genuine enthusiasm; all unselfish devotion, patriotism, philanthropy, art; all self-sacrificing zeal, whatever its object, — partakes of the nature of religion. Its essence is, —

> "Forget, forswear, disdain
> Thine own best hopes, thine utmost loss and gain,
> Until at last thou scarce rememberest now
> If on the earth be such a one as thou;
> Nor hast one thought of self-surrender — no!
> For self is none remaining to forego."

In the narrower and technical sense, religion may be roughly defined as homage paid to surperhuman power. And this definition holds good, albeit religions exist in which the objects worshipped are not superhuman, but infra-human, — religions in which homage is paid to brute creatures and inanimate things. These objects are conceived as superhuman by the worshipper. When the Negro of South Africa prostrates himself before a block of wood, he confesses as sincerely a superior to himself as the Parsee when he bends in adoration before the rising sun, as the Christian when he worships the invisible Lord. He has not yet learned the greatness that is in him, and is therefore ready to acknowledge in any creature a greater than himself. The eternal Mystery which all souls reverence looks out upon him from the senseless block; and that is what he really adores. And that is what we also adore, more worthily conceived, but can we say more exactly understood? Must we not say, as incomprehensible to us as to him?

The motive which prompts this homage is one of the primary forces of the soul. There is nothing more radical in man than religion; nothing more capable, more commanding. Stated or spasmodic, quiescent or flamboyant, in calm or storm, it builds by turns, and fires the world: in its pureness, the ornament and strength of society (*decus et præsidium nostrum*); in its fall and perversion, the scandal and scourge of nations. Its scope is the measure of history. It supplied the first rudiments of civil society; it forecasts the social destination of man. Wherever humanity is found at its highest, religion has been the motive-power, — leader in all progress; home-guard of all stability; source of revolutions the most prevailing; champion and prize of the boldest adventures; pioneer more eager than commerce; explorer more patient than science. Religion is acknowledged the mother of arts: she reared the temples that make Egypt venerable, and shaped the marbles that made Greece renowned. She lighted the eyes of the Sistine Virgin, and unrolled the "Divina Commedia," and inspired the strains of Handel and Bach. In private life she has been the authoritative teacher, comforter; lifting the soul above the dust, purifying the heart by faith, eliciting the spirit of self-sacrifice by which society subsists, cheering the sufferer in mortal pains, redeeming and renewing the world.

While gratefully acknowledging this multifold service of the great benefactress, we cannot forget the mischief and the woes that have often accompanied these gifts and goods. We cannot forget that religion has been a worker of evil, — one of the greatest of the workers of evil. No agent that has wrought in earthly scenes has been more prolific of ruin and wrong. The wildest aberrations of human nature, crimes the most portentous, the most desolating wars; persecutions, hatred and wrath and bloodshed, more than have flowed from all sources beside, — have been its fruits. The victims of fanaticism outnumber those of every other and all other passions that have wasted the earth. Pining in dungeons, hunted like beasts of prey, stretched on the rack, affixed to the cross, — their sufferings are the horror of history. No high-wrought fiction, recounting imaginary woes, can match the colors of their authentic tragedy. A corruption of the text of the Vedas has cast thousands of Hindu widows alive on the funeral pile. An interpolation of two words in the service of the Eastern Church has driven whole villages in Russia into fiery death. A sentence in the Book of Exodus has been a death-sentence to millions of hapless women. And who shall compute the sum of the lives that have furnished the holocausts of the Inquisition?

"Tantum religio potuit suadere malorum."

In this tale of sorrows we must reckon, moreover, the melancholy and madness religion so often engenders, — religious mania, which, where it does not impel to self-slaughter, oppresses the soul with dull despair, or pierces it with mortal anguish. It is fearful to think that man, in addition to the necessary burdens of life and all inevitable ills, should be subject to these ideal woes; that so many fine spirits should suffer blight through their own diseased imaginations; that to so many noble minds the light that is in them should be made darkness through superstitious doubts and fears; that so many innocent hearts should bear the burden of self-imputed guilt and doom! No region of the earth, and no plane of life, is secure from this plague. Bayard Taylor found in the track of the missionaries beyond the Arctic circle the same spiritual ails that have desolated polished lands. "The soul," says Novalis, "is the most active of poisons." Religion is the soul of mortal life: when mis-directed or over-urged it becomes, instead of an animating force, a consuming fire.

Considering these harms, one is tempted to question if religion, on the whole, has been a blessing to mankind. To that question the answer must be sought in the infinite possibilities that lie in the idea of God, and the infinite dearth of spirit involved in the want of that idea, without which life would seem to be the sport of lawless power, — no reason in its origin, no meaning in its course, no hope in its end. Given that idea, all things desirable are possible.

Meanwhile, our business at present is not with the moral but with the historical aspects of the subject.

The history of religion is the history of man; not of nations, but of man. The chronicles of nations, made up as they are of wars and revolutions, political formations and decays, dynasties and parties, institutions affecting the temporal and material well-being of their subjects, — these and the like of these, which figure so largely in the volumes of historiographers, are properly no part (or a very subordinate part) of the history of *man*. They are accidents, not substance; episodes, not method. The true history, the thread on which these are strung, is that progressive life of the spirit which binds the nations in one Providential order, and which alone gives meaning to man's being in time. Without this, what we call history is a mere compilation of anecdotes, which may entertain the curious, but which leads to no rational result. Reason demands, as the end and destination of man in society, a state in which the divine law shall organize itself in civil polity, and form the basis and determine the conduct of social life: in other words, a theocracy, or Kingdom of Heaven.

Such being the end, the history of man must be viewed in relation to that end; so viewed, it assumes a sacred character. With all its contradictions and immoralities, which do but furnish the antagonism necessary to all development, the history of man is the history of religion: the main epochs in the one are identical with those of the other. Accordingly, it is no one-sided or bigoted view of human things which has led Christian nations to date the world's history with their religion. The chronology is true to the absolute fact as well as to Christian consciousness. Christianity dates, because it determined, the course of time. The supreme moment in the ever-proceeding revelation of God, it became the confluence of the two main streams of civilization, — the Semitic and Japhetic. Uniting these, it forms the one river of modern history. Christendom is no provincialism; it is the world's highway.

In tracing the course of religious development, our first business is to ascertain the law and method by which that development proceeds. On this point theology and science are at variance. Where theology says "revelation," science says "law;" and each supposes an antagonism between the two, as if one of these methods precluded the other. In the view of theology, the idea of a law of development militates with the supposition of the present immediate action of the spirit of God. And, on the other hand, science mistrusts the term revelation, as seemingly opposed to that constant order which it loves to find in all the succession of the ages of man. As usual in such controversies, both parties are right, and both are wrong. There is a law of development in the history of religion, and there is revelation. In the realm of spirit, as well as in the kingdoms of unconscious Nature, God acts by law. His revelation of himself is not spasmodic, but methodical, continuous. Christianity, the highest instance of that revelation, is no episode, but a necessary part of the Divine method. The old way of treating the subject regarded Christianity as an afterthought of Deity, an amendment of the programme of Providence, necessitated by the miscarriage of former methods, "an act supplementary to an act," instead of the original design provided for in the constitution of things. The Mohammedan poet was nearer the truth: —

> "The world's end and beginning are the same,
> And Jesus entered it when Adam came."

All such views of all such subjects are fast disappearing in the light of modern thought, which postulates law instead of arbitrary will as the fundamental reason of things. It is the business of science to trace that law; in all that exists to ascertain the normal principle by which it exists, and in virtue of which it could not be other than it is. Science knows nothing fortuitous and nothing arbitrary; she finds necessity in the most exceptional as well as the most stated ; in a shower of meteoric stones as well as the precession of the equinoxes ; in spasms of wind and storm as well as the regular alternation of the tides ; in the flaming aurora as well as the motions of the planetary system. In the very madness of nature and of nations she sees or divines an overruling method, and knows that the wildest excesses of either must work in the traces of Omnipotent order, — as the caracoling steeds in Guido's great fresco are harnessed to the chariot of the constant sun, and lead the measured dance of the Hours.

We express in one word the characteristic difference between the ancient and the modern view of the universe, when we say *Law*. In every realm of human converse the scientific view has replaced the mythical. The world as viewed by the ancient mind was the product of caprice. Gods and demigods ruled it at will. Egyptian droughts were figured as the death of Osiris slain by the hand of Typhon. Returning fertility was ascribed to Horus, the immortal youth who conquers Typhon, — type of Nature's rejuvenating power. The disproportion of the lunar to the solar year was expressed by the threat of Sol to Rhea, that no month of the year should be allowed her for the birth of her child. The difficulty is adjusted by Hermes, who plays at dice with the Moon, and wins from her the five supplementary days with which the improved calendar eked out the three hundred and sixty of the original year. The term "Milky Way" in sidereal astronomy recalls the mythical explanation of the nebulous streak in the heavens so named; the word "volcano" suggests the stithies of Vulcan and the Lemnian fires. History was handled in the same fashion: demonic caprice was its motive power; its processes were the freaks of Divinity. The progress of civilization from Asia to Europe was conducted by Zeus, who crosses the Hellespont in the form of a bull bearing the daughter of Agenor or Canaan. Semitic culture conducted by conscious intelligence is Bunsen's exposition of the myth. Where ancient philosophy allegorized, the modern intellect formulizes. Where the ancients saw will, the modern sees law, — law from whose dominion human agency is no more excluded than the kingdom of unconscious life. If there is any product of civilization which might be supposed to be irresponsible and accidental, it is language. But language is shown by modern glossologists to be subject to laws as inevitable as those which regulate all the processes of Nature. For this, too, is a process of Nature. It is not a human device, but a growth. The Roman Emperor might extend to whomsoever he pleased the right of citizenship, but he could not naturalize a vocable.

If, then, history and language are necessary products, if the deeds and the speech of men in the gross are subject to law, it may be presumed that religion — the gravest and deepest of human concerns, the consummate product of humanity — is no exception to the general rule. We cannot suppose that the progress of religion, any more than the secular progress of human kind, is surrendered to accident; that the mind acts less methodically in this than other manifestations; or that Destiny is less concerned in this than in others. We must suppose a Providence in it; that is, a Providential education of the human race in religion, and an ordained method or necessary order by which it proceeds. That necessary order, viewed on the human side, we term the law of religious development. That such a law exists as part of the reason of God, as a mode of the Divine wisdom, there can be no doubt; the only question is whether it is discoverable by man. Can it be ascertained by philosophic inquiry? Our answer to this question at present must be an empirical one; we cannot answer it dogmatically. We cannot assume to demonstrate the entire law of religious development; we can only indicate, as facts observed, or as inferences from them, some of the principles involved in it.

I. In the first place, then, we observe three

stages of religion answering to the ages of human life: childhood, youth, maturity, — a period of the senses, one of sentiment, and one of ideas. Each of these stages has its own appropriate faith and worship; and so we distinguish three fundamental forms of religion: realism, personism, and spiritualism, — the worship of things, the worship of persons, the worship of spirit.

These stages are not sharply discriminated, but overlap one another like childhood and youth, or like youth and manhood, in the human individual. Accordingly, the several religions corresponding with them shade one into another by such nice gradations, and are so immixed in practice, that the lowest form of Nature-worship is not without some gleams of spiritual life, and the purest of historical religions is not without some taint of fetichism. All that can be fairly maintained is the prevalence of one or the other at different stages of human progress. There have even been cases of national religion in which the three forms co-existed, — as in Egypt under the Sesostrids, where the grossest fetichism alternated with Osiris-cult in the practice of the laity, while the finished epopt, under priestly training at Sais, was initiated in the truth of pure theism.

Under the heads which have been named, there are several subdivisions and many distinct phases of religious life. Realism includes fetishism, the worship of earthly creatures, and what is called "Sabaism," the worship of the heavenly bodies. Personism embraces the religions of Vedism, Brahmanism, Hellenism, and Odinism. Spiritualism comprehends the highest phases of all the revealed religions.

II. The threefold division which graduates the religious progress of the human race repeats itself in particular dispensations. Most historical religions have their sensuous, their sentimental, and their spiritual or spiritualizing period;[1] they exhibit phases of realism, personism, and spiritualism. Either of these phases is more or less marked according to the general character of each religion, but in none are they wholly wanting. No religion is through all its periods entirely exempt from fetishism, and none is quite destitute of spiritual life.

Take an example from Judaism.

In the earlier history of the Hebrew people, before the establishment of the temple-worship,

---

[1] Not always indeed in the chronological order corresponding with childhood, youth, and manhood. The origin and earliest childhood of revealed religion is spiritual. Christianity especially had such an origin, and preserved for a time its spiritual childhood. But in its decline and subsequent revival, Christianity also exhibits the three phases above named. We note in it sacramental realism, idolatrous personism, and restored spirituality.

we read in the national Scriptures of a certain consecrated chest, or "Ark of the Covenant." This structure was held to be the dwelling-place of Deity; it was borne in solemn procession on great occasions, and formed, with the associations and traditions attending it, the prominent feature of Israelitish worship. This institution the Tribes appear to have derived from the Egyptians, in whose religion *kibotism*, or ark-worship, was also a leading rite. We find traces of it in other ancient nations. They seem to be in some cases reminiscences of the preservation of a human pair, by means of a box or rude craft, from the waters of a deluge. There are Greek medals representing a chest in which two individuals are floating on the water, with a dove and an olive-branch and a sacrifice supposed to be offered by the rescued pair after the subsidence of the waters. The ark on one of these medals bears the Greek name of Noah (Noe). Whether or not the service of the ark in the countries in which it was practised had this origin, it appears to have prevailed not only among civilized peoples, but also to some extent among barbarous tribes. Sir Joseph Banks, who accompanied Captain Cook in one of his voyages, found on an island of the Pacific a chest resembling the Ark of the Covenant as described in the Old Testament, with rings and poles for carrying it.

It was called by the islanders, "The House of God."

Now the Ark of the Covenant was essentially fetish. It was supposed to be the medium of Divine power and blessing. When the Tribes crossed the Jordan, it was carried in advance, and miraculously divided the waters. It was borne in procession around the walls of Jericho, and caused their downfall. After temporary disuse, it was brought out again in the time of the Judges, on occasion of an engagement with the Philistines. "And the Philistines were afraid, for they said, God is come into the camp. Woe unto us! for there hath not been such a thing heretofore." They rallied, however, and not only repulsed the Israelites, but even took the Ark of God, brought it to their city of Ashdod, and placed it in the Temple of Dagon. The consequence was that early on the morrow, "Behold, Dagon was fallen on his face before the Ark of the Lord." At the same time, and owing to the same cause, we are told that the city was visited with a sore epidemic. Altogether, the presence of the ark proved so disastrous that the Gentiles were fain to be rid of it; and after some consultation brought it to Kirjath-jearim, and deposited it in the house of Aminidab, where it lay for twenty years. When David ascended the throne, and established the seat of government at Jerusalem, he undertook the removal of the ark to that city. The first attempt was unsuccessful, resulting in the death of the man employed in its transportation; whereat David was so disgusted that he abandoned the enterprise, until he learned that Obed-edom, in whose house the ark had been stored, was miraculously prospering through the influence of the charm. He then appointed a new commission, and the ark was brought into the city with great pomp, the king himself heading the procession with a dance, — which "excited some remark."

This is the last act of homage to the ark in Hebrew history. When Solomon's Temple was completed, it was deposited in the Holy of Holies, where it thenceforth remained an obsolete sanctity. It perished with that temple, and that is the last we hear of it. So completely had it dropped from the use and consciousness of Jewish worship, that, when after the Captivity a new temple was instituted, no attempt was made to restore it. Ark-worship had died out: a new phase of Judaism had succeeded. The presence of Jehovah had disengaged itself from the "Mercy-seat between the Cherubim" which surmounted that time-honored box: it was no longer associated with any material thing. The devout imagination had outgrown that conception, and replaced it with the

4

notion of a potentate enthroned in the heavens. "It is He that sitteth above the circle of the earth, and the inhabitants thereof are as grasshoppers." The God of this period, though far surpassing the divinities of Gentile worship, — distinguished from them by onliness, as sole governor of heaven and earth, and by holiness, as exercising a moral jurisdiction over moral agents, — was still conceived under human limitations. He is still a national God, the God of Israel, with a special affection for Mount Zion.

A third, and the supreme stage of Judaism, begins with the settlement of Jewish colonies in Alexandria and Asia Minor, where contact with Greek wisdom stimulated the action of the national mind, and gave the religious consciousness its final development. In this stage, the idea of God is entirely divested of local and national limitations. The Alexandrian translators soften down, as far as possible, the anthropomorphic expressions of the Hebrew text. Jesus, the son of Sirach, evades the theophanies. It is no longer the Lord himself whom Moses saw face to face, "as a man talketh with a friend," but only a part of his glory. And where the Book of Exodus speaks of the thick cloud in which was God, Ecclesiasticus mentions the cloud without affirming that God was in it.[1]

[1] Nicolas, "Des Doctrines religieuses des Juifs."

The God of Ecclesiasticus is a God whose "spirit fills the earth."

III. The progress of religion, like all human development, proceeds by action of antagonistic powers. The antagonisms most noteworthy are those of Faith and Reason, and those of Sense and Conscience.

Religion, in its first manifestation, is an act of pure faith. The worshipper embraces without question the object on which it is directed, be it fetish or person. Whoever professes to represent that object is received as infallible authority. Where this principle is dominant, it begets a corresponding form of social polity, — hierarchy, or theocracy, such as we find in the earlier periods of Egyptian history, in Brahmanical India, and among the Druids. In this polity the priest is before the king, and the State a function of the hierarchy. The principle of theocratic or hierarchical government is implicit faith; its consummation is the institution of an hereditary priestly caste, whom the people regard as not only mediators of Godhead, but as being themselves divine. This institution still survives in the Brahman of Hindostan. "The birth of the Brahman," says Menu, "is the eternal incarnation of justice. For the Brahman born for the execution of justice is destined to identify himself with Brahm." "The Brahman is sovereign Lord of all beings; all that the world contains is his property. By his primogeniture, by his eminent birth, he has a right to all that exists." To this day, in Bengal, the lowly Sudra crawls on his knees to kiss the feet, or beg parings of the nails, of an individual of the priestly class nowise superior to himself except in the article of birth. The homage is not rendered to wealth or power — the object of it may be destitute of either — but to the portion of divinity supposed to reside in the favored caste, indicated by the bit of sacred cord which denotes the twice-born man. There is no servility in it, but simple reverence, — pure, unquestioning faith.

When, in the course of popular development or military reaction, faith becomes modified by never so little intellectual activity, the secular interest begins to assert itself. By-and-by it conquers a position beside, and co-ordinate with, the sacerdotal; and finally obtains supreme command, subordinating the sacerdotal, and controlling its functions.

The first stage in this process of secularization is exemplified in the empire of Japan, where the secular and ecclesiastical powers act with parallel function. Also in Thibet, where, if the Dalai Lama is theoretically incarnate Deity, the particular incumbent of the office for the time being is appointed by the secular power; that is, he is one of three Khubilkans, or twice-born children, nominated by the Chinese Court, or accepted by plenipotentiaries of that government residing in Thibet.[1]

The next degree of secular encroachment is reached, when the temporal sovereign assumes the patronage and visible headship of the Church, — as does the English Crown of the ecclesiastical establishment of Great Britain, and as Peter the Great put himself at the head of the Orthodox Church of Russia.[2]

The third and last stage of secularism in civil society is entire separation of Church and State, and the irrecognition on the part of the ruling powers of any particular religion as divine or more obligatory than any other. This is the position of the Government of the United States, which knows no religion as possessing any other claim than that of the numerical majority of its disciples for the time being. It recognizes the present fact, nothing more. The Government appoints chaplains; and the chaplains thus far have been Christian, for the reason that the subjects to whom they minister are Christian. But nothing in the Constitution

---

[1] Köppen, "Die Lamaische Hierarchie und Kirche."

[2] He is said to have thrown his hunting-knife on the table, saying to the assembled clergy, "There is your Patriarch."

of the United States forbids the appointment of Mohammedan chaplains; on the contrary, the principles of the Constitution would seem to require the appointment of such, or of those of any other faith whose disciples should happen to constitute the majority of the population to whom the chaplain was to minister. Ours is, perhaps, the only Government in Christendom in which Christianity is not formally recognized; the only one which absolutely discharges itself of all preference for, or interest in, any particular religion as possessing a supreme claim.

Beside the antagonism of faith and reason, parallel with it, is the conflict of sense and conscience, of the outer and the inner life. Hence the distribution of religion in two great classes, — polytheism and monotheism, or natural and revealed. The principle of polytheism is Deity in Nature; — in Nature, not as God's handiwork, the witness of his skill, but as God's embodiment, as divine mediation. The principle of monotheism is God in the conscience, — moral obligation divinely imposed. Accordingly, Mosaism, the earliest historic embodiment of that principle, is termed "The Law;" and Mohammedism, its later product, takes the name of Islam, "Righteousness."[1]

---

[1] So Emanuel Deutsch explains the term.

Religion begins with the worship of things; from fetishism it advances to personification of natural forces, and proceeds in the direction of personism, until some quickened and reflective soul, — in the language of theology, some divinely-missioned individual, — through predominance in him of the moral sense, arrives to the truer conception of Deity as moral lawgiver, and adores the God of conscience above all gods. Then commences, for the age and people in which such prophet appears, the reaction of the inner life; the soul asserts its supremacy over Nature; religion becomes internal, reflective, moral, protestant. Christianity consummated that reaction, completely abolishing the Nature-worship and polytheism of the Greco-Roman world. The two main streams of ancient religion, Hellenism and Semitic monotheism, — themselves the *débouchures* respectively of other, elder, Phœnician, Egyptian, and Persian faiths, — found their confluence in the Christian dispensation. Hellenism was completely merged and lost in it. Semitic monotheism, after delivering its "tribute-wave," has preserved an independent existence, and still survives in the Judaism of the "Dispersion;" still flourishes in Mohammedism, one of the most wide-spread of existing religions. This, and the elder religions of Central and Southern Asia, — Brahmanism and Buddhism, — still sway the major portion of the human race, but with such fixity, such incapacity of growth or effective reformation, as must needs neutralize their historic influence, if it does not abridge their duration. Extensive and prevailing as they seem when measured statistically, they are still but bounded provincialisms when viewed in relation to cosmopolitan humanity.

Christianity is the solvent of other religions, and may be regarded as the ultimate religion of man. In Protestant Christianity, religion has reached the extreme limit which divides it from pure science; in its latest development it seems to portend the union of the two. Further than this religion cannot go in the direction of reason, — in the rational apprehension of spiritual truth. There can be no progress out of Christianity into any new religion; unless, indeed, we give that name to some future dispensation of science, applying ascertained laws and scientific demonstration to the ethical and social relations of man.

Here, then, we have the entire cycle of religious development, the outline and ground-plan of the religious history of human kind. It begins with the worship of irrational objects, and proceeding through the various stages of naturalism, symbolism, personism, ends in the worship of pure spirit.

IV. The transitions from natural to revealed religion are mediated by extraordinary personalities, — exceptional individuals, — who accordingly are known as mediators in religion, and whose names are indelibly written on their respective faiths. "Personality," says Bunsen, "is the lever of the world's history." This is true of the secular, but far more true of the spiritual, history of man. When we say Moses, Zoroaster, Sakya-Muni, Jesus, we enunciate systems, civilizations, æons.

Far back in the impenetrable twilight of prehistoric time, as reflected in Hebrew tradition, occurs the name of SETH, which — whether it stands for an obsolete divinity, as recent criticism conjectures, or whether it represents a son of Adam, according to the current interpretation — possesses a deep religious significance. With this name, — as father, or creator, of ENOS (man), — there connects itself in the Biblical record the remarkable statement, "Then men began to call upon the name of the Lord." These words shadow forth some irrecoverable gospel, some long-perished revelation, some reaction against primeval superstition, of which but this mystic cipher survives, — sufficient to show how deep and aboriginal in human nature is the protest of the spirit against the aberrations of sense.

Emerging from this shadow-land of antediluvian

tradition, the first religionist who meets us on the borders of recorded time is the patriarch Abraham, — a name of measureless import in the annals of humanity as well as a cardinal date in the history of religion. Abraham is the first distinct historic personality.[1] Not the first historic personage, for Egyptian history was old, and had dragged the chain of its successive dynasties through long centuries, when the great Chaldean pitched his tent on the plains of Moab. But Egyptian history in all those ages presents no defined individuality, no character sufficiently marked "to point a moral or adorn a tale." The dynasties evoked by the Egyptologer out of the dim past, like the phantom-succession of Scottish kings evoked from the dim future by the witches in Macbeth,

"Come like shadows, so depart."

Dates and names and shadowy outlines are all that Egyptology has raked "from coffined clay." Egyptian history, like its perished forms whom we dig out of their crypts, is a bloodless mummy, with no expression in its faded lineaments, — important only as a measure of time. The first defined personality, the first live figure, the first blood-

[1] This was written before Herr Goldziher's work on Hebrew Mythology. There is nothing in that work which alters the opinion expressed above.

warm individual known to history, is also the first reformer, the first monotheist, — the patriarch Abraham. It is noticeable, by the way, that the reformers in religion, — Abraham, Zoroaster, Mohammed, Luther, — are historic characters, while the authors of idolatrous systems have left no trace of their personality. Or, to put the same thing in another way, the known founders of religions are all reformers. So much more difficult is it to abolish falsity and establish truth than to authorize and propagate error! Such work demands a virtue and a force which stamp themselves indelibly on their time, and secure to the reformer a permanent place in the world's records.

Abraham is the first reformer in religion, the first protestant. High above the mythical formations of his own and subsequent times he lifts his sublime head, and displays the deepest faith of the soul, — as geology finds on the highest mountain-tops the deeper layers of the earth's crust.

An anecdote which Biblical tradition has preserved, but which, I fancy, has been misconceived, and therefore misrepresented in the process of transmission, reveals the nature of the man, and comes to us charged with typical import. Settled in a land where universal custom required the sacrifice of the first-born, whether of brute or human parentage, he is tempted, after the example of the worshippers of Moloch, to make an offering of Sarah's first-born, the son of his hopes, to the Lord. But a truer feeling corrects this impulse, and stays the filicidal hand. If the piety of custom seemed to demand the sacrifice, the piety of the heart forbade it. He had courage to believe that the God of his devotion did not require the monstrous act. It was not his readiness to make the conventional sacrifice, but the courage that refused it in spite of custom and tradition, that proved his faith. He dared to live by faith, and was counted just in so doing.

Four thousand years later, when Luther, a pilgrim in Rome, in compliance with the painful fashion of his time was climbing on his knees the Santa Scala of the Lateran, there rushed on his soul that saving word, "The just shall live by faith." It was the spirit of Abraham come again in the person of a German monk, that moment new born of the lineage of faith.

This, then, is the import of the story; and this is the import of Abraham to us and to all time,— the voice in the soul correcting tradition; thought purifying faith.

III.

THE WAY OF HISTORIC CHRISTIANITY.

CHRISTIANITY must be studied in its social developments, — must be studied as an organized and organizing power in human society, — in order to a right understanding of the real import of the Christian faith.

Only through its history can Christianity or any religion as a social movement be truly known. Whatever develops itself in time requires for its full comprehension to be studied in its processes; that is, historically. Even animal, even vegetable, natures require to be so studied. It is with strict philosophic accuracy that we speak of "Natural History," in reference to such studies. The nature of the bird is not exhausted by the study of the egg, or the plumage, or the note, or the anatomy. To these must be added the knowledge of its habits, its relations to its kind and to other kinds, its movements and migrations: in a word, its history. To know the oak, it is not sufficient to study the acorn or the sapling. We need for that purpose the full-grown tree, with the wear of centuries chronicled in its annual rings. More emphatically, of man our best knowledge is not derived from a physical analysis of the human frame, or metaphysical analysis of the human mind. We may know every bone and muscle in the body, and we may know every faculty and law of the mind, and still be very ignorant of human nature until we study it as it manifests itself in action, and trace its action through successive ages. Our best anthropology is learned, not from Haller or Hunter or Kant, but from Tacitus and Gibbon. Of institutions, human and divine, of systems of belief, of religious dispensations, of the Christian dispensation in particular, the same law holds: they are known by their history. Christianity is known by its history. As a sentiment affecting the individual soul, as a doctrine determining individual faith, we may learn it from the Gospels; but not as a world-dispensation involving the spiritual destiny of many generations. Christianity in that sense can no more be known from the Gospels than the oak can be known from the acorn; than the river that traverses continents, that feeds itself with streams from a thousand hills, and bears half the commerce of the world on its bosom, can be known from the trickling rill or sequestered pool to which curiosity has finally traced it. Rather the pool itself would be unknown, except to the heron that dips her wing in its wave, or the deer that browses by its marge, had not the marvel of the river first directed inquiry to the marvellous source. It was Christianity, already established in the world, that led to the study of the Gospels; not the study of the Gospels that revealed Christianity. The gospel itself — I mean the gospel record — is the product of Christian history, not its source. Who knows how much or how little of the observation and experience of the actual eye-witnesses of the ministry of Jesus has come down to us? It is impossible to say to what extent the views and theories and disputes of more than one generation of believers, — party interests and ecclesiastical policy, — may have modified those venerable and priceless records which bear the titles of Matthew and John, and which, whatever their origin and composition, are traceable in their present form to within a century only of the events they commemorate. The value of the record is nowise impaired by this uncertainty. The scriptures of the New Testament contain enough of the mind of Christ to serve as a standard of Christian truth, and to furnish a well of refreshing in which a corrupted and penitent Church may wash and be clean. But they do not contain the sum of Christianity, no more than the acorn contains the oak.

It is a mistake to suppose that the Apostolic age

was the perfect age of the Church, and every subsequent age a wider departure from the truth, a steady progress in corruption. A truer idea of the Christian dispensation is expressed in the word *development*. Christianity is not a fixed but a flowing quantity and power. It is not to be found complete and entire in any scripture, church, or age, but unfolds itself successively through many scriptures, churches, ages. It is not a totality, but a process; a process of which the Church — that is, Christian society — is at once the medium and the exponent, and ecclesiastical history the report. Let ecclesiastical history, then, understand its function to be that of exhibiting the progress of Christianity as it organizes itself in human society, and the progress of society as organized by Christianity.

This twofold process is subject to laws without which, and the belief in which, all history is a mere collection of dead facts without sense or purpose. These laws in the sphere of the Church are all comprised in that Providential agency which theology terms the "Holy Spirit." The action of the "Holy Spirit" is the fundamental postulate, the organic hypothesis of Christian Church-history, without which the study of that history is meaningless and valueless.

I propose to consider this agency which shapes

and constitutes the history of the Church, in some of its aspects.

It manifests itself, in the first place, as *Ordination*,—a divine necessity directing and controlling the order of events. In history as in Nature there is nothing fortuitous, nothing wilful, nothing that could have been other than it was. Human free-will is the instrument employed; but the result is necessary. Every finite will is divinely circumscribed; and the sum of all wills is comprehended in the orbit of the Universal Will, and resolves itself into that. This first and vital principle of all historical science applies with peculiar emphasis to the history of the Church, and is all the more important to the right understanding of the facts, the more the facts appear to contradict it.

To the superficial glance, the history of the Church appears to be a tissue of accidents, a wild and wayward deviation at every step from the probable and looked-for and natural direction.

A native of Palestine, and destined in the views and expectations of its first teachers to occupy that soil with its supreme power and central life, Christianity soon became an alien in the land of its birth. Of oriental lineage, it never perceptibly influenced the civilization of the East; but casting aside its oriental costume, which survives only as a fossil relic of Biblical archæology, forgetful of its Asiatic blood, it turned its back on ancestral Shem, and settled with the children of Javan who divided the isles of the Gentiles. The seed of Abraham identified itself with the uncircumcised West. Entrusted to simple provincials whose little world was all contained between Lebanon and Carmel, whose highest conception of their mission was to reinstate the Judaic dynasty, it was suddenly snatched out of their hands by a daring outsider who had never known Christ in the flesh; who boasted that *his* Christianity was an independent revelation, and would take no instructions from those who had the gospel direct from its author; who magnificently set aside the foremost of them all, and withstood him to his face; who called himself an Apostle, but was not so regarded by the other Twelve; who gave the religion an entirely new aspect, and yet came to be regarded as its authorized and principal exponent. It began with announcing a heavenly kingdom, and hastened to establish an earthly one. Instead of erecting, as was fondly expected, its throne on Zion, it selected for its capital the mother of abominations, the Babylon of the Apocalypse. It began with establishing social equality, even to community of goods; but soon developed a priestly aristocracy, the most complex and oppressive the world has ever known. It began with hereditary horror of graven images, and came to be the horror of Ishmael for its idolatry. It began with worshipping Spirit in spirit and truth, and it came to worship a morsel of bread.

If we come to *doctrines*, we find equal cause for surprise in its wide and apparently wilful divergence from the primitive faith, and in the trivial causes which decided the prevalence of the one or the other opinion in the Church. Compare the discourses of Jesus as reported by the evangelists, or even the confession of faith known as the Apostles' Creed, with the doctrines propounded by the Councils of the fourth and fifth centuries, with the "Summa" of the thirteenth, with the Tridentine decisions of the sixteenth; and see how huge a nimbus of ecclesiastical orthodoxy envelops how small a nucleus of primitive faith. The christology of the Church, for more than a century, fluctuated between Athanasian orthodoxy on the one hand and Arian, Nestorian, and Eutychian heresies on the other. The decisions of the Councils did not always coincide with the general opinion of Christendom at the time; and only the accidental circumstance of imperial patronage, concurring with the views of interested prelates, prevented the decision of the fourth Council from being reversed by another in the brief period which intervened between the fall of the Western Empire and the schism of the Churches, and left the doctrine of Latin Christianity respecting the nature of Christ where the middle of the fifth century had placed it. The policy which fixed the faith of nations was not always regulated by the piety and wisdom of those who would seem most fit to direct it. Cabal and intrigue, the accidents of life, court patronage, intimidation, and even armed force have sometimes carried the day in the action of the Councils and the conduct of the Churches. The turbulent ferocity of Cyril decided the issues of the Council of Ephesus, and gave a goddess to the Christian world. The sister of one Cæsar caused the triumph of the Arians, and the sister of another procured the defeat of the Nestorians. The death of two emperors,[1] leaving their orthodox widows on the throne, established the worship of idols in the East. The perfidy of another instigated the reformation in Bohemia, the forerunner of Protestantism and the parent of one of the purest of existing sects. The want of a marriage license drove Popery from England; a failing exchequer drove Protestantism from France.

From these and numberless other instances it might seem as if the course of ecclesiastical his-

[1] Leo and Theophilus.

tory, and with it the fortunes of Christianity, were left to chance and human caprice; as if the condition of Christianity at any moment were the mere fortuitous result of such agencies. But no one can suppose this, who considers for a moment the consequences implied in it. Such a supposition is fatal to any rational idea of Divine revelation.

For why do we believe in a self-revealing Spirit? Why believe that the heavens in man were opened, and a fresh word from the bosom of the Everlasting interpolated in the groping intellect's uncertain process, but because we see such apocalypse to be needful for the future and constant guidance of the race? And how is that end to be accomplished except by the stated, normal action of the same Spirit which evolved that gospel in the fulness of time, and which never, in all time past, had left the world without witness and without mediation of the godhead, and without a word proportioned to its day? There are Christians who seem to think of the Holy Spirit as the ancients did of their Astræa. They suppose that it had its dwelling on this earth in the golden age (the apostolic age) of the Church, but fled up to heaven in the brazen and iron ages which succeeded, and has been to the Church ever since but a distant star in the zodiac of old traditions. I believe, on the contrary, that the Holy Spirit, — in whatsoever manifestation or disguise, illumination or occultation, —has never been wanting to the Church of Christ; has been in sunshine or in shade, in triumph or in passion, the "effectual working in the measure of every part," to "the increase of the body" and the "edifying of itself in love;"—now emerging into solemn epiphany in seasons of "refreshing from the presence of the Lord," now engulphed in disastrous twilight; but still there, still active, though all its action may, at some dear crisis, have been confined to one poor, hunted, cowering sect, or folded up in a single agonizing breast. Whatever reason there is for supposing a revelation at all, for believing in divine dispensations of truth, the same reason compels us to believe that such a dispensation, once initiated in human society, is not left to itself to take what direction chance may impart, to prosper or fail as chance may decide; but in all its developments and phases is still subject to the same Power, and still directed by the same Wisdom, which dispensed the original word, and planted a new heaven and a new earth in the human breast. Without the supposition of the Holy Spirit as its method and law, there is no ecclesiastical history that deserves investigation.

Another aspect in which this agency presents itself is *Education.* We have viewed it as divine necessity, we have next to consider it as divine beneficence. The Spirit not only appoints, but appoints with a purpose, — a wise and benevolent purpose directing the order of events, and causing them to co-operate in promoting the spiritual growth of society; that is, in educating society. There is and can be, in the nature of things, no absolute demonstration of such a purpose. It is pure hypothesis, which the consummation of all things alone can verify. But the need of this hypothesis to rationalize the portents and enormities of history, to bring them into harmony with any intelligible, conceivable order of the universe, the atheistic alternative of no purpose and no Providence involved in its rejection, — these are its warrant and abundant justification.

History, or the world of conscious, voluntary agencies, is more prolific, as might be expected, in disturbances and anomalies, in horrors and atrocities, than the unconscious, involuntary world of Nature. But geology knows that the earth of to-day, — our human earth with its apt appointments and nice accommodation to human uses, its stratified mountains and alluvial valleys, its granite and slate and coal and iron, — is the product of those stupendous revolutions that perplexed the Saurian nations of pre-Adamite time. And humanity trusts that the deadly encounters, the atrocious wrongs, the persecutions and fightings, the blood and crime of past societies shall furnish the necessary social deposits, the historic strata and ecclesiastical alluvium of future composed and tranquil ages, when our present imperfect organizations shall be known only as steps toward a new and replenished earth.

Nowhere is the dark side of history more prominent than it is in the annals of the Church. And what to Christian faith is more perplexing than the horrors of Christian warfare, than Christian persecutions, and all the atrocities committed in the name of religion, is the wide and seemingly wilful divergence of the doctrine and practice of the Church from the precepts of the Gospel. When we turn from the teachings of Jesus to John-of-Damascus's or Anselm's doctrine of Redemption, or St. Thomas's doctrine of Sacraments; from the *Agapæ* of the Apostles to the High Mass; from the Council at Jerusalem to the Council of Constance, — we are conscious of a gulf imperfectly bridged by the Christian name. I have often thought that if I were to undertake, as an exercise of ingenuity, to construct a system of religion as far as possible removed from the Christianity of the Gospel, without abandoning the Christian name, I should be likely to invent some such system as that of the Church of Rome. And certainly many of the doctrines and practices of that Church, — such as indulgences, transubstantiation, penances and masses for the dead, — must be regarded by all but Romanists themselves, however liberal and philosophically tolerant, as inventions and corruptions which have foisted themselves on the primitive faith. But to say that the entire doctrine and practice of the Church, whereinsoever it departs from the Gospel record and the teachings of the Apostles, — that is, where Gospel and Epistles, as we understand them, furnish no basis for such doctrine or practice, — is sheer corruption, this is to adopt a position which I find it impossible to reconcile with any worthy or tenable view of Divine revelation. It supposes Christ to be defeated by Anti-Christ; it supposes revelation to be a failure, and the Word of God to return unto him void, not having accomplished the thing which he pleased, nor prospered in that whereunto he sent it. The idea of Divine revelation involves as its necessary corollary a Providential oversight of that revelation, a Providential order in its developments. And if we allow a Providential order in the history of the Church, we concede to it the order best adapted to the spiritual wants of the time and the education of the human mind. The religion of the Middle-Age is certainly not the Christianity of the New Testament; but we are not therefore authorized to pronounce it unchristian or antichristian. The New Testament is the highest, but by no means the only, authority in matters of Christian doctrine. To maintain that it is so, is an error of Protestantism, which a candid and enlightened Protestantism in this age of the Church should reconsider and renounce. It is an error involving consequences as grave as the Catholic theory of tradition to which it was opposed. We cannot claim inspiration for the Scriptures and deny it to the Church. The former depends on the latter. It was the Church that decided, and that after much controversy, of what books the New Testament should consist. And all the books of our present New Testament were not embraced in the canons either of Laodicea or of Carthage.

I do not say that the Church was infallible in her speculative views, that she had sight of the absolute truth, or came so near to it as enlightened individuals who in all periods have dissented from her judgments, — the heretics of elder and more recent times. But I believe that the Church was wise in her practical decisions, wiser even than she knew; wise with the unconscious wisdom of spiritual instinct. In other words, she was inspired. Even in those cases in which her decisions seem most repugnant to reason, her course may have been divinely shaped in accordance with ends divinely ordained. The truths of the time are not always truths of pure reason; and still they are truths.

One or two cases may serve for illustration.

The earliest doctrinal decisions of the Church are those which assert the deity of Christ. Whatever may be our private convictions regarding this doctrine, whatever we may think of the evidence for it or against it in the writings of the New Testament, thus much is certain, — that the deepest consciousness and truest life of the Church in the fourth century were with the doctrine and for it.

Equally certain is the wonder-working influence of this idea on the heart of Christendom, when once by faith it became a constituent of the mental life of the Church. It brought the individual mind and heart into close, immediate, and even sensible communion with God; it made the Church the veritable kingdom of God to believers; it gave her a sense of Divine authority and sufficiency, of saving necessity and absoluteness, which satisfied her own consciousness of rightful sway and carried conviction of that right to others. It was not enough in rude ages to be intellectually assured of the truth of Christianity as a system of faith and practice; it was necessary to have a God historically present and verbally speaking to the soul. On the other hand, the philosophic mind, impatient of propositions which it cannot range and schematize in its own fashion, may find in the very terms which formulate this dogma in the language of the Councils a way of escape from any violence done to the understanding by an indiscreet presentation of the subject.

Nowhere, it seems to me, is the guiding Providence of God in history more conspicuous than it is in the wording of the final *dictum* of the Councils respecting the nature of Christ. The christology of the Church was the growth of centuries. The homoousian theory passed through several stages before it was perfected and given to the world in the form which remains to this day the genuine "Orthodox" view of Christ, though very unlike the *soi-disant*, Patri-passian Orthodoxy of our time. The first four œcumenical councils represent its principal phases and successive modifications, as developed by the exigency of different periods and conflicting minds. The Council of Nicæa decided that Christ was one with God in substance; that of Constantinople reaffirmed this consubstantiality and applied it to the Holy Spirit. At Ephesus it was determined that in Christ two natures unite in one person; and finally, at Chalcedon it was concluded that, though the person be one, the natures remain two natures still. This was the final triumph of Athanasian orthodoxy over the heresies opposed to it. It was well for the Church and well for humanity that this view prevailed as against the Arian and against the monophysite. Both these doctrines flout the humanity of Jesus. The monophysite perceived only deity in Christ. The Arian saw neither God nor man, nor a God-man, but a hypothetical being who is different from both,—a sheer invention, an unintelligible ghostly chimera, whom one can neither repose in as true God nor sympathize with as genuine man. The Athanasian doctrine preserves the humanity intact, and even guards it with jealous care, leaving me at liberty, as my spiritual wants or mental habits incline, to fasten on the human or divine in the hypostatic union,—*οὐδαμοῦ τῆς τῶν φύσεων διαφορᾶς ἀνῃρημένης διὰ τὴν ἕνωσιν, σωζομένης δὲ μᾶλλον τῆς ἰδιότητος ἑκατέρας φύσεως, καὶ εἰς ἓν πρόσωπον καὶ μίαν ὑπόστασιν συντρεχούσης.*

The Catholic or Orthodox christology is precisely that which, by the comprehensiveness and impartiality of its statement, allows the largest liberty of speculation, and admits of the greatest diversity of view. It merely affirms what every one believes, who believes in Christianity at all,—that God and man wrought together in

Christ for the regeneration of human kind. In what way and measure these two agencies combined in the one *πρόσωπον*, it does not undertake to determine. Your faith may prefer to dwell on the God in Christ; my spiritual wants may need the man. Here is that which gives to each what each demands, unprejudiced and unimpaired: *salva proprietate utriusque naturæ; verbo operante quod verbi est, et carne exsequente quod carnis est.* The Arian doctrine, on the other hand, is a rigidly defined, abrupt hypothesis, intractable, insoluble; to be taken bodily, if at all, and held by an act of volition as a stubborn anomaly which the mind can neither historically adjust nor philosophically assimilate.

Another instance in which the historical issue conflicts with the rational, Protestant judgment is that of the Council of Ephesus, which asserted the godhead of the mother of Jesus by the title of *θεοτόκος* (God's mother), and deposed the patriarch Nestorius for disputing that phrase.

When we read in the Gospel the story of Jewish Mary, the descendant of forty generations of monotheists and idol-haters, the meek girl betrothed to one as lowly as herself, the fond mother whose whole future is concentrated in her first-born, the careful housewife intent on domestic offices; when, with this conception in our mind, we turn to the fifth and following centuries of the Christian Church, and find this Galilean woman converted into a goddess, the foremost figure in the Christian ritual, — this daughter of a nation whose prophets denounced the vengeance of God on the recreant women of the tribe for burning incense to the "Queen of Heaven," herself transfigured into a Queen of Heaven, and receiving incense in that name, — we are conscious of a startling discrepancy between the Gospel and the Church. We perceive that, in migrating from its native fold in the bosom of Israel to alien Gentile climes, Christianity cast aside the sacred traditions of its Hebrew ancestry, and compounded with the profane Roman and Greek. Our first feeling is one of indignation and disgust at what seems a gross and wilful perversion of the purpose and spirit of our religion. But when we consider all that the Virgin was to the Church of the Middle Age, — how, when in the lapse of time and the absence of the Scriptures the Son of Man had receded so far into absolute godhead that, though theoretically human still, his humanity and with it his mediatorial character had quite faded from the popular mind, — how, then, the Mother replaced the Son, and became the acknowledged mediatrix between God and man; when we consider how this radiant figure of the mediæval cult embodied to the popular mind, together with all that is holy and reverend in Deity, all that is congenial and kindly in man, and especially all that is pure and tender in woman, — that in her, as never before and nowhere else, were impersonated spiritual beauty and celestial love, — that in her for the first time the world possessed a moral ideal, and with it a triumphant vindication of womanhood; when, above all, we reflect that the Virgin was the only intelligible manifestation and representative of Divine grace, that in her and through her the pardoning mercy of God was revealed and dispensed to an age incapable of apprehending spiritual ideas which were not embodied in a sensuous type; and when we think of the mighty influence which such a personality, which the constant presence of such an idea, must have had in refining and educating the mind of the time, — our disgust will be changed to admiration of the Providential wisdom which furnished so important an aid to spiritual culture and devout aspiration in the wreck of conventions, the dissolution of manners, the shock of lawless violence, the triumph of brute force, the desolation and disorganization which succeeded the decay of the old civilization. Over all the tumult and tempests of that wild time this gentle and benign form brooded like a dove, rebuking violence, compassionating sorrow, calming grief, refreshing hope, attracting devotion, forgiving penitent guilt; everywhere composing, encouraging, reconciling. It is true the Mother in a measure supplanted the Son and even concealed the Father, filling up the whole field of the Christian's heaven, receiving the honors and apparently fulfilling the functions of the godhead. The creature was preferred before the Creator: so far the action of the Church was seemingly a return to heathenism. Yet it was no heathen goddess which the Church adored in the person of Mary, no imperfect creature disfigured by human frailties and passions, but the very beauty of holiness; a faultless image invested — so far as the mind of that age could apprehend them — with the veritable attributes of Deity. Practically it was God himself whom the mariolater addressed, — the Eternal, with a tenderer name and more intelligible accidents and more defined personality. It is the nature of devout sentiment, when once it becomes dominant in the mind and acts independently of the understanding, to body *forth* the object of its devotion, to give form and feature to the infinite, to humanize if not to idolize its God. We may well pardon mediæval devotion, which gave its God the form most intelligible to its own thought and most grateful to its own feeling. So far as the religious life of the individual is concerned, it matters less to what idea of divinity we pray (so it embrace our highest conceptions of the holy and the good), than it does that the prayer itself be fervent and true. It would seem as if the Almighty had purposely shrouded himself behind this effulgent image, and thrust it ostensibly forth as the fittest demonstration and truest embodiment of those attributes of divinity which it most concerned the popular mind to believe and to cherish, — especially of divine grace, which having been excluded from the creed of the Church, except as a special distinction conferred on certain elect natures, reappeared in its mythology. It was the most effectual if not the only way in which the characteristic grace of the Gospel could be presented to the unreflecting mind of the time.

Nestorius and his party were burned and persecuted, not for refusing homage to the Virgin, but because they protested against the title by which it was proposed to designate the new divinity, — a severe measure, seeing that the protest probably sprung from a truer piety than that which dictated the dogma. But this historic wrong, if we so regard it, was historically righted and compensated in the final event. The pious patriarch died the victim of unjust persecution; but his party survived, and with them his faith and name. The Nestorians became a large and powerful sect independent of the Catholic Church. They spread through Assyria, Persia, Egypt, Arabia, India; they crossed the Imaus and established a church in Tartary. The Christians of St. Thomas, on the coast of Malabar, are their descendants. They are still extant in various parts of Asia. In their origin the most primitive of Christian churches, older than the Roman, more eastern than the Greek, they have perpetuated Christianity in the land of its birth.

I will cite but one more instance in which the course of ecclesiastical history appears at first to contradict our ideal, but is found on reflection to justify itself as Providential wisdom. My third example is the stubborn policy of Rome, which created, or which failed to heal, the successive ruptures of the Church. Beside the Nestorian schism and other lesser fragments, Christendom is now divided into three great sections, — the Greek, the Latin, and the Protestant Churches. This division, of which Rome lays the blame on those whom she excluded, is in fact her own work, — the result of that imperious absolutism with which she has always trampled on the private conscience, and required unconditional surrender of opinion. This policy ecclesiastical Rome inherited from pagan Rome. The Emperor Trajan established the principle, not unknown to modern and even republican legislation, the precise enunciation of which he owed to Pliny, — that whatsoever the private convictions of a subject, whether right or wrong — *qualecumque esset quod faterentur* — the obstinate persistence in it, contrary to the will of government, was a punishable offence; *debere puniri.* In conformity with this principle, Rome in the fifth century not only repudiated the imperial *Henoticon*, which aimed to restore the integrity of the Christian communion, but excommunicated the Greek churches through their patriarchs for their complicity in that instrument. In this spirit she cast out the Iconoclasts in the eighth century, and broke with Eastern Christendom in the ninth and the eleventh. And when in the fifteenth, at the Councils of Ferrara and of Florence, the attempt was made to reconcile and reunite these severed fragments, the project was frustrated by Rome's insisting on the recantation and renunciation by the Greeks, of the principal points of difference between them. With the same pervicacity she turned a deaf ear to the cry for "reform in the head and members," which went up from the heart of Christian Germany with the dawning of the *Rénaissance*, set up Councils in opposition to the reform Councils of Constance and Basil, and forced the Protestant schism by excommunicating the reformers of the sixteenth century, who wished to purify, not to divide, and would have given their lives to preserve the unity of the Church, would Rome but consent to have it purged of its corruptions. And finally, when forced by the pressure of the North and West to call the Council of Trent for the express purpose of reforming abuses and recovering by reform the Protestant secession, her intrigues brought about the contrary effect, perpetuated the most offensive features of Romanism, and established an irreparable breach between the Roman and the Saxon mind. Better break than bend; better a divided Church than the smallest concession; better lose a kingdom than abate a tittle of her arbitrary will, — has been from the beginning the one unvarying principle of Roman policy.

Our moral sentiment of course condemns this policy, so far as the spirit and temper of Rome are expressed by it. But considered as the means and condition of spiritual development and human progress, our riper judgment will rejoice in it. The idea of catholicity, of ecclesiastical integrity, of a single individual church whose heart shall be the metropolis and whose extremities the outskirts of civilization, which shall clasp the world with its binding sacraments, and string the nations like beads on the thread of a common confession: one Lord, one faith, one baptism, — this idea is pleasant to the mind and dear to the heart of humanity.

When we consider what such a church might accomplish for the civilization and sanctification of human kind, no wonder that the instinct of early Christendom demanded it! No wonder that earnest spirits in all time have striven for it as the true fulfilment of the gospel's mission, the realization of that divine word, "That they all may be one, as I Father in thee and thou in me, that they may be one in us"! Unquestionably, a Catholic Church, in some sense, is the rightful heritage of the Spirit, the consummation to which Faith may legitimately look, the ideal which Faith is bound to cherish.

But here, as everywhere, the ideal and the actual are wide asunder. It is a long way between the conception and the consummation; and not only long but devious, circuitous, oftentimes seemingly retrograde. The path which may ultimately lead to the goal tends meanwhile in a contrary direction. Whoever studies attentively the times of those schisms, and the nationalities divided by them, will perceive that temporary separation, if not final divorce, was required in order that each new era might develop itself freely, unhampered by the old.

The real quarrel between the Greek Church and the Latin, if I rightly interpret it, was not the worship of images, nor the use of unleavened bread, nor the different procession of the Holy

Ghost; but something more latent, unknown to either party, and undefinable, It was the difference which divides the youth from the child. Latin Christianity was rapidly developing a subjectiveness and a sentimentality unknown to classic antiquity, and which bred disaffection toward the sensuous, objective Greek. The Greek, on the other hand, always deficient in inwardness, had no taste for Western devotion, and no sympathy with Western romance. This antagonism, which displayed itself so glaringly in the time of the Crusades, was sufficiently developed in the eighth and ninth centuries to render impossible a cordial union and harmonious co-operation between the two churches. The mutual excommunications and formal separations of that crisis did not originate but only declared a breach beyond the power of synods to repair.

Six centuries later, there arose between the Latin and the German nationalities a feud analogous to that which divided the Latin and the Greek. As that was a rupture between boyhood and youth, so this may be designated as a revolution separating youth from manhood. In the former case it was a new æon, an age of romance disengaging itself from the sensuous world of antiquity; in the other it was also a new æon, an era of science emancipating itself from the age of romance. Then it was sentiment contending against sense; now it was science in conflict with sentiment.

In the fourteenth and fifteenth centuries, when Europe began to weary of the saddle, when gunpowder was exploding feudalism, and when the printing-press was striking off the first proofs of a new dispensation, — the awakened intellect, hitherto the docile pupil of the Church, and the faithful vassal of suzerain Rome, became conscious of a want which the Church could no longer supply; became conscious of a mission whose supreme function was to summon Rome herself, and all things else in heaven above and on the earth beneath, to its own inexorable bar. Accordingly, the alternative of the sixteenth century was not simply whether Rome should reform specific abuses or Protestantism secede, but whether Rome should lay down her assumed infallibility, or the human intellect forego its appointed career. And since neither course supposed in this alternative was possible, a schism was the inevitable result. Rome might reform specific abuses, and behooved to do so; but she could not renounce her assumed infallibility without a suicide involving the downfall of the entire fabric of the Latin Church, — an event which, in that day, would have been as perilous to Protestant Christendom as to Catholic. But neither, on the other hand, could the intellect renounce its divinely-appointed career, nor pursue it in subjection to papal authority. Science could not stoop to prince or pontiff for leave to see and to say what she saw. She could not sit at the feet of Holiness to know if the sun stood still, or the earth was put together in six times twenty-four hours, or Moses and Matthew composed the writings which bear their names. It was necessary that Rome with her authority and Protestantism with its science should part company, that each might unfold its own life and fulfil its mission independently of the other, and both in their several and separate spheres work together for the common end,—the education of man.

Thus we have in the three great sections of the Christian world three epochs of Christian history, representing three life-periods,—childhood, youth, and full age; the periods respectively of Sense, of Sentiment, and of Science.

To the spiritual eye these superficial antitheses of Greek Church and Latin, Catholic and Protestant, are resolved in the higher synthesis of a common origin and a common Lord; a Christendom whose Head is one though its polities are many, and whose kingdom is entire however its communion be divided. The Holy Catholic Church, which Faith demands and expects, is no illusion; it exists already in the catholizing consciousness of true piety. Wherever there is a catholic mind, there, subjectively, is the Catholic Church.

I have spoken of historic Christianity as the process of the Spirit by which the divine idea of the Gospel is to be realized in time. We have viewed it in its two aspects of necessity and beneficence, with the two corresponding functions, divine ordination and divine education. But the action of the Spirit is not exhausted in these functions. There remains a third. It lies very near; it is prefigured in the view which the Christian world entertains of the person of Christ.

Universal Christendom holds that, in some sense or other, God and man were united in the person of Christ. I say universal Christendom, because, historically, the exceptions are not worth noticing. Whether we state it in the language of the Scripture, "In him dwelt all the fulness of the godhead bodily," or adopt the Orthodox phraseology of two natures in one person, or say with the Unitarian that Christ was divinely inspired, especially inspired, possessed of the Spirit "without measure," — the truth received is practically the same: the difference is in breadth of statement, not in substance of doctrine. But Christ, as the Head of the *Ecclesia*, is the prototype of the Christian world, the representative of the new heaven and new earth, the spiritual cosmos which the Christian ages are expected to unfold. Whatever was true of Jesus historically is theoretically and prospectively true of Christianized man. Christianization is mutual adoption of God and man.

The consummation of this process would be to realize in all men the same union of the human and the Divine which the Church ascribes to its Head. Historic Christianity is the movement of society in that direction, with all the hindrances and contradictions and deviations and retrogradations which attend it, and which checker and date the course of time. It is the progress of society in that union with God which humanity has in Christ.

Accordingly, the third function of ecclesiastical history to which I allude is expressed by the term *Incarnation.* God incarnates himself in human society just so far as the kingdom of God is established in the world. Every triumph of truth and right which Christianity achieves over the selfish passions of men, like the abolition of slavery and the emancipation of woman; every principle of justice which gains ascendancy in human legislation, which incorporates itself with civil government and becomes an organic element of society, such as political equality; every institution which labors in the name of Christ for the relief of human misery and the furtherance of human well-being, such as hospitals for the sick and insane and ministries to the poor, — is a step in that progressive incarnation of divine attributes in human kind, which illustrates and fulfils the prophetic prayer of Christ, "That they all may be one in us."

Christian history, — that is, the written history of Christian society, — exhibits but little progress as yet in this direction. And had we no other data from which to judge of the future of humanity than what is chronicled in the books, one might almost despair of the gospel and of man. So many centuries has the name of Christ been graved on the forehead of society, and with all reverence named of men, and so little has the thing, the spirit, prevailed which that name imports! So many centuries has Christianity builded its churches and administered its sacraments and published its scriptures, and so little as yet has been seen and felt of Christ! The written chronicle seems rather to conceal than to reveal him, and the first impression of humanity regarding it might well find vent in the cry, "They have taken away my Lord, and I know not where they have laid him!" But this first impression is founded on a very superficial view of Christian history and the Christian world. The written chronicle is necessarily a very imperfect account of what has been effected by the gospel. This is not what the records have usually undertaken to exhibit. They report the exterior constitution of the Church, not its interior life. They chronicle the successive organizations and varying costume of the Spirit, not its essential growth. It would not be difficult to trace through all these centuries of revolution and misrule, of strife and oppression, of theological hatred and priestly persecution, the secret windings and subtle ramifications of a sacred artery, a spiritual aorta, connecting the heart of Christendom with its uttermost fibres, and filled with the blood of Christ. It would not be difficult to show that each century in turn has eaten of the flesh of the Son of Man, and had his life, however latent, abiding in it. And in this our day, amid all the indifference and supineness, the scepticism and the scorn, the madness and the crime, which meet and appall us on every hand, it would not be difficult to discover unmistakable signs of deeper earnestness and truer devotion, of a more thorough penetration and occupation of this age by the spirit of Christ, than any past time has known.

The only philosophy of history which satisfies mind and heart is optimism, — the belief that all things tend to good and produce good in the final result; and that if — in the lofty language of

Leibnitz — "we were sufficiently acquainted with the order of the universe, we should find that it surpasses all the wishes of the wisest, and that it could not be better than it is, not only for all in general but for ourselves in particular." Christian history, especially, is studied to little purpose unless we learn from it the Christian lessons of patience and hope. It reveals not only an unlooked-for power of self-recovery in man through the agency of the Holy Spirit, and shows how impossible it is for God to withdraw or man to drive that Spirit from the world, and what "a charmèd life old goodness hath," and how the deeper shades of moral corruption appear so only through the light that limits them; but it also discloses to careful observation a steady progression in good hitherto, which points to a future better than this present and better than all the past, — a height and breadth of social development, a spiritual maturity of human kind, which secular philosophy concurs with divine revelation in predicting, and to which both have assigned the august title, "City of God."

IV.

THE WAY OF HISTORIC ATONEMENT.

A RELIGION wide as the widest outlook of the modern mind; a religion free as human thought, concurrent with reason, co-ordinate with science; a religion in which the present predominates over the past, and the future over the present; in which judgment tops authority and vision outruns tradition, — this is the instant demand of a liberal faith.

Two ways appear of meeting this demand, two distinct postures of the mind toward it, among those who equally urge the claim. The one undertakes to supplant, the other seeks to unfold. The former renounces, and declares its independence of, ecclesiastic and historic Christianity; disallows its hereditary title, and rejects all claim of its record to any admissions which conflict with the every-day experience of men, which offend the sensuous understanding, or transcend the methods of science. It culls from the sifted gospel some golden grains of ethical import, and embodies these in a theory of life and man which may or may not, according to circumstances, call itself Christianity, but which claims to be its essence, and offers itself to the Church as such.

The other position respects the claim of ecclesiastic continuity, and seeks in Christianity itself, — in historic Christianity, — a meaning and a purpose so wide as to throw its orbit outside of the most elliptical radicalisms that traverse its spheres: as the sun, which seemed to the early Copernicans stationary, is judged by sidereal astronomy to have an orbit of its own, which includes the aphelia of all the comets; and not only so, but carries them with it in its grander sweep.

It is not pretended that this comprehensiveness lay in the conscious thought of the apostles and first teachers of Christianity; enough to suppose that it lay in the mind of the Spirit which edited the gospel out of the deep of its own idea. Of this supposition there is and can be, in the nature of things, no positive proof. Those who adopt it may, with the easy self-deception of speculative zeal, unwittingly transfer to the gospel a conceit of their own engendering. And certainly the Christianity of those who conjure into it whatever their fancy affects, is quite as arbitrary in one way as, in another, the Christianity of those who conjure out of it whatever their fancy distastes. The *plus* and *minus* are equally wide of the truth.

But who shall undertake to say, on historical and

critical grounds, precisely how much or how little lay in those utterances of the early Church which have come down to us, and what were the absolute limits of their vision? In the writings of St. Paul there are indications of a mind that out-travelled the perceptions of his contemporaries, and saw in Christianity a possible solution of quite other problems than the rehabilitation of the Jewish State. The thoughtful reader, in some of these Epistles, and especially in that to the Romans, comes upon traces of an intellectual survey which took in a good deal more than the civil world of that time. St. Paul was the first interpreter of Christ, who seems to have divined his historic significance. To the Palestinian apostles the Christ was but the fulfilment of the hope of Israel. To the author of the fourth Gospel he was only a bodied Word, a demonstration of godhead on a spiritual plane for spiritual ends. Paul brought Christianity down from heaven to earth, as Socrates did philosophy, and brought it out of the little sanctum of Judaism into the broad scene of the nations. Christianity, in his view, was the universal mediator, the reorganizer of universal history. A Jew by descent, but a citizen of the world in his new-born consciousness, he credited the gospel with cosmopolitan aims. And one of those aims, — the one which includes all others, — he expressed by a term which is rendered "atonement" in our English version of the text. This brave English word, in its literal and etymological sense, is itself a contribution to theology to be received with all thankfulness. No modern language, that I am aware of, possesses a word of precisely the same import. Nay, the word "atonement," I suppose, though it seems presumptuous and sounds paradoxical to say so, expresses more exactly than even the original Greek the essential point in Paul's doctrine of reconciliation. It expresses the result of that process of which the original Greek and the corresponding word in other versions suggest the method.

Atonement is one of those ideas which have suffered much belittling in ecclesiastical hands. It has never, since Paul's day, had justice done to it in systems of theology. Theologians, especially Protestant theologians, have belittled the idea by a capital misconception, which makes atonement a private concern of the individual soul, a private adjustment of the soul with God. Nothing could be more foreign to Paul's view and the views of the early Church, nothing more foreign to the spirit of the gospel, than Calvin's idea of "Particular Redemption." Paul, if I rightly conceive him, would have utterly repudiated such an idea; — a redemption determined by personal favoritism, — a redemption accorded to a favored few, himself being one of the few, and denied to the rest of mankind. He who wrote, "I could wish that myself were accursed from Christ for my brethren, my kinsman according to the flesh," was not likely to limit the grace of God by personal preference, or to put *selection* in the place of the *election* which he taught. That election itself he saw to be only initial, and neutralized by the new dispensation: "Blindness in part hath happened to Israel until the fulness of the Gentiles be come in, and then all Israel shall be saved. For God hath concluded them all in unbelief, that he might have mercy upon all."

The error of particular redemption, like so many others in theology, has arisen from the transference of the operation and fruits of the atonement from this earthly world to a life beyond the grave. The antichristian absurdity of such a redemption appears the moment the doctrine is applied to human life. The atonement comtemplated by Paul is no private privilege, and no transmundane acquisition; but a public grace, of which the individual becomes partaker through his social relations and not by private negotiation, and the realization of which is society itself in the measure of its moral and Christian progress.

The apostle, cherishing the analogy of Judaism, connects this idea with that of sacrifice in the death

of Christ, — whether in the way of cause and effect, or of typical demonstration and ecclesiastical parallelism, we need not stop to inquire. The idea of sacrifice is an ineradicable element in religion, and could not fail to be retained as an image and object of contemplation when it ceased to be a ritual function. The Church of Rome has made the image itself a part of its ritual, in the elevation of the host; that is, in the presentation by the priest to the worshipping assembly of a wafer which represents the host or victim offered for man in the person of Christ. By the daily repetition of this pantomimic sacrifice, the Church of Rome symbolizes the perpetuity of that atonement which is not a single but a constant operation of the one sacrifice which, as the writer to the Hebrews says, Christ offered once for ever. In that dumb show, when the priest at the tinkling of the bell uplifts the sacred monstrance, according to the theory of Roman symbolism, the breach that sundered heaven and earth is momentarily evened, and God and man are atoned.

Rome symbolizes the perpetuity of the atonement in the ecclesiastical sense of sacrifice for sin; but, not divining its deeper sense and its application to human society, Rome has failed to represent what is more important than its perpetuity, — viz., its progressiveness. A progressive reconciliation

MiCU

of the earthly and heavenly in human life, — a mutual interpenetration of the two, — this I conceive to be the real import of the doctrine of atonement. An historic process, not a theological device, is what I find in it.

The general formula of earthly and heavenly includes many opposites, or supposed opposites, which constitute accordingly the several topics of atonement, — natural and supernatural, finite and infinite, temporal and eternal, God and man, the Church and the world, mortal and immortal. It is the tendency of false religion, in all dispensations, to emphasize and magnify these antagonisms. A true religion tends to harmonize them. Therefore we say, "The atonement in Christ;" inasmuch as the reconciliation of these antitheses is the consummation of the Christian idea. I select for present consideration one or two of the more significant.

I. Natural and supernatural. The antagonism here is not in the thing, but in the thought. It is a classification, under these two heads, of ordinary and extraordinary phenomena and powers. The term "natural" is used to denote the stated and intelligible facts of human experience, — those which have been investigated, referred to known agencies, and ranged under formulas which we call laws. Together they constitute the "System of Nature," so called; which of course can mean nothing more than our observation or systematization of Nature. The system is in us, and not in the things themselves. Whatever transcends these familiar experiences, — facts which are not embraced in this system, and seem not to tally with it, — are either denied, or classed as "supernatural." They are denied by those who cannot tolerate that their little system, with which so much pains has been taken, should be proved imperfect by facts or alleged facts which it will not take in. It is the feeling of the child who fancies he has made a perfect figure with the bits of ivory in his Chinese puzzle, and subsequently discovers that one of the seven pieces has been left out. He would fain suppress the refractory piece. It is certainly more agreeable to question the facts, than to entertain the suspicion of the "more things in heaven and earth" of which the poet speaks. Nor is any thing gained, that I can see, by admitting the facts, so long as they are excluded from the sphere of Nature, to which humanity with its destinies belong. The term "supernatural" supposes two distinct agencies, Nature and God; that is, it separates Nature from God, — it makes Nature godless, — and so introduces into the scheme of religion a dualism which is Manichean and antichristian. The progress of Christian thought will abolish this dualism, will teach that the ordinary and extraordinary in human affairs are equally natural and equally divine. All phenomena are natural, and all causes that produce them are natural. A genuine miracle would be the most natural of all; it would be Nature in her immediateness, Nature unveiled, without the illusion of statedness which so befogs poor human wit, and stands instead of Nature in the vulgar mind. The spirit is Nature's innermost life: he who has most of it is most natural. Who so natural as Jesus? The miracles recorded of him are proofs of his naturalness. Suppose them mythical, they would still in a certain sense be illustrations of it, as legitimate impressions of his great nature on contemporary minds. Whoever shall attain to the same spirituality will experience that *rapport* with the central Power which the record ascribes to Jesus; he will have that sympathy with the universal Will, that shall make all things possible which seem desirable. If miracles show themselves in him, they will be the most natural things which he does. In proportion as men grow towards spiritual maturity, it will come to be seen that there is but one power in the greatest and in the least, — in the resurrection of the dead and the shooting of a grain of wheat. In the fulness of that spiritual maturity the godless distinctions of false religion will be done away, and natural and supernatural be atoned.

II. God and man. Religion begins with a huge separation between these two. In its barbarous stage, where it takes the form of fetishism, that with which man has least sympathy is most likely to serve him as God. His god must be a fright to command his homage. A monster will answer that purpose better than a human model of power and goodness. He will sooner bow to a crocodile or misshapen stone than to any fellow of his tribe. And so, at the other end of the spiritual line, monotheism in its earlier forms, Hebrew monotheism, determined an absolute separation, an impassable gulf, between God and man. God was in heaven, and man on the earth: the only relation between them was legislation on one side and subjection on the other; arbitrary exaction there, unconditional obedience here; commandment above and fear below, and burning and thundering Sinai between. Theology before the Christian era had outgrown this view, and sought to correct it with the notion of a second God, not quite so distant as the awful first, — a kind of prime minister of the Majesty on high, intermediate between Him and this earthly world. The Christian Church took up the idea, applied it to Christianity, and turned it about and about, and worked it this way and that way, to see if a bridge could be made of it to span the supposed gulf between God and man. The attempt was a failure: the bridge would not reach. If the second God is a creature, as the Arians affirmed, there was still a gulf between him and the first. If he is no creature, but consubstantial, "very God of very God," as the Athanasians claimed, then there is a gulf between him and man. Say with Apollinaris, that he took the place in Jesus of the human soul; then Jesus was no man at all, but God appearing in a human form. Say with Theodore of Mopsuestia, that God was united to a genuine human individual in Christ; and the statement, if analyzed, can mean no more than that God was associated with Jesus and co-operated with him, — both uniting in one effect: which is true enough, but if predicated of Christ alone constitutes no substantial union of God with man, and leaves human nature where it was before. Practically, the second God is no nearer to man than the first. The gulf is still unbridged. The Holy Spirit which proceeds from both might supply the missing link, were it not that the Holy Spirit is conceived by one party as a priestly charm, by another as a fitful gust from the heavenly shore. Neither the second God nor the third can quite reach to bridge the gulf. The Trinity sits throned on high, — man grovels below. Theology can mediate no real union between the human and divine.

What theology did not finish, religion had already found in the consciousness of Christ. "I am in the Father, and the Father in me." "He that hath seen me hath seen the Father." "I and the Father are one." Here is no doctrine, but a human experience. To make theological capital of such language, to coin this high utterance into dogma, is almost a sin against the Holy Ghost. It is no dogma, but the ecstasy of religion; which, as we saw, having begun with the widest separation of the human and divine, ends with declaring the absolute union of the two. What Jesus affirms of himself he prophesies and implores for all his followers: "As thou, Father, art in me, and I in thee, that they may be one in us." Theology has never done justice to this saying, has never fairly faced it, has never dared to appropriate its awful import. The contrast between the idea of humanity one with God, and the actual world of any past time, has seemed so monstrous, that the words have remained a dead letter as to any serious application of their import. The world, no doubt, is very godless; society everywhere far below the Christian ideal, — yet somewhat less so than in ages past. Assuredly the humanities have made some progress. The relief of want, the instruction of ignorance, the reform of vice, are more and more objects of care and effort in Christian society. And these humanities are also divinities. All agencies and organizations based on purely moral ideas, and working in the spirit of faith and love for moral ends, are the very presence and inworking of God in society. Thus God progressively incarnates himself in human life; and thus human life, with progressive edification, builds itself up into God. In the measure in which these agencies accomplish their design; in the measure in which sin and wrong are weeded out of the walks of men, in which the law of love asserts its sway and extends its empire over human life, in which the face of society conforms to the image of Christ, — in that measure the atonement proceeds until God and man are one; one not only in community of purpose and identity of will, but one in the consciousness of mutual, perfect, and unchangeable love. "All mine are thine, and thine are mine," "thou in me and I in thee," must be the confession, must express the consciousness of collective humanity, if the kingdom of heaven is any thing more than a Jewish chimera or a waking dream.

III. As the greater includes the less, the union of God and man involves the resolution of all the other antitheses named; and especially that of temporal and spiritual, or the Church and the world. The line of that division bisects all religions and civilizations hitherto. The more immature, the more crude and idolatrous the faith of an age or people, the more it has emphasized and organized this dualism. In the elder faiths it developed an hereditary priesthood and a hieratic government, and culminated in the deification of the spiritual function; as witnessed to this day in the twice-born Brahman of India, and the Khubilai Khan or Lama-God of Thibet. The separation of sacred and profane in human life bears an inverse ratio to the progress of religion. The ruder the religion, the wider the separation.

The genius of Christianity, as shown in the Gospels, is wholly and gloriously adverse to such separations. While it sanctifies the world, it secularizes the Church, and looks to the doing away of all distinction between the two. Jesus was emphatically a man of the world. The daily walks of men were familiar to his feet; their daily joys and sorrows, and all their wants, familiar to his heart. When he went to the marriage feast, he went as a wedding guest, and brought his own contribution, material as well as moral, to the general joy. When he went among publicans and sinners, he sat at their tables without reserve, and shrank from no contact with the daughters of vice. Religion might flaunt her sanctimonies, — he wore no phylactery but his native holiness; he suffered no sabbath to check his humanity, and no tradition to bound his freedom. The genius of Christianity abhors professional sanctity; it abhors a priestly caste.

But the genius of Christianity is one thing; its historic envelopment, another. Christendom hastened to establish a priesthood; the priesthood hastened to invest itself with exclusive and magical powers. Professional Christianity hastened to separate its holies from the profane world. Into the desert and into the cell, into sackcloth and cowl, went all the religion, and starved and scourged and tormented itself, until piety and penance were synonymous terms, and a wasted, woe-begone figure, bending over a death's-head or clasping a crucifix, became the exponent and symbol of devotion. With equal zeal, in the opposite direction, the secular interest hastened to withdraw from the ghastly presence of the sons of God. Into the saddle and into the field and into the pirate ship, into violence and blood and lawless rapine, rushed the godless outside world, and knew no religion but the most external, — passive reception of sacraments that kept the Devil, who was also external, at bay.

All through the centuries of the middle age, this sheer separation of the spiritual and temporal prevailed. Religion was a specialty, a distinct profession, nowise incumbent on the world at large. The very word became a synonyme of separation, — as in Southern Europe to this day a religious person denotes a monk or a nun. The institution of chivalry was a kind of mediation between these extremes. When martial prowess was married to saintly devotion, when the swordsman became a missionary of righteousness, a limit was set to the reign of brute force on the one hand, and of ghostly pretension on the other. This beautiful growth of the middle age is the type of a still continuing mediation between the Church and the world, represented in our day by practical philanthropy and social reform. For still the separation continues, — in Protestant Christendom still continues. Religion is still a specialty, a distinct concern. A sharply dividing line, in most Protestant sects, distinguishes with superior holiness the sheep of the inner communion from the necessary but unsanctified goats of the outer fold. These distinctions, whatever their value in view of the present state and stage of Christian culture, are nevertheless proofs of an immature Church and imperfect atonement. "When that which is perfect is come, then that which is in part shall be done away." The Church as at present interpreted, is a partiality; religion, as now understood, is a partiality: partialities which are providential, indispensable hitherto; the abolition or disuse of which would only leave us the opposite partialities of worldliness and irreligion uncorrected and unchecked. Better that the Church and the world, spiritual and temporal, business and religion, should stand opposed to each other as now, than that the world and its temporalities should stand alone, and Church and religion have no standing. Nevertheless, it must not be forgotten that the perfect state is the interpenetration of these opposites; that the true Church is society informed by the Spirit of God; that true religion is the health of the spirit manifest in healthy and beneficent action. All other religion, — religion that detaches itself from the business of life, — however commended by saintly precept and illustrated by saintly example, is disease, or at best a provisional experience. The sanctities of man are not his separations, but his communications; and, as language itself instructs us, holiness and wholeness are one. Atonement will not be complete until the distinction of sacred and profane, temporal and spiritual, business and religion, the Church and the world, is practically neutralized; until these dislocations of human nature are healed, these severed parts and processes atoned in one undivided and absolute life.

IV. That absolute life, that mighty solvent in which flesh and spirit are resolved, and natural and supernatural fused in one, — shall it not also fuse and resolve the last and longest contradiction of time, the contradiction of mortal and immortal, the here and the hereafter, earth and heaven in the local sense of those terms? "The last enemy that shall be put under is death." The apostle who wrote thus had a vision of a state in which death should be no more. The popular belief transfers that state from this human earth to some unknown region beyond; and Christians talk of "going to heaven" in much the same way that the ancients talked of going to the place of departed souls: with this exception, that the going in the one case is a going up, in the other it was a going down; but with this advantage on the side of the ancients, that they had a distinct conception of the whereabouts of their imaginary world, and the route by which it was reached. I see no reason for this translocation; no reason for supposing that the sphere of planetary attraction ceases with the dissolution of the animal frame; no reason for supposing that the planet's hold of its own is bounded by the animal life. On the contrary, it accords with reason to believe that the soul — which makes the individual, and which must not be confused with the accompanying spirit, which is not individual —

is a part of the planetary life, and can never, while that life endures, be divorced from the system to which it belongs.

It may be that the human body, without the intervention of death, will one day become so etherealized as to be impervious to death, — will become death-proof; that in this way mortal will put on immortality. However this may be, I am persuaded that dying is not migration, that this earth is man's future and eternal abode, and that in the course of human development the time will come when death shall no longer occupy the place it now does in the human economy; but, if in any sense it continues to be, will be practically, as an enemy, put under. In the final and consummate atonement, this last antagonism of mortal and immortal, earth and heaven, will be atoned. There will be no talk then of "going to heaven," as in the Gospel there is no such word. We do not go to heaven, but heaven comes to us. They whose inner eye is opened see heaven, and they who see it are in it, and the air to them is thick with angels, like the background of Raphael's "Mother in glory."

I have dwelt on those topics of atonement which seemed to me most significant, and which best illustrate the practical working and thoroughness of the great historic process. It might seem that the survey should embrace, among other adjustments, the reconciliation of science and religion, — the two interests which divide the mental life of the age, and whose growing antagonism has been to many good people a source of uneasiness in recent time. But this antagonism belongs rather to the realm of thought than to that of actual life, with which our view of the atonement is mainly concerned. As such, it is properly included in that of natural and supernatural.

The opposition of science and religion is discrepance of method, rather than contrariety of aim. Both are ministers of social well-being, and therefore co-agents in the work of atonement; for whatever promotes the general well-being is an agent in that work. Both seek the good of society, but in ways how different! The one by unfolding and applying the laws of Nature; the other by revealing and applying the laws of the soul. The one by facilitating social converse; the other by ennobling its quality. The one by evening physical obstructions and extending the material comforts of life; the other by eradicating moral evils and deepening the import and consciousness of life into life everlasting. Both look to human well-being; both, if genuine, end there. But here is the rub! The action and success of religion depend on certain ideas and beliefs which science, if it does not impugn, mistrusts and discredits, because unable to verify them by its own methods,—methods approved in its own domain. Such ideas as Providence, Revelation, or God in history, Immortality,—nay, the idea of a God, in any proper sense of the word,—is out of the domain of science, and is only admitted, if at all, on the ground of the moral sense.

The stupendous successes of science in her own dominion have emboldened her to claim jurisdiction over territory not amenable to physical authority, and to war against dynasties that sit "on no precarious throne, nor borrow leave to be." Religion acknowledges with all thankfulness the share in the atonement which science may rightfully claim,—her mediatorial agency in the sensible world, where her ministry is always a ministry of reconciliation, smoothing the hostilities, adjusting the alienations, yoking the contrary forces, compelling the antagonisms of Nature, and stretching the electric cord of intelligence from city to city, and from land to land, across all solitudes and under all deeps. Subsidizing for that purpose the swiftest of material agents, by a kind of earthly omnipotence, she compels the lightnings to be our couriers, and drives them by the wondrous road she has built for their journeyings along "the bottom of the monstrous world," where, since the birth of time, no sentient heart ever beat, no voice ever broke the eternal silence, no thought ever penetrated but the omnipresent thought of God! Through those untrodden and sunless realms a road has been built for the lightnings to go upon and to carry intelligence and conscious thought and purpose, and tidings of war and peace, and solemn greetings, across the unsympathizing vastness, virtually annihilating the hostile element, and so fulfilling the prophecy, that there be "no more sea."

Religion accepts with all thankfulness the mediations of science; but religion will not suffer science to dictate her beliefs, or to strike from her creed whatever the text-books fail to explain. When M. Renan declares it to be an absolute rule of criticism to admit no miracle in history, because the condition of a miracle is faith, religion is content that men should render to Criticism the things which are Criticism's, and to Faith the things which are Faith's. But when he insists that "the faith of humanity" rests on a fancy of Mary Magdalene, religion can but smile at the huge inconsistency which, seeking to escape an improbability, tumbles into a tenfold greater, and which sacrifices the real order of Nature to an idol so named. Of the real order of Nature, the first principle is, that every effect must have an adequate cause. The Christian Church was founded in the belief of the resurrection of Christ. What was the cause of that belief? To rest the growth of ages on a woman's delusion, is a greater invasion and inversion of the order of Nature than any miracle recorded in the New Testament. It is one of the mistakes of the time, to overrate the authority of physical science, whose judgments are valid only on purely material ground, and lose their conclusiveness when a spiritual factor intervenes. To deny the spiritual factor is the instinct of science, but also her weakness; an unconscious confession of her own limitation, which many mistake for the limit of truth. In the world of phenomena, science is queen; in the world of causes, she is a bungler and an alien. It is only within her proper and bounded domain of physical inquiry that she can claim to be interpreter of the methods of God. It has been said that religion has no function "which may not be discharged by science." If so, let us hasten to make up for lost time, for wasted hours of worship, since the foundation of the world. Let us straightway convert our temples into lecture-rooms. Cease idle prayers, cease drivelling praise! Henceforth let the weekly holy-day be devoted to scientific investigations. Let the children of the Sunday-school repeat for litany the multiplication-table instead of the Lord's Prayer. Let anatomical and physiological demonstrations replace the broken body of the Eucharist and the waters of baptism. Let font and chalice be sent to the curiosity-shop, and shelved with Chinese joss-sticks and hideous Indian gods. Vanish, ye dim surmises of a supersensuous world! Vanish the Holy Ghost! Let serviceable gases entertain the well-spent hour!

Science can do much; but there are functions of religion which cannot be discharged by science. Not yet has science succeeded to the throne of God in the heart of mankind. We are no nearer to God in our knowledge than in our ignorance, unless to the knowledge of Nature be added the knowledge of spiritual truth. On the contrary, without the spiritual complement, the more scientific, the more atheistic. Science can do much; but there are straits in life where science can afford neither counsel nor aid. Standing by the bedside of his dying mother, says a German humorist, "I thought over all the great and little inventions of man, — the doctrine of souls, Newton's system of attraction, the Universal German Library, the *Genera Plantarum*, the *Magister Matheseos*, the *Calculus Infinitorium*, the right and oblique ascension of the stars and their parallaxes. But nothing would answer. And she lay out of reach, lay on the brink, and was going; and I could not even see where she would fall. Then I commended her to

God, and went out and composed a prayer for the dying, that they might read it to her. She was my mother, and had always loved me so dearly; and this was all I could do for her. . . . We are not great, and our happiness is, that we can believe in something greater and better."

I said there are two ways of meeting the demand for a truly liberal and rational religion; — two ways of meeting, but only one way of solving, the problem. Not in the way of denial, but of faith, the solution must come, if at all. Faith in Christ as the type of consummate humanity; faith in humanity as prefigured in Christ; faith in God as humanity's fulness and justification; faith in reason as God's interpreter; faith in revelation as reason's consummate flower; faith in society as ever-progressive realization of reason and of God, — is not this the desired solution?

The Christian confession need not bound our religious sympathy. All religions that devoutly aspire, all religions that diligently labor, all religions that minister to human weal, deserve our sympathy and claim our respect. But Christianity is more than religion; it is history's highway, humanity's thoroughfare. The paths that diverge from it will return to it again, or lose themselves in nothingness. Whatever dissents from it is partiality and limitation; in it is wholeness, and the widest vision, and the largest liberty.

V.

THE NATURAL HISTORY OF THEISM.

A GLANCE at the world acquaints us with the prevalence of worship, consequently of some conception of Deity, in human society.

We cannot indeed say what used to be said, what Plutarch and Cicero so confidently affirmed, that belief in God is found wherever man is found. A better-informed ethnology contradicts that assertion. There are certainly peoples in whose life, if travellers report them truly, this element is altogether wanting. The natives of the valley of La Plata and of Paraguay, according to Azara, were entirely destitute of any religious beliefs or rites when he travelled among them. The missionaries who visited those tribes, supposing that they must have some sort of religion, took for idols the figures carved upon their pipes and bowls, and burned those implements accordingly. Others, seeing them beat the air on the appearance of the new moon, imagined that they worshipped that luminary. "But the positive fact is," says Azara, "that they worship nothing in the world, and have absolutely no religion."[1]

According to Crantz, the Greenlanders had no religious ceremonies, and exhibited no sign of religious life. Schoolcraft describes the Camanches as equally godless.

Sir John Lubbock has accumulated a mass of testimony to the same effect from travellers in regions inhabited by savage tribes. M. Bik inquired of the Arafuras what power they invoked in time of need when their fishing vessels were overtaken by storm, and no human aid could save. The answer was, that they knew not on whom to call in such straits; did he know? and would he be so good as to inform them? The Zulu chief when he heard of God would transfix him with his spear. "And yet this was a man whose judgment on other subjects would command attention." Very pathetic is the Kaffir's confession: "I ask myself, Who has touched the stars with his hands? on what hills do they rest? The waters are never weary; they know no other law than to flow without ceasing from morning till night, and from night till morning; but where do they rest, and who makes them flow? The clouds come and go, and burst in water over the earth; whence come they,

[1] See "Voyages," II. 3, 137. Quoted by Schelling, Philosophie der Mythologie, 73.

and who sends them? . . . I cannot see the wind; what is it, and who makes it blow? . . . Do I know how the corn sprouts? Yesterday there was not a blade in my field; to-day I returned and found some. Who can have given to the earth the wisdom and the power to produce it? Then I buried my face in both my hands."

These exceptions do not disprove an innate tendency to worship in man; they only show that this tendency is not always active, that certain conditions are required for its manifestation. Its state of abeyance in the South American savage no more disproves its existence in him, than its state of suspension disproves its existence in the secularist or unbeliever of Christian lands. Still Cicero's assertion, that no people is so rude as not to have some notion of Deity, must be taken with this qualification, that religion is *usually* found in the savage state, and *always* in civil society.

We may say, then, that belief in Deity is natural to man; is one of the primary forces of the soul.

The origin of this belief is a question of wide dispute. The "*fecit timor*" of the atheist poet, the "*notio insita*" of Cicero, the original-revelation theory of Cudworth and later divines, represent the range of opinion concerning it. Hume was the first to distinguish between the "foundation in reason" and the "origin in human nature" of the idea of God.[1] He supposes polytheism to have preceded monotheism in the course of human development. And this supposition is confirmed by ethnological research. On the other hand, a not unreasonable prejudice in Christian lands has leaned to the opposite view. Reasoning from our idea of God and the seeming necessities of human nature, one might presume that the Being of whom the knowledge is so essential would make Himself known to man in the beginning, that this knowledge would enter into Nature's dower, would form a part of the primal outfit of human kind. And such has been the presumption of most Christian writers who have treated this topic prior to Hume. They have held that the first of mankind were endowed with this saving knowledge; that a revelation of the Godhead was made to original man, which soon waxed dim, was gradually perverted and finally lost; that all polytheisms — Indian, Phœnician, Grecian, and others — are disintegrations and corruptions of an aboriginal monotheism.

To this hypothesis there are grave objections, not to speak of the *a priori* difficulty of supposing that so essential a good once possessed could be lost to all but a fraction of the human race. A revelation which could be so easily forfeited must

---

[1] Natural History of Religion, Introduction.

have been quite inadequate; and, if thus inadequate, why bestowed? Why did not the God who gave it maintain it, or immediately replace it when lost? Polytheism is no more deducible from monotheism by division and dissolution of unity, than monotheism, as some have maintained, is derivable from polytheism by concentration and absorption of the many into one. Each has its own independent origin.

Certain it is that history knows nothing of the primal revelation which this theory affirms. History finds men in the earliest ages which its scrutiny has yet reached, possessed with the crudest conceptions of Godhead, — the earlier, the cruder, the farther from the truth. It finds savage tribes or incipient nations involved in thick midnight of spiritual ignorance, blindly feeling after something divine.

And yet if we inquire whence the thought, the presentiment of any thing divine to feel after, we shall have to admit some innate impression, some dim, instinctive sense of Deity, antecedent to even the most imbecile groping after God. So much must be conceded in order to account for the first and feeblest essays in that kind. An intimation of Deity[1] implanted by Deity's self in the human constitution. We cannot call it an idea, for ideas are

[1] "Notio Dei insita." Cicero.

perceptions, and cannot be properly said to exist where the object is not consciously present to the subject. And yet it is something more than mere perceptivity; it is preparation to perceive and the certainty of perceiving whenever the requisite conditions shall concur, — external suggestion and internal demand. It is with the discovery of God as it is with the discovery of self. The infant has no idea of self, and yet that idea is sure to arise in the mind in due course of development. It is not communicated from abroad, but generated within. It may therefore be said to pre-exist as impression before it exists as idea.

The ancients, especially the Platonists, recognized this mental condition, and called it "prolepsis," anticipation. Cicero defines it as an antecedent notion,[1] requiring further development, and so applies it to the being of God. He speaks of a God who reposes in the notion of the mind [2] as in a track or impress he has made of himself.

To civilized man the idea of God arrives with instruction, which does but fructify a pre-existing germ. Without instruction, the idea is certainly not developed in the individual mind with the same

---

[1] "Notionem appello quod Græci tum ἔννοιαν tum πρόληψιν dicunt. Ea est insita et ante percepta cujusque formæ cognitio enodationis indigens." Topica 7.

[2] "Deus ille quem mente noscimus atque in animi notione tanquam in vestigio volumus reponere." De Nat. Deorum, I. 14.

inevitableness with which the mind develops the idea of self. But taking the whole of humanity, we may say that the idea of God is as proper to the race as that of self to the individual. A human being cast from infancy upon absolute solitude, might not have the idea of Divinity in any sense or shape awakened within him. If he did, it would in all likelihood be not the monotheistic idea, but some low form of polytheism or fetishism. Yet even that would be impossible without an innate aptitude for Theism in the soul. Without a prepared niche in human nature, no image occupying the place of Deity and receiving divine honors would ever have been set up. It is idle to talk of fear as possessing this deific power. Fear can make bugbears, but can never convert the bugbear into a God. The brute fears, but the brute knows no God. The brute shuns the object of its fear; in man there is a principle which, in spite of fear, impels him to draw near to some dreaded object with reverential homage. Fear alone would never do that. Fear alone would never have invented worship. It may cringe, but not adore.

The fact is, human nature, prior to all teaching, is conscious of a want which Deity alone can satisfy. It seeks its own complement when it prays; and were there not some affinity between the human and the divine, the soul would never have dreamed so much as the wildest African dream of the unknown God. Human nature requires a God, and prior to all teaching, with no guide but vague anticipation or unreasoning instinct, blindly gropes after something to fill that place in the soul which enlightened Theism fills in civilized man.

Now where will this groping first alight? What being will man first embrace as divine? Will it be one of his own kind; some select individual eminently wise and good? Obviously not, for the reason that humanity lies too near. The savage knows it only in its weakness and imperfection. In the greatest of his tribe he sees only his like. But religion's first impulse is to seek in God something foreign and very different. For this, man is thrown upon irrational Nature. There he encounters the unknown Power whose presence the rudest feels, and endeavors to fix before he is able to reason about it or to state it distinctly to himself. It is not that he infers an intelligent Maker from the wondrous works which meet his eye. That is the act of more advanced reason, to which the idea of God is already familiar. But he feels a Presence in Nature transcending human powers. That silent Presence which we all feel, and feel most profoundly in the deepest solitude, the feeling of which gave birth to Arcadian Pan, the instructed monotheist refers to the one all-present God, the Maker and Father of all. The savage has no such idea, but he has the same feeling, and has it more intense. He is haunted by that felt Presence. In the heart of the forest, on the lonely shore, he feels that he is not alone, that very near him is a Greater than himself. The Power that works in the processes of nature, that breathes in the wind, that drives the cloud, that roars in the thunder, that watches in the stars, — this unseen Power, his undeveloped thought has not yet learned to generalize. With him it is not the one pervading Spirit of whom and by whom are all things. He can only lay hold of it in particular phenomena; he must individualize it, must vest it in some palpable object. And the more grotesque the object, the more abhorrent to taste and reason, the more likely it is to stand for Deity in his conception, as appealing more forcibly to his imagination than nobler and comelier natures. Some misshapen tree or stone that caught his eye at some critical moment of danger or deliverance, of good or ill success, becomes to him an object of adoration, which may or may not be adopted by the tribe. The tribe is more likely to fix on some monstrous or dangerous animal — a serpent, a crocodile, a tiger.

There is no caprice in this, no wilful perversion or turning aside from the truth, no corruption of degenerate humanity; but human nature in its first incipient aspirations, feeling after God, "if haply" it "may find him." The history of religion begins in this way. This is the first, initial act of that spirit which sang the Hebrew litanies and dictated the "Revelation of St. John the Divine." This is what man first finds when he feels after God; he passes by the sun and stars and the upright human form, and lights upon a serpent or a stone. These are objects which millions of human beings worship at this day. Nor are these monstrosities altogether confined to savage tribes. Fetishism mingles with the rites of nations full-grown and refined. It is found in Egypt contemporaneous with the worship of Osiris and the splendors of Luxor and Thebes. It is found in Assyria in the palmiest days of Chaldean civilization. In the most magnificent of cities, in the most flourishing period of its history, the chief object of worship was a serpent, — not a carved symbol, but the living beast, — not as typifying any thing beyond itself, but as actually divine. Arnobius, a Christian convert of the fourth century, relates that in Africa, where he resided, he never, before his conversion, saw a stone on which oil had been poured without paying it homage.[1] Stones smeared with oil and called "Betyls" were among the earliest

[1] Adv. Gent. I. 39.

objects of devotion. The patriarch Jacob, grandson though he was of the first-recorded monotheist, made a "betyl" of the stone which had served him for a pillow in the place where he dreamed the dream of the ladder reaching from heaven to earth. Aerolites were deemed by the ancients especially sacred. The world-famed temple of Diana at Ephesus commemorated one of these meteoric stones.[1] The black stone of the Kaaba at Mecca is also, it is supposed, an aerolite. Devoutly kissed by annual thousands of Mussulman pilgrims, it remains to this day a relic-fetish in the midst of the purest monotheism.

The next stage in the religion of Nature, still within the sphere of realism, is separated by a wide remove from the first in dignity and import, — Sabaism,[2] or more properly Astrolatry, the worship of the heavenly bodies.

The most positive of natural phenomena, the most universal and appreciable of natural benefits, is light. It is no mere figure of speech to call it the "life" of the world. It is precisely that. The difference between light and no light to the eye is the difference between the visible all and noth-

---

1 Διοπετοῦς, Acts xix. 35.

2 According to Chwolsohn, the use of this term to designate a form of religion is incorrect. Die Ssabier. Vorrede, 19.

ing. Historically, it is the difference between creation and no creation, between cosmos and chaos. Without it no vegetable, without it no animal, no organized life. Without it, —

> "The world was void:
> The populous and the powerful was a lump,
> Seasonless, herbless, treeless, manless, lifeless;
> A lump of death, a chaos of hard clay."

The old astrolaters may not have had sight of the whole of the truth poetically imaged by Byron, and scientifically expounded by Moleschott and Tyndall; but they saw enough to satisfy them that light is the greatest of material benefactions. What wonder that the sun, the prime source of that light, should be worshipped as the prince of the heavenly powers, and the other luminaries, in their several degrees, as blessed and divine! "Hail, holy Light," is the matin song of religion emerging from the night of fetishism. Hallowed be sun and stars! and hallowed be fire, the earthly antitype of heavenly light and heat! Fire, the purifying power, from which the word "pure" is derived, which separates the ethereal from the earthly, and re-unites it with its kindred sky! Fire, in its finished form of flame, expresses aspiration: it suggests the pyramid; may it not have suggested the earliest use of that structure? The pyramid is a petrified flame.

But sun, stars, and fire are not the only benefactions of Nature. Thought pauses upon these as the most commanding; but religion finds other kindred objects of devout contemplation. Holy, also, is the vaulted sky outstretched as a tent, the sun's tabernacle; holy the circumfluent air, the fitful winds, the stedfast earth. With the glowing appreciation of the powers of Nature, with the action of the plastic imagination upon them, they come in time to be personified and worshipped as personal agents: and so the next step in the progress of natural religion [1] is impersonation of natural powers resulting in mythology. Of this impersonation the hymns of the Rig-Veda represent the initial stage; of this we have in the Osiris-cult [2] of ancient Egypt, the first fully developed mythology: Bramanism is its greatest social product; Greek poetry and art, its noblest intellectual creations.

One step farther brings us to the top and consummation of natural religion. The elements are great; the natural man renders them instinctive homage: but to cultivated, self-possessed

---

[1] I use this phrase in the sense of Nature-worship, not in the current sense of rational religion, which seems to me a misuse of the term.

[2] According to Bunsen, the Osiris-cult preceded Egyptian zoolatry; but this can be true only of its adoption by the priesthood, not of its intellectual genesis. See Gott in der Geschichte, Vol. II. 27.

thought there is something greater than these. Conscious intelligence, reason, — in a word, the rational soul, is more than sun or stars, or wind or flood. And the rational soul is man. Unconscious Nature is great; but man is greater. Not man as we commonly behold him, the drivelling imbecile of every-day life, but man as poetic imagination apprehends him, — the ideal man, divested of earthly limitations and imperfections, superior to accident, unvexed by care, impregnable to fear, invulnerable, immortal, rejoicing in eternal youth. What image of Divinity can equal this? What impersonation of elemental powers, rude, Titanic, hundred-handed, can vie with this glorified human type? Surely, if there be gods, they must be divine men. The Greeks saw this. They alone, or they first, of ancient nations — the Athenians especially, with their democratic leanings — perceived the import and worth of man, and embodied that perception in their divinities. They expressed it in two immortal myths; one retrospective, the other prospective. The first is the conquest of the Titans by the Olympians, "the younger gods;" the second is the Chained Prometheus. The former demonstrates the superiority of conscious intelligence over lawless, however gigantic, force, — cosmos mastering chaos; the latter typifies the present abeyance, premonitory of the ultimate triumph, of humanity, — the triumph of right over will, of reason over fear, of the rational service of human kind over all religion in which the moral principle is not supreme.

We will call this last and highest stage of natural religion Theanthropism. The Greco-Roman and the Scandinavian mythologies — Hellenism and Odinism — are its two historic examples. Theanthropism is partly a development of the antecedent stage, — the impersonation of natural forces, — and partly the addition of a new element. The Greek divinities were mostly impersonations, but impersonations stamped with a human type and subordinated to it. Other religions had developed gods that were partly human. Such were the Crishna of the Mahabharatta and Egyptian Osiris. What distinguishes Hellenism is its preponderant humanity. Indian and Egyptian worship still clung to the symbol, and often, in accommodation to the symbol, merged the human in the monstrous. Crishna appears with more than the human complement of limbs, Osiris is figured with the head of a bird, Isis with that of a cow, in pictorial representations. The Egyptians had no such impression of the dignity of man as would make the human form the most fitting embodiment of Deity. The human was no more divine in their estimation than the brute, — was even less so, because more familiar, less seemingly mysterious. It is an alien spirit that looks through the eye of the serpent and the ox, and, because alien, mysterious, unfathomable. The more alien, the more divine, in the apprehension of the pre-Hellenic world. With the Greek, on the contrary, the original symbol representing elemental powers was merged in the human person, or retained only as adjunct and decoration, like the bow in the hands of Phœbus, or the winged sandal on the feet of Hermes. Zeus, the divine impersonation of the sky, is a human being of immortal mould. He bears in Homeric verse the epithets of cloud-gatherer and thunder-rejoicing; but the bolt in his right hand is the only visible sign which distinguishes the god from the man.[1]

Moreover, the Greeks introduced a new element into religion, — the worship of actual historical characters, of departed worthies, heroes whose virtues had raised them to the level of the gods. This was something very different from the worship of ancestors, of which traces appear in many of the ancient religions. That was a family rite,

---

[1] It may be objected that the Greek mythology differed from those of India and Egypt, not in its essence, but only in its artistic representations; that its human aspect is only a concession to the claims of art, which abhors the monstrous. But art with the Greeks was the product of religion, and must be regarded as the exponent of pre-existing ideas. It represented conceptions which religion had inspired.

having no connection with public worship, and therefore not in the line of that historic development which I am tracing. The hero-worship of the Greeks and Romans was a part of that Theanthropism which constitutes a distinctive feature of their religion. This I regard as the culmination of the natural religions; just as Christian Theanthropism, springing from a different root, is the culmination of the spiritual or "revealed." To that different root let us now direct our attention.

We have traced the progress of the idea of God in the way of natural religion through the several stages of Fetishism, Astrolatry, Impersonation of physical forces, and Theanthropism; God as terrestrial creature, God as celestial radiance, God as personified elemental power, and God as man. Observe that these different conceptions, with only a partial exception in the case of the last, have one trait in common, one capital defect; to wit, the absence of that moral element which makes the distinguishing feature, the very foundation, of those religions which we call "revealed." Even in Hellenism, the moral element is found only as an incidental trait, like the chastity of Artemis and the avenging function of the Furies; not as a necessary constituent. Even in Theanthropism the moral is subordinate to the physical.

The reason is obvious. Natural religion is derived from the contemplation of external Nature; but external Nature exhibits no trace of moral life. There is no apparent sympathy in Nature with moral ends, no faintest intimation of the moral law. The elements are no respecters of persons: they know neither sinner nor saint. The sun smiles alike on the evil and the good. The same moon lights the robber and the minister of mercy on their several ways. The same breeze propels the merchant's and the pirate's sail. Traitor and patriot, murderer and missionary, cannibal and Christian, all have the same Nature for their heritage, and find in Nature the same accommodation. The blue sky bends over all, the hospitable earth entertains all, — all are served by Nature's laws.

How, then, should natural religion attain to the idea of the moral law? The deep saith, "It is not in me;" earth and sky have not found it. But is not the moral law written in the heart of man? Religion has only to look there, has only to look within, to find moral obligation, and from it to infer a moral Ruler of the universe, the holy and just God of monotheism. True, and this is precisely what distinguishes natural religion from "revealed." When man looks within, looks deep enough to find moral obligation, and to refer it to the power and law of which it is the witness, the whole system of natural religion is done away. A revelation has been made in him of the one true God. Revelation is not from without, but from within: it is moral intuition. God reveals himself, not by sensible apparition, but by his witness in the soul. That testimony, first heard by elect individuals, — meditative men, like Abraham, Zoroaster, Moses, Jesus, — and declared by them, becomes what we call a "revelation," or divine dispensation of religion.

Monotheism, then, comes not by the way of natural religion, seeking God without and fusing its many gods into one, but by reflection seeking God within; and *the difference between natural and revealed religion consists in this, that in the former the religious sentiment is turned outward, and that in the latter it is turned inward.*

Quite otherwise, the phrase "Natural Religion," or, more properly, "Natural Theology," is commonly used to designate those primordial verities which constitute the substance of monotheistic religion. This use of the term dates from Raymond de Sebonde,[1] who wrote, in the beginning of the fifteenth century, a work which Montaigne, at the

[1] "Theologiæ naturalis nomine primus usus est Raymundus de Sebonde, natione Hispanus, ineunte, sec. xv. auctor libri primum editi Daventriæ et Theologia Naturalis, sive Liber Creaturarum inscripti." Wegscheider Institt. Theol. See Herzog's Real-Encyclopädie for an elaborate account of this work.

instigation of his father, turned into French, and to whose defence he devoted the most elaborate, though not the most edifying, of the immortal Essays. The design of Raymond was to vindicate the truths of "Revelation" by proofs and illustrations drawn from Nature. But illustration of a truth by the facts of Nature is one thing, the discovery of it from the contemplation of Nature is another. The phrase "Natural Theology" is an unfortunate one, as fostering the delusion, so widely spread, that the contemplation of Nature teaches monotheism, would teach it to sagacious minds where other teaching has not anticipated that result. The contemplation of Nature teaches no such thing. Nature, the arena of antagonistic forces, the scene of perpetual conflict between good and evil, — Nature, with her sunshine and calm of to-day, her earthquakes and tornadoes of to-morrow, suggests dualism or polytheism, not the one God, the Creator and Father of all. Uninstructed by other teaching, and without monotheism already in the mind, who would ever divine that the desolate crag or blasted volcano was moulded by the same Power that flings the rainbow over it? Who would ever conclude that the scorpion and the bird of Paradise have one Father? Monotheism is not an inference from Nature, but the gift of Tradition, or an intuition of the private soul divinely touched, brooding over its own deep. The first monotheist was one who withdrew his gaze from the starry heaven and the creaturely earth, and found in the secret of his own thought the divine "I am." What they mean, or should mean, who speak thus of "Natural Religion," is that system of truths which Nature studied in the light of revelation confirms, — not the system which Nature teaches. "Rational Religion" would be the fitter term.

To find the one God in Nature, man must first have found him within. The religious mind turned inward encounters another Divinity than the aspects of Nature had suggested to uninstructed contemplation. It finds in the dictates of the moral sense, in imperative warnings and obligations, in the consciousness of spiritual wants and aspirations, a God unknown to natural religion, — a God who is not mere Power and Intelligence and commanding Will, but Goodness, Holiness, Truth, Love. These constitute the God of moral intuition, — a God self-evident, and One in the double sense of onliness and unity. The very idea of such a God excludes multitude. There can be but one absolute Good. Hence revealed religion is necessarily monotheistic. The natural religions, on the other hand, seeking God outwardly, and based on the assumption of a separation in space between God and man, are polytheistic. So long as the divine is conceived as existence *in* Nature instead of Nature's continent, there is no ground for unity in the Godhead. On the contrary, many gods, in that case, will be required to match the many-sidedness of Nature.

Other characteristics follow from this one. The natural religions are sacrificial, the revealed are ethical. The natural are hierarchical, the revealed are congregational. The natural are idolistic, the revealed are scriptural. I speak of tendencies, not of uniform results. In practice these tendencies are often modified by counter influences, by corruptions and perversions. When revelations expand and harden into ecclesiasticism, they sometimes assume the characteristics of naturalism : they become sacrificial, hierarchical, and here and there degenerate into fetishism.

Revelation must not be confused with systems of religion based upon it. Revelation, as such, is purely individual experience; the revealed religions, such as Jehovism, Parsism, Christianity, Islam, are providential and historic growths, which may or may not ensue from that experience. Revelation there has been in the midst of polytheism, and through all the course of human history. For the truths of the Spirit have no date, although the "dispensations" which embody them, like other social products, are subject to historic necessity, and must bide their time. Revelation in individual seers, like Pythagoras, Socrates, and Isaiah, may antedate by centuries the organization of its truths in ecclesiastical polities. It depends, not so much on the clearness and fulness of the revelation, as on the personality with which it is associated, and, of course, on the providential order of events, whether or not the revelation shall become an historic dispensation. The moral intuitions of Plato far transcended those of Mohammed; but the moral force, the momentum of personality, the quality of soul in Mohammed, exceeded the genius of Plato. Adopted by Providence, the slender thought and vast soul of the Arab have rallied around them a fifth part of the human race, whilst the fuller revelation of the Greek could only modify Gentile and Christian theology with its intellectual leaven.

The history of religion is a record of man's search after God. It begins with the lowest, and ends with the highest; it begins with the most foreign, and ends with the most interior; it begins with stones and the beasts of the field, and ends with the Spirit. Every step in this process is divine education. Nature-worship had its meaning and embodied an essential truth. The presence of God in Nature, the sacredness of Nature, is the truth deposited in the human mind by natural religions.

The supremacy of Spirit is the lesson of the revealed. And so the history of religion repeats the story of creation: first that which is natural, then that which is spiritual. The natural man seeks God in Nature; first in the creaturely forms around him, then in the skies. The spiritual knows that the Supreme Presence is not a question of topography; that the throne above the skies is but the last resort of realism; that neither up nor down, nor in any outward direction, but inward and ever inward, is the way to God.

VI.

CRITIQUE OF PROOFS OF THE BEING OF GOD.

THE traditional idea of God is that of a superhuman, extramundane Being, combining in himself all conceivable perfections: from whom, as cause and ground, all other being is derived; on whom, as the universal Providence, all creatures depend; whose will, as moral ideal, is the highest law for intelligent natures.

An idea of such transcendent import could not fail to stimulate in philosophic minds the attempt to verify it by scientific demonstration. Much labor and learning have been expended in such essays; but still the strongest proof of the Being of God is his idea in the universal consciousness of man. I say universal, because the exceptions — of savage atheism at one extreme of humanity, and of philosophic antitheism at the other — do not materially invalidate the fact. God in this idea is his own witness, and asserts himself with a weight of evidence which no resistance of denial, and no ingenuity of speculation, can quite countervail. Attempts to demonstrate the truth of this idea from external data have not been successful. Proofs from Nature may entertain the faith of believers, but cannot conquer unbelief. For though, to predisposed minds possessed with the idea, Nature confesses God with the manifestations, everywhere obvious, of intelligence and law in all her processes and functions, these manifestations carry no conviction to the atheist, who sees in them nothing more than the necessary conditions of being. In the strictness of logic, they have not the binding force of demonstration which the advocates of Theism profess to find in them.

Theology claims that Theism is the best solution of the question, Whence this universe of things? But the truth of an hypothesis which seems to solve a given problem is not established by that solution, unless the solution is complete, and leaves no question unanswered. If it fails to satisfy that condition, it is simply the best hypothesis, nothing more.

What evidence have we of the being of God as a real existence essentially distinct from other being?

The demonstration of Deity attempted by Theism has developed two sorts of proof, known as *a posteriori* and *a priori;* the proof of God from the world, as effect presupposing a cause, and the proof of God from his idea in the mind. The proof *a posteriori* has been subdivided into cosmological and physico-theological. The *a priori* is termed ontological.

The cosmological proof is derived by different theists from different premises. Locke starts with the consciousness which every man has of his own existence. Leibnitz, in his "Confessio Naturæ contra Atheistas," argues from the fact of motion. But, in each and every case in which this mode of reasoning is employed, the gist of the argument is, that all sensible phenomena and all finite existences must be referred at last to an infinite and immaterial Being, as their first cause: inasmuch as every phenomenon and every finite existence is known to be an effect of some antecedent cause, and that cause again an effect of another antecedent, that of another, and so on *ad infinitum;* which gives a beginningless sequence of cause and effect,—as Sir William Hamilton says, "an infinite non-commencement." But that is found to be an absurdity and an impossibility. Therefore, it is argued, we must suppose, as the cause of all, a Being outside of this series, from whom it originates: omnipotent, as being the source of all power and all things; intelligent, because intelligence exists, and cannot be supposed to be derived from the unintelligent,—or, as Locke expresses it, "the cogitative from the uncogitative." Philosophers who rest in this argument, and especially the two that I have named, express the uttermost confidence in its validity. Says Locke (Essay, book iv. ch. 10), "Though this [viz., the being of God] be the most obvious truth that reason discovers, and though its evidence be, if I mistake not, equal to mathematical certainty, yet it requires thought and attention, and the mind must apply itself to a regular deduction of it from some part of our intuitive knowledge. . . . To show, therefore, that we are capable of knowing, *i.e.*, of being certain, that there is a God, and how we may come by this certainty, I think we need go no further than ourselves, and that undoubted knowledge we have of our own existence. I think it is beyond question that man has a clear perception of his own being: he knows certainly that he exists, and that he is something. . . . In the next place, man knows by an intuitive certainty that bare nothing can no more produce any real being than it can be equal to two right angles. . . . If, therefore, we know that there is some real being, and that nonentity cannot produce any real being, it is an evident demonstration that from eternity there has been something; since what was not from eternity had a beginning, and what had a beginning must be produced by something else." He then proceeds to show that "that eternal Being must be most powerful," "and most knowing," "and therefore God." Immaterial, because the "cogitative" cannot have been produced by the "uncogitative."

Leibnitz, after showing that every moving body must derive its motion from some other body, and that, as no body can, by its nature and definition, be self-moving, so no infinite series of moving bodies can explain the origin of motion, — concludes that motion must have originated from a Being who is not body, *i.e.*, from an immaterial and omnipotent First Cause. He thereupon declares his astonishment that this method of demonstrating the existence of God has occurred to no other philosopher of his day. "Et miror neque Gassendum, neque alium inter acutissimos hujus seculi philosophos, præclaram hanc demonstrandæ divinæ existentiæ occasionem animadvertisse."

My reverence for Leibnitz and Locke is as great as any man's, "*sed magis amica veritas.*" I cannot admit the force of either demonstration. Grant that an endless chain of existences, — each antecedent producing its consequent, — an endless sequence of causes and effects, is inconceivable, I cannot see that cutting the knot by the supposition of a self-existent Being outside of that sequence proves the existence of such a Being. It is assumed that every effect must have a cause; then, from the fact that single existences are known to us as effects, it is inferred that the entire universe is effect, and must have a cause outside of itself. To meet this necessity, the argument assumes something outside of the universe that caused it. But what caused the cause? The answer is, It caused itself; it is at once both cause and effect. But, so far as the argument intends the solution of an ontological difficulty, it fails by substituting a greater difficulty for a less. If inconceivableness is the difficulty to be remedied, a self-existent Being outside of the universe, is, to say the least, as inconceivable as a self-existent universe, and burdens us with the additional difficulty of conceiving a point of connection between two beings which, by supposition, are alien the one to the other. The word "omnipotence," or "infinite power," does not explain the difficulty; for all that we know of power is the action of body or spirit on a given object to change its condition. Of its action on any thing not given, *i.e.*, of its action on nonentity to produce entities, we have no knowledge, and can form no conception. We can judge of infinite power, only by what we know of finite power. It must be essentially the same with finite power, differing only in degree, if it be any thing of which we can form any notion, or have any logical right to affirm any thing. If infinite power can out of nonentity produce a universe, finite power should be able out of nonentity, at least to produce some infinitesimal fraction of a universe. But no power of which we have any experience can do this. Strange that so cautious and acute a thinker as Locke should rest in such a conception, or rather in a phrase which conveys no distinct conception to the mind; that, forsaking the sure ground of experience in which his philosophy loves to dwell, he should link his proof of the being of God with so questionable a notion as that of the creation of matter by infinite power. "Is it not impossible," he asks, "to admit of the making of any thing out of nothing, since we cannot possibly conceive it?" and he answers, "No, it is not reasonable to deny the power of an Infinite Being because we cannot comprehend its operations." Here the good man's faith gets the better of his logic. His proof of Deity rests on the inconceivableness of an uncreated universe; nevertheless he acknowledges that creation out of nothing is utterly inconceivable. All that is valid in Locke's demonstration is the first step; viz., that as something now exists, and as nothing cannot produce something, it follows that something must always have existed. Between that and his idea of God there is an unbridged, and, by that method, unbridgeable, gulf. He fails to prove that the universe itself may not have existed from all eternity. "Inconceivable," yes; but creation out of nothing is equally so. "The cogitative cannot have sprung from the uncogitative." Granted; but does it appear how the uncogitative can have sprung from the cogitative? or why both may not be coeternal? The argument, I repeat, gives us a greater difficulty for a less. Either the infinite Being is a part of the series of existences to be explained; and then it would be a simpler solution of the difficulty in question, and an easier cutting of the knot, to suppose, with Spinoza, a self-existent, infinite substance, uniting both attributes, the cogitative and the uncogitative; or else the infinite Being is outside of, and distinct from, the series of existences to be explained, and then the only connection between it and those existences is the arbitrary and unintelligible notion of power.

The demonstration of Leibnitz is liable to the same criticism. It substitutes a greater difficulty for a less. The motion of moving bodies cannot, he contends, be explained by the action of bodies, since no body is self-moving. Therefore we must suppose a Being who is not body, to account for the origin of motion. But how explain the origin of that Being? "*Ratio conclusionis*," he says, *tamdiu plane non reddita est, quamdiu reddita non est ratio rationis*." Here, again, it is a cutting of the knot, which might also be cut by supposing an eternally existing, self-moving world.

Kant (Kr. d. r. V.) charges the cosmological argument with being the ontological in disguise. Accordingly, his refutation of it attacks the alleged ontological character, which I cannot find to be in its intent, whatever there may be of such a character in its essence. But he says of it, moreover, that it hides a whole nest of dialectical assumptions, which transcendental criticism may easily detect and demolish. For example, from contingency it infers causality. But the principle of causality is applicable only to the sensible world: it has no meaning, and we have no criterion of its use, outside of that world. But in this case it is used for the very purpose of transcending the sensible world. In like manner, the inferring of a first cause from the alleged impossibility of an infinite series of given successive causes is not authorized by principles of reason, even within the sphere of experience; much less have we any right to extend the inference beyond that sphere into a world to which the chain does not reach. It is a false self-contentment of reason to regard this series as completed by the final abolition of all conditionality; and then, when nothing further can be idealized, to accept that as the consummation of one's idea. Moreover, the argument confuses the logical possibility of an idea, — the idea of a Being in whom all reality combines, with no internal contradiction, with the transcendental; whereas, the practicability of such a synthesis demands a principle which again would be applicable only within the field of possible experience." "It may be allowed," he says, "to adopt the hypothesis of a Being of the highest adequacy as the cause of all possible effects, in order to facilitate the unity of explanation which reason demands. But to take upon one's self to say that such a Being exists necessarily, is no longer the modest expression of an allowable hypothesis, but the bold assumption of apodictic certainty; for, of that which one professes to cognize as absolutely necessary, the cognition also must carry with it absolute necessity."

The other *a posteriori* argument to be examined is the so-called Physico-theological, more commonly known in English theology as the Argument from Design. The argument is this: Whatever is by its constitution adapted to a particular end supposes contrivance, and hence a contriver. Natural objects, and especially organized creatures, are adapted to certain ends; they must, therefore, be the product of a Being who contrived them for the ends to which their adaptation points. Furthermore, as the means by which those ends are effected far surpass all human power and skill, it is argued that their contriver is a Being whose power and skill are infinite. Everywhere in Nature we see what seems to us design. Only infinite power and skill could plan and execute the nice adaptations by which vegetable and animal organs are severally adapted to the wants of each creature, and perform their life-sustaining and life-propagating functions. Look at the human eye, says the theologian; examine its complex apparatus of layer, lens, and humors, its adjustment to the light without and the optic nerve within, observe its capabilities and defences; and say if any cause but a God of infinite wisdom can explain the miraculous organ? Man was designed to see, and this is the wonderfully skilful device by which that end is accomplished. The argument is a strong appeal to a principle in human nature which prompts us to infer an intelligent author wherever, in any object, we see fitness and use.

Let us see what degree of validity is fairly attributable to this demonstration, and how far, in itself, without aid or support from any other source, the argument from design is conclusive of the being of God.

It should be premised that the argument originated with those who, by inheritance and without demonstration, were already possessed and convinced of the truth to be established. This circumstance would not invalidate the argument, if otherwise conclusive, inasmuch as the aim is not to show that men get their idea of God in that way, but that the given idea may be thus scientifically legitimated. Nevertheless, there is a difference of cogency between the reasoning by which a truth is discovered, like the truths of astronomy, and that by which it is attempted to defend it. If it could be shown that an intelligent unbeliever has been in any instance converted by it, or a competent reasoner, who (if such a thing were supposable) had never heard of a God, has been made a believer by it, the fact would add greatly to the strength of the argument. What is that argument?

Whenever we behold a use resulting from the constitution and arrangements of a complex object, we infer design, and consequently a designer. So far as this inference applies to objects which are not products of Nature, — to artificial creations, so called, — the inference is warranted by experience. Have we any logical right to transfer the conclusions of that experience to natural products, to the operations of Nature? To establish that right, to authorize that transference, there should be, I think, not only an incidental resemblance, but a perfect analogy between the two. But what is the fact? The works of man and the products of Nature resemble each other in a single point; in all others they are utterly dissimilar, — dissimilar in their origin, dissimilar in their conditions, dissimilar in their history. In one point, viz., the adaptation of means to ends, they coincide: the points in which they do not coincide are infinite. Look at the works of man. The human artificer takes the requisite materials which he did not create, but which are furnished to his hand; he fashions and puts them together in certain combinations, and constructs a machine; let us say a watch, a thing that, by operation of a mechanical law, which man again did not create, but which is given him, carries an index around a dial-plate. The watch is said to measure time. Properly speaking, the watch does no such thing. All that the watch does, is to carry two pins, one faster, one slower, around a graduated circle. The maker has fixed the rate at which they move from figure to figure. The possessor notes their position on the dial, and by it measures time. Now, what analogy is there between this structure and an apple-tree, or the human eye, with which Paley compares it? What analogy between a manufacture from given materials, and the growth that secretes its materials as it proceeds. How the eye is formed is a question to which physiology can give only an approximate answer. All we can say is that its formation is not a manufacture, but a growth; that, by the action of certain forces, certain organic filaments and particles arrange themselves according to a given type. Whence that type, physiology cannot say. The theist believes it to be devised by an infinitely wise Being, the God of theology. But this belief is a foregone conviction, which he inherits by tradition. He brings it to the contemplation of Nature, and finds it confirmed: but it is not the product of that contemplation; no *a posteriori* reasoning can originate it, or demonstrate its truth. For observe that, when we say design, we beg the question. All we see in the case of the eye is adaptation; a certain co-ordination of parts which seem to condition the act of seeing. The idea of design is purely subjective,—an idea derived from human workmanship, which we apply to Nature. Were we not already possessed with the idea of God as the Author of Nature; and were it not for our irresistible propensity to anthropomorphize, to ascribe human methods to the God of our belief,—I doubt if we should ever have come upon this mechanical view, this cunning-device theory of natural products. I doubt if we should view them as workmanship at all. We see how human creations are formed: we know what study and calculation go to the making of a watch or steam-engine; we know that the more complex and effective the mechanism, the greater the ingenuity of the author;—and we anthropomorphize, we carry our joiner-view of creation into Nature, and represent to ourselves a planning, contriving intellect as the antecedent Power, from whose skilful adjustments and nice calculations Nature had its rise. If we came to the contemplation of Nature without the idea of God in our minds, we should not, I suppose, view it as cunning mechanism, or at all as something created by antecedent power, but rather as a self-subsisting whole. The question of its origin would hardly force itself upon us: we should accept it as it is, and suppose it to have been always as it is, and self-perpetuating. The curiosity of its structure, if it came at all into consideration, would not compel, nor even, perhaps, suggest, the idea of contrivance by an artificer external to itself. We should view the adaptation of organ to function and part to part in any individual portion of it, as we should the whole, as necessarily so constituted, — as something which could not be otherwise, if the whole was to be at all. This, I think, is the natural, unbiassed view of the universe: this is the way it would strike us, were not the idea of God given in human nature. And this is what Hume means when in his "Dialogues concerning Natural Religion," the most sincere and original treatise on the subject in English literature, he makes Philo, one of the speakers, say, that the world bears a greater resemblance to an animal than it does to a machine.

Does the physico-theological argument disprove this view? I cannot see that it does. Paley, the Bridgewater essayists, and others of that stamp, have not disproved, if even they have fairly considered it. They have done nothing to prove the existence of God to the satisfaction of a really logical unbeliever, competent to weigh evidence and to judge of the force of arguments. They have come to the contemplation of Nature, not to ascertain an unknown fact, but to justify an assumed one; not with a view to an impartial examination of different cosmogonies, but with a cosmogony fixed in their minds which they were to verify, with a foregone conclusion to be confirmed. They had a case to make out, and in that they have not succeeded. What they have done is worthy of all praise. They have brought to view the exquisite adaptations of Nature, and, *on the supposition of a God for its author*, have abundantly illustrated the wondrous skill of the Creator. But the pivotal point on which the whole question hinges, this sort of demonstration fails to substantiate. That point is that the aptitudes of Nature, or what seem to us such, prove design in the sense in which the adaptations of a sewing-machine prove design in its author. To impute design where we recognize use in Nature is, I repeat it, a begging of the question. The design we impute is something appertaining to ourselves: it is our own subjectivity which we import into Nature.

It has been surmised that what we regard as design in Nature may be a necessity inherent in the nature of things. "It is observed by arithmeticians," says Hume, "that the products of 9 compose always either 9 or some lesser product of 9, if you add together all the characters of which the former products are composed. Thus of 18, 27, 36, which are products of 9, you make 9 by adding 1 to 8, 2 to 7, 3 to 6. Thus 369 is also a product of 9, and if you add 3, 6, and 9, you make 18, a lesser product of 9. By a superficial observer, so wonderful a regularity may be admired as the effect either of chance or design; but a skilful algebraist immediately concludes it to be the work of necessity, and demonstrates that it must for ever result from the nature of these numbers. Is it not probable, I ask, that the whole economy of the universe is conducted by a like necessity, although no human algebra can furnish a key which solves the difficulty. And, instead of admiring the order of natural beings, may it not happen that, could we penetrate into the intimate nature of bodies, we should clearly see why it was absolutely impossible that they could ever admit of any other disposition?"

This suggestion, it may be said, can only be regarded as an exercise of ingenuity, a trick of fence intended to rebut the aggressive dogmatism of theology, not as pretending to be a sufficient account of the order and fitness apparent in creation; that it cannot be supposed to be the view sincerely entertained by a sound and seriously disposed mind, of the constitution of things. It may be so: I only cite it as showing that design is not the only supposable explanation of the aptitudes in question. And here let me say that I am far from denying the *theological* value of the argument from design; its theological value is great: my criticism concerns only its speculative claims. And, speaking in the interest of speculative philosophy, I further contend that, though we grant to this argument the fact of design, and therefore a designer, as the true and only explanation of natural phenomena, there is still an immense gulf between that conclusion and the fact of an infinite and perfect Being which Natural Theology pretends to deduce from it. How does the argument bridge this gulf? The great Contriver is seen to be very powerful and wise; and therefore, for aught we know, he may be infinitely so. "It is a power," says Paley, "to which we are not authorized by our observation or knowledge to assign any limits. . . . It cannot with respect to us be distinguished from infinite."

So much we may readily admit. But to metamorphose this modest negative into that transcendental positive which Theism affirms, to exalt the absence of known limitation into categorical infinity, to read in the marks of power and wisdom surpassing human art omnipotence and omniscience, is an intellectual *tour de force* which sober logic is compelled to disown. When the argument has shown a contriver of incomparable skill, it has reached the bounds of legitimate induction. The step from that to the God of theology — a God not only powerful and wise, but just and merciful and true — is not an induction, but a leap. More glaring still is the failure of this demonstration when, from certain satisfactions for which provision has been made in the constitution of sentient Nature, it argues a Being of infinite benevolence united to infinite power. The satisfactions of Nature are many and great: enjoyment abounds; but suffering also abounds, if not in equal measure, yet in a measure which physical theology leaves unexplained. Evil pervades the system of things. Every stage in the ascent of animated Nature, from the polyp to man, is an increment in the scale of suffering, which challenges Theism with an ever louder and angrier Why? and which the physical contemplation of the universe can never adjust with the theory of omnipotent Love. What infinite Benevolence wills, that infinite Power might accomplish. Infinite Benevolence must will the happiness of sentient beings: why then a world so cumbered with enormous woe? is the everlasting protest of heart and flesh against the positions of Natural Theology. There *is* an answer to this protest; but the argument from design is not that answer, and cannot furnish it. That argument can only plead that the arrangements of Nature were planned to give pleasure, not pain: if pain in any case results from them, it is not a designed but an incidental consequence. But the incidental consequence, if it does not impeach the goodness, would seem to impeach the wisdom of God, which failed to provide against such incidents. "The teeth," says Paley, "are contrived to eat, not to ache. Their aching now and then is incidental to the contrivance, perhaps inseparable from the contrivance;" and he adds that they may be "a defect in the contrivance."

It is easy, no doubt, to exaggerate the evils of life and their damaging effect on the cause of Theism. The sceptic in Hume's Dialogues, I think, overstates the theological dilemma when he says, "Allowing, . . . what you never can prove, that animal or at least human happiness in this life exceeds its misery, you have yet done nothing. For this is not by any means what we expect from infinite power, infinite wisdom, and infinite goodness.

Why is there any misery at all in the world? Not by chance surely. From some cause, then. Is it from the intention of the Deity? But he is infinitely benevolent. Is it contrary to his intention? But he is almighty." And he adds: "Nothing can shake the solidity of this reasoning, so short, so clear, so decisive, except we assert that these subjects exceed all human capacity, and that our common measures of truth and falsehood are not applicable to them." I believe, on the contrary, that this reasoning may be very easily refuted. But Hume is entirely right in what he so much insists on, — that though the contemplation of the world as it is, with its manifold imperfections, would not invalidate the doctrine of an almighty, all-wise, and benevolent God, were it otherwise established on independent grounds, the contemplation of the world as it is, does not, of itself, suffice to establish that doctrine.

A curious illustration of the influence of abstract speculation on the thinker's practical estimate of life is given in the views of the two English writers whom I have quoted, — Paley and Hume. Paley revels in the contemplation of the happiness which beams upon him from all the aspects of Nature and life, and exultingly points to the marks of divine benevolence in the constitution of brute and man. "It is a happy world after all. The air, the earth, the water, teem with delighted existence. In a spring noon, or a summer evening, on whichever side I turn my eyes, myriads of happy beings crowd upon my view." And in human life, he is sure "that the common course of things is in favor of happiness; that happiness is the rule, misery the exception." Hear how Hume, on the contrary, or the speakers who may be supposed to represent him, intone the wretchedness and sorrows of life. "I am persuaded," says Philo, in the Dialogues, "that the best and indeed the only method of bringing every one to a due sense of religion is by just representations of the wickedness and misery of men." "The people, indeed, replied Demea, are sufficiently convinced of this great and melancholy truth. The miseries of life, the unhappiness of man, the general corruptions of our nature, the unsatisfactory enjoyment of pleasures, riches, honors, — these phrases have become almost proverbial in all languages. And who can doubt of what all men declare from their own immediate feeling and experience? . . . As to authorities, you need not seek them. Look round on this library of Cleanthes. I venture to affirm that, except authors of particular sciences, . . . there is scarce one of these innumerable writers from whom the sense of human misery has not in some passage or other extorted a complaint or confession of it." "And why should man pretend to exemption from the lot of all other animals? The whole earth . . . is cursed and polluted. A perpetual war is enkindled among all living creatures. Necessity, hunger, want, stimulate the strong and courageous; fear, anxiety, terror, agitate the weak and infirm. The first entrance into life gives anguish to the new-born infant and to the wretched parent. Weakness, impotence, distress, attend each stage of that life, and it is at last finished in agony and horror." "All the goods of life would not make a very happy man; but all the ills united would make a wretch indeed, and any one of them almost, (and who can be free from every one?) nay, often the absence of one good, (and who can possess all?) is sufficient to render life ineligible. Were a stranger to drop on a sudden into this world, I would show him, as a specimen of its ills, an hospital full of diseases, a prison crowded with malefactors and debtors, a field of battle strowed with carcases, a fleet foundering in the ocean, a nation languishing under tyranny, famine, or pestilence. To turn the gay side of life to him, and give him a notion of its pleasures, whither should I conduct him? — to a ball, to an opera, to court? He might justly think that I was only showing him a diversity of distress and sorrow." "There is no evading such striking instances," said Philo, "but by apologies which still further aggravate the charge. Why have all men, I ask, in all ages, complained incessantly of the miseries of life? They have no just reason, says one: these complaints proceed only from their discontented, repining, anxious disposition. And can there, possibly, I reply, be a more certain foundation of misery than such a wretched temper?"

On comparing these opposite views of the value of life, the suspicion may arise that a radical difference of temperament in the two witnesses has colored their respective and conflicting reports. But Hume was not a morbid man. He says in his life of himself: "I was ever more disposed to see the favorable than the unfavorable side of things,—a turn of mind which it is more happy to possess than to be born to an estate of ten thousand a year."

The physico-theological argument, then, whatever of practical and theological value may be conceded to it, breaks down in the attempt to throw a bridge of logic across the chasm which divides the finite in human experience from the infinite of human thought. To say nothing of the many instances in which the alleged fitness in the arrangements of Nature is apparently wanting, and where a different arrangement would seem to be more conducive to animal weal; to say nothing of the subterfuge contained in the plea of "general laws" by which it is attempted to cover such cases, and to which the obvious answer is, If general laws will not protect individual well-being, why are not special arrangements provided for that end? to say nothing of all this, — the argument is unsatisfactory as failing, in the first place, to prove from the aptitudes of Nature the fact of design in the sense in which it is claimed; and, secondly, as failing, if design be allowed, to prove from that the infinite and perfect Being whom Theism affirms.

Kant's critique of this argument is interesting, both as logical authority, and as indicating a struggle between moral predilection on the one hand, and the incorruptible judgment of the thinker on the other. "This demonstration," he says, "deserves always to be named with respect. It is the eldest, clearest, and best suited to the common reason of man. It animates the study of Nature, as in turn it owes its own being to that, and through it obtains for ever new force. It carries purpose and design where our observation would not of itself have discovered them, and enlarges our knowledge of Nature by the guiding thread of a special unity, whose principle is outside of Nature. This knowledge, again, reacts on its cause, — that is, the idea which gave rise to it, — and so increases faith in a Supreme Author to an irresistible conviction.

"It would therefore be not only disconsolate, but altogether in vain, to attempt to detract any thing from the authority of this demonstration. Reason, unceasingly elevated by such mighty, and, under its manipulation, ever-increasing, although merely empirical, topics of proof, can never by doubts of subtile, abstract speculation be so depressed as not to be roused from every fit of brooding irresolution, as from a dream, by the first glance which it throws on the wonders of Nature and the majesty of the world-fabric, and to lift itself from grandeur to grandeur up to the highest; from conditioned to condition, up to the supreme and unconditioned Author of all.

"But although we have nothing to object to the reasonableness and utility of this procedure, but, on the contrary, have to recommend and encourage it, we nevertheless cannot approve the claims which this demonstration would make to apodictic certainty, and to an acceptance needing no favor or foreign support. And it can do no injury to the good cause to tone down the dogmatic language of scornful reasoners to that of moderation and the modest expression of a faith which suffices to pacify, though it may not command unconditional subjection. Accordingly, I maintain that the physico-theological demonstration alone can never demonstrate the existence of a Supreme Being, but must always leave it to the ontological (to which it but serves as introduction) to supply that defect."

Then, after showing how the argument, even if successful in proving the contingency (or derivative character) of natural forms, and thence a world-architect, fails utterly to prove the contingency of the substance of Nature, *i.e.*, to prove a world-creator; after showing how those who employ it, in defiance of logical authority, jump from their conclusion of a potent and wise artificer to that of an infinite and perfect Being,—the peerless critic concludes with saying, that "The physico-theologians have therefore no cause for their coyness toward the transcendental demonstration, and for looking down upon it with the self-conceit of clear-seeing masters of natural lore, as on the cobweb-fabric of benighted dreamers. For, if they would examine themselves, they would find that after they have travelled a considerable way on the ground of Nature and experience, and found themselves as far as ever from the object which gleams upon their reason, they suddenly quit that ground and pass over into the region of mere possibilities, where, on the wings of ideas, they hope to reach that which had eluded their empirical investigation. And when, at last, after this mighty leap, they think they have got firm footing, they extend the now determined conception (which they have come into possession of they know not how) over the whole field of creation, and illustrate their ideal, — at bottom the product of pure reason, — poorly enough, it is true, and far below the dignity of the object, by experience, without being willing to confess that they have come to its cognition or assumption by any other path."

The main defect, and the fatal defect, in both of the arguments which have been examined, is the want of a logical synthesis between eternal existence in the one case, or the fitness of creation in the other, and the infinite Being, the almighty, all-wise, and beneficent Person, whose existence the argument aims to establish. The source of each argument is a mental necessity which constrains the theist to connect in the one case the evident dependence, in the other the appearance of design in creation, with the preconceived idea of God. He carries into Nature what he had in his mind, and what he carries that he finds.

We come now to the *a priori* or ontological proof, known also as the proof by "aseity," *viâ aseitatis*, which means the demonstration of God from himself (*a se*), from the nature of his idea. This argument was first suggested, so far as we know, by a godly Italian, a pupil of the Norman Lanfranc, and his successor, — first as prior of Bec, then as archbishop of Canterbury, — St. Anselm, a man in whom the philosopher and the devotee, simplicity of faith and activity of intellect, were strangely combined, and who heralded the great revival which scattered the sleep of the Dark Ages, and irradiated Europe with the dawn of intellectual light. The account which his biographer gives of his discovery of this demonstration adds to its interest, if not to its weight. It came into his mind to inquire if all that we believe and predicate of God might not be proved by one brief argument. The thought haunted him by day and by night; it invaded his rest, it even disturbed his devotions; until once, in the midst of a self-imposed vigil, the thought occurred which he endeavored to embody in his "Monologium," and afterwards in the "Proslogium," or "Fides quærens Intellectum." This is the famed ontological proof. We believe that God is something than which nothing greater can be imagined. But that than which nothing greater can be imagined cannot be in the intellect alone: it cannot be a mere thought of the mind; for, if it were only a thought, it might be conceived as existing, and that would be something greater. If, therefore, that than which nothing greater can be imagined existed in the mind alone, a mere conception, then that very thing than which nothing greater can be imagined would be something than which something greater *could* be imagined, which is contradictory.

This argument, with some modification in the form of it, was revived by Descartes five centuries later, was confirmed by Spinoza, and has been approved by some of the foremost of German metaphysicians, — not indeed as logically conclusive against atheism, but as weighty and profound, evincing a true conception of the nature of that idea in which thought and thing, subjective contemplation and objective necessity, are so inextricably blended. Leibnitz says of it, "I do not contemn the argument invented some centuries ago by Anselm, which proves that the perfect Being exists necessarily; although I find this defect in it, that it presupposes the possibility of the perfect Being. If this one point can be established, then the whole demonstration will be complete." Hegel finds this in it, that, as thought and being are antithetical, a Supreme Being who is only thought is finite, and therefore not really the Supreme Being.

The ontological argument came to be misrepresented, and is still understood to affirm necessary existence on the simple ground of perfection in the object of thought. We have the idea of a Being embodying all perfection; but existence is necessary to perfection, therefore our all-perfect Being must exist. Even Leibnitz seems, in the passage I have quoted, to have construed it thus. It is against this perverted argument that the mighty polemic of Kant is directed; at least, it is only against this perversion that his polemic is valid in the whole extent of its demonstration. But against the argument so understood his critique is conclusive. Kant objects, 1st. That existence is not a predicate, not one among other qualities appertaining to a thing, but merely a putting of the thing with all its predicates. It may make some difference with me, practically, whether or no I have the hundred pounds which I imagine; but it makes no difference as to the idea of the hundred pounds. 2d. He objects that necessity affirmed of a logical conclusion is a very different thing from necessity of being. If I entertain the idea of God at all, I must needs ascribe to him such and such predicates, — omnipotence, omniscience, and necessary existence among the rest. I may say, the idea of God implies these attributes, — that, if he exists at all, he is self-existent; but I can, nevertheless, reject the idea altogether, with all its belongings.

But Anselm's demonstration is not the ontological argument which Kant assails; it is not at all the absurd syllogism which some would make of it:

that God is a being possessing all perfections; but existence is one perfection, therefore God exists. Anselm does not reckon existence among the divine perfections, and thence conclude that the being whose idea embraces all perfections must needs exist. He compares two modes of conceiving the all-perfect Being,—that which conceives him simply as an object of thought, and that which conceives him as really existing; and he maintains that, so long as God is conceived only as an object of thought, —*i.e.*, as a product of the human mind,—we do not conceive that than which nothing greater can be conceived, in which consists the true definition of God. And as to the objection, that a given idea is no more perfect for representing an actual existence than if it were merely a fiction of the mind, Anselm would say that this may be true of finite things: they may be conceived as existing or not existing; necessary existence is no part of their idea. Not so with the idea of God: in that idea is given something which cannot be conceived as not existing; but which, if conceived at all, must be conceived as that necessary existence on which all other existence depends. Otherwise, it is not the idea of that than which nothing greater can be conceived.

It must be allowed that this demonstration expresses a true perception of the grounds of certitude by which the existence of God is assured to those who have the idea, and seek confirmation of its import. But it has no validity as addressed to unbelievers. All that it really proves is, that, given the idea of God, it is that of a necessarily existing being. The idea is presupposed as something given by religion. The argument rests on the postulate of faith. Hence, the title of Anselm's treatise, "Fides quærens Intellectum." Descartes, who repeats the argument, places its whole force in the consciousness we have that our idea of God must have God for its author. "Tota vis argumenti," he says, "in eo est quod agnoscam fieri non posse ut existam talis naturæ qualis sum, nempe, ideam Dei in me habens, nisi revera Deus etiam existeret. Deus, inquam, ille idem cujus idea in me est." But this conviction does not admit of being logically legitimated; and whilst we feel, as certainly a majority of the deepest thinkers have felt, the substantial weight of the ontological argument, we cannot, in the cause of Theism, employ it against systematic atheism. In that service it avails as little, perhaps even less, than the *a posteriori* proof from design. "The really profound thought it embodies," says Hegel, "has acquired a false and shallow aspect from being forced into the form of a conclusion of the understanding."

Kant, who rejects, in his "Kritik," &c., the ontological proof, on the ground that you never, as he says, can thresh or shell (*heraus klauben*) existence out of thought, had previously attempted an argument somewhat resembling it in his "Einzig möglicher Beweisgrund zur Demonstration des Daseins Gôttes." He there offers a demonstration, — or, to state it more exactly, the ground of a demonstration, — which, whilst in abstruseness and subtlety it exceeds that of Anselm and Descartes, holds less of spiritual reality, as it seems to me; and, if more logical in form, is less weighty in substance, and therefore less convincing than the one we have just been considering. The demonstration is based on the abstract notion of possibility. Possibility is relation to something given: it therefore presupposes existence. Something is possible: therefore something exists which makes it possible. If all existence is denied, there is no material for supposing any thing; and consequently all possibility ceases, — possibility being the supposition of a supposable thing. Here, at the very threshold, a criticism suggests itself. What we mean by possibility is the perception of agreement between given ideas: it resolves itself, at last, into a state of the thinking mind. Not only, therefore, does possibility cease when existence is denied, but it ceases also if intelligence is denied. We might, therefore, on Kant's premise of interior possibility implying existence, shorten the process, and say at once, that possibility implies intelligence. Kant seems to treat the notion of possibility as something objective, — something distinct from thought. There is no contradiction, he says, in denying all existence; only we cannot deny existence and still retain possibility, because then there would be no material for thinking. But suppose I deny possibility, as well as existence, what becomes of the argument? It is true, the denial of possibility presupposes existence as well as the affirmation of it. It presupposes the denier. Here we come at once to Descartes' *Cogito ergo sum;* and it does not appear why this is not a better, because a nearer and more appreciable, point of departure, than the abstract notion of possibility. We need not follow the process by which, from existence presupposed in possibility, the argument deduces a necessary Being, and then logically demonstrates the unity, the simplicity, the unchangeableness, the eternity, the supreme reality, of that Being. But, when in the *Vierte Betrachtung* the author proceeds to show that the necessary Being is a spirit, it is curious to see how he slides into the inductive, and falls plump on the very satisfactory cause-and-effect argument whose validity in this application he afterward, in the treatise of "Pure Reason," disallows. "The properties of a Spirit, Understanding and Will, are of such a kind that we cannot conceive any reality which would compensate a Being for the want of them. And since these properties are those which are capable of the highest degrees of reality, and are at the same time among the possible, it would follow [that is, if we deny them to the Supreme Being] that understanding and will and all the reality of the spiritual nature are, through the necessary Being as a ground, possible in others, whilst yet they are not to be found, as belonging to its nature, in that Being itself. Accordingly, the effect would be greater than the cause." Most true! But this conclusion is not the legitimate yield of the *a priori* method hitherto pursued in this demonstration. The author ascribes understanding and will to the necessary Being, not because he finds them in the nature of that Being, but because he finds them in finite and contingent being, and cannot account for them there except on the principle of cause and effect.

It has seemed to me that an argument simpler than that of Kant, and equally rational, might be drawn from the nature of space. Space is that which cannot by any possibility be conceived as non-existent. We may imagine every thing out of space, every space-occupying thing annihilated; but space will still remain. But space, says Kant, is relative: it cannot be conceived without conceiving something else. If, therefore, space remains, though all *space-occupying* objects be supposed non-existent, the something else must be a subject *not occupying space*, — that is, spirit: or, to put the thing in a different shape, space has no existence except as contemplated; it is, in its essence, external. If, therefore, space must have always existed, there must also have been always a contemplating subject. We cannot conceive of space antecedent to all created being, without also conceiving an intelligent mind. We cannot deny its essential externality, implying a conscious subject to which it is external. Say, if you will, that the mind itself, in attempting to conceive of pure space devoid of all created being, by a necessary act of imagination constitutes itself the conscious subject contemplating space, and then by a trick of subreption substitutes God in the place of self. That very necessity, which is nothing less than a law of the mind, is presumptive evidence in favor of the truth that a conscious subject must have preceded all objective finite being, which truth is the very kernel of Theism.

Kant affirms that the cosmological, the physico-theological, and the ontological proofs are the only possible methods of demonstrating the existence of God. Yet Kant, in his "Critique of Practical Reason," suggests another more potent than these, derived from the moral law; whose empire in human nature implies an authority above nature, a divine Lawgiver.

I think there is still another, which I will briefly indicate. To make it intelligible, we must first disabuse ourselves of a very ancient and inveterate prejudice, — the most obstinate of all our prejudices, — that which supposes the existence of an external world subsisting by virtue of a certain substratum to which we give the name of matter, and which, though as commonly conceived it has the reputation of something pre-eminently solid, as if it were solidity itself, every thinker knows to be the merest fancy that ever got named in human speech. Schelling, in the Introduction to his "Transcendental Idealism," says, "The one ground-prejudice to which all others may be reduced is none other than this, that there are [material] things without us; a belief which because it rests on no reasons or conclusions (for there is not a single proof of it that will bear examination), and yet does not admit of being eradicated by any proof of the contrary, lays claim to immediate certainty. But since it relates to something by supposition entirely different from ourselves, — nay, opposed to ourselves, — of which it is impossible to understand how it can enter into our immediate consciousness, the belief must be regarded as nothing more than a prejudice, — an inborn and original prejudice, it is true, but not the less a prejudice on that account." He afterward finds the proposition, "There are things without us," to be practically identical with the proposition, "I am." It is one of the curiosities of psychology, that this emptiest of all abstractions, a pure creation of the human mind, — the notion of matter which Leibnitz defines as the sleep of the Monads, and Hemsterhuys as spirit curdled, Schelling as spirit in equilibrio, — that this conceit should have dominated, not only natural science, where it has its uses, but also theology and philosophy, where it is a senseless obstruction, a hindrance to all right perception. The belief in matter, as it lies at the foundation of most of the atheism in the world (not indeed of Schopenhauer's, who believes in no such thing), so it also underlies most of the attempted demonstrations — I mean, the *a posteriori* demonstrations — of the existence of God. Those demonstrations presume the existence of matter, — a *tertium quid*, something intervening between God and the finite mind; but leave us in the dark as to whether the supposed matter, the material of creation, was created before the forms of which it is supposed to be the stuff, and then moulded into those forms as the potter moulds his clay, or whether it was created simultaneously with those forms. In either case, since matter by supposition is a substance distinct from God, these arguments involve the inconceivableness, not to say contradiction, of the origination of substance out of no substance, — something out of nothing.

Let us, then, dismiss from our minds the notion of matter, and view the phenomenal world as a sequence of mental experiences, — seeing, hearing, feeling, tasting, and the like. I inquire the origin and ultimate ground of those experiences. My consciousness tells me that I am not their author. I do not cause, but receive them. In some of them I am entirely passive; in others, my action is one, but not the sole, factor. The experience refers me to a cause without, and the cause must be adequate to the effect. And here is where all material explanation fails: for matter, by supposition, is inert and powerless; it could not of itself, were there any such thing, produce an effect. The cause must be a power, and the power must be equal to my uttermost experience. If I have an experience which I call seeing a star a hundred million of miles removed, the power must be equal to that effect. Again, a portion of those experiences I classify as intelligent and sentient beings like myself. On comparing my experience with theirs, I find an almost uniform agreement. What is white to me is white to them, what is black is black; we agree in square and round, in hot and cold. Hence I infer the unity of the power which creates these experiences in different minds. Following this line of induction, I arrive to the idea, not precisely of the God of theology, but yet of a Being resembling that as nearly at least as the Being demonstrated by the physico-theological argument.

The demonstration which I have indicated is substantially Malebranche's doctrine of seeing all things in God. After showing that we perceive objects not in and through themselves, but by means of their ideas, Malebranche says, "It is certain that ideas are effective, because they act upon the mind. . . . Now, nothing can act immediately on the mind, unless superior to the mind. Only God can do that." "Rien ne le peut que Dieu seul. Car il n'y a que l'Auteur de notre être qui en puisse changer les modifications" (Recherche de la Vérité, L. III. ch. vi.). I shall not pursue the argument: I only suggest it. I do not affirm that it has the force of absolute demonstration. But I think I may claim for it as much of validity at least as logical analysis finds in the stock arguments of Natural Theology. Those arguments attempt to prove the existence of God from *things;* but the existence of things, as Descartes has shown, is less certain than that of God. The certainty of things depends on the certainty of God.

The fact is, the belief in God precedes and underlies all the attempts to prove his existence, and vitiates all the reasoning in such demonstrations. The idea being given, to defend it by reasoning is one thing, to discover it by reasoning is a very different thing, and a feat that was never yet accomplished by mortal wit. The idea is given, a glance at Nature confirms it, and all that is essential in the argument from design is the feeling which demands intelligence as the co-ordinate of being. It is not the wonders of anatomy or cosmology, as portrayed in the Bridgewater treatises, that compel belief: they are simply responses to, or reflections of, the God-idea; all the cogency they have in the way of proof, the simplest existences have as well. For of all existence the correlate in reason is absolute Being,—*i.e.*, God. He to whom Nature undissected is not the immediate presence of God will never reach him by dissection. When Vanini was arraigned before the Senate of Toulouse on the charge of atheism, he picked up a straw from the floor, and said to his judges: "This straw compels me to confess that there is a God." A straw is as much a witness of God as any process of animal life. On the ground of the argument from design, we want a God as much for the first filament of incipient organization as we do for the finished curiosity of the human hand, as much for a blade of grass as we do for a star, as much for a single wild-flower of the woods as we do for the arch flower of creation. And, on the ground of the cosmological argument, we need him as much for a chaos as we do for a cosmos. The first aspect of Nature suggests a God, not on the principle of cause and effect, but because it reflects to us the idea in our mind. A glance does that as well, or even better, than an anatomical demonstration. "We murder to dissect;" and he who does not, like Adam in Paradise, hear the voice of the Lord God walking in the garden, will never find him by following the anatomist along the paths of dusty death.

To the question, Is there any proof of the existence of God? I answer without hesitation, There is none in the sense of syllogistic demonstration,— none which has the force of a mathematical conclusion,—none in which logic may not detect some flaw, some vulnerable point, some tendo Achillis exposed to the shafts of criticism. Is it asked why a truth so fixed in human faith, and so essential to human well-being, should not admit of irrefragable proof? I answer that its very certainty precludes demonstration. There is nothing of which you are more certain than you are of your own existence; and nothing which you would find it more difficult to prove, *in words*, to one who, for the sake of argument, should undertake to deny it. Your subjective certainty, expressed by the *Cogito ergo sum* of Descartes, you would find it difficult by any process of logic to convert into objective certitude. All attempts to prove the existence of God labor with this difficulty, that the thing to be proved is more certain than the topics of proof by which it is attempted to prove it. We know God, if at all, not by inference, but by direct intuition. So Norris argues in his "Theory of the Ideal World." "God is seen by his own light." "If God," says this brave Platonist, "as being pure Act [for which he quotes Thomas Aquinas], be the most intelligible object, then he must be intelligible in the most perfect manner, or else he will not be what we suppose, — the most intelligible object. But now it seems plain, that for a thing to be intelligible by another thing is not to be intelligible after so perfect a manner as to be immediately intelligible in and by itself. And, therefore, whatever necessity there may be of ideas[1] for the understanding of other things, we have reason to conclude that God is by himself immediately intelligible, and to be seen by

[1] That is, representative ideas. The author, as idealist, supposes that sensible objects are seen by representative ideas; but God, he argues, is seen without the intervention of these, — is seen by immediate intuition.

his own light as being himself that pure and perfect light in which there is no darkness at all." In other words, God is his own witness; and his witnessing of himself in every unsophisticated mind and every sound heart is the surest and most satisfactory proof we can ever have of this primary truth. If God exists, it is incredible that the Being so named should not give assurance of himself to intelligent thought, should not bear witness of himself in intelligent minds. And, on the other hand, the most philosophical, the only rational, way of explaining the general, not to say universal, belief in God, is the supposition of an object corresponding to that belief.

"I have not," says Kant, in the preface to the "Einzig möglicher Beweisgrund," — "I have not so high an opinion of the utility of an undertaking like the present as to suppose that the most important of all our cognitions, There is a God, is insecure without the aid of metaphysical investigations. Providence has not willed that those perceptions most necessary to happiness should rest on the subtlety of fine conclusions; but has given them directly to the natural, common understanding, which, if we do not confuse it with false art, will not fail to lead us to the true and the useful, so far as it may be most needful for us."

VII.

ON THE ORIGIN OF THINGS.

A BEGINNING of being is inconceivable; a beginning of existence there must have been. I use with distinction two words which are commonly regarded as synonymous. For ordinary purposes, they may properly enough be so regarded. But in strictness of thought they are not synonymous; the things signified are not identical. A distinction of ideas is implied in the fact of two different words in the languages of civilized peoples. Existence presupposes being; but being does not necessarily include existence. Being is the ὄντως ὄν, existence the ἄλλως ὄν, of the Platonists. Being is universal; existence is particular. Being is absolute; existence is relative. Being is eternal; existence is transient. The one is insensible and unsearchable; the other comprises the sensible universe of things.

And the sensible universe had a beginning. The whence, the how, and the why of that beginning is the ever-disputed problem of ontology.

Time was when men were content to accept the world as it is, — to look upon it as self-existent, — without inquiring its cause or ground. But when advancing culture stimulated intellectual curiosity, philosophy began to speculate on the origin of things. Observation of natural processes, — birth and death, change and decay of visible forms — suggested the thought that all things are in flux. "*Πάντα ῥεῖ*," said Herakleitos. But an everlasting flood supposes an everlasting fountain. A never-beginning series of transient existences is an impossibility. There must have been a first, and, before that first, an unbeginning something that gave it birth. The conviction arose of a Power behind this world of shows, — unseen, unknown, but absolute and eternal. This Power might be conceived as single or as dual, or even as plural; for the "Elohim" of the Pentateuch expresses an indefinite number, and the "Atoms" of Epicurus, which represent in his system the invisible agency, are supposed innumerable.

The two ideas, — the eternal and the temporal, the infinite and the finite, — being given, creation would seem to be the logical relation of the one to the other. Intelligence in the finite would seem to be best explained by the supposition of creative intelligence in the infinite. Spinoza neutralizes the distinction between the two by making the finite a mode of the infinite, and endowing the latter with the two attributes of thought and extension. And Fichte, in the spirit of Spinozism, pronounces the idea of creation to be the ground-error of false metaphysic.[1] But "creation" is a word of wide significance; formation by a conscious, intelligent Will,—the traditional view of Theism,—is not the only conceivable genesis. Others have been propounded. The various attempts to formulate the copula between being and existence have given rise to so many distinct theoretical cosmogonies, the more important of which may be classed under the following heads: Creation by chance; creation (divine) by proxy; creation by emanations; creation by God out of pre-existing matter; creation out of nothing; creation out of spiritual substance; and, lastly, ideal creation.

Creation by chance, in the Epicurean cosmogony, postulates two conditions,—an infinity of atoms, and motion. The atoms set in motion, being furnished with hooks,—or, in modern phrase, having mutual affinities,—must needs combine. Out of an infinite variety of possible combinations, there was but one that would give the result of a life-sustaining, self-propagating world. If the

---

1 Schelling, with truer consistency, affirms that no idea of Godhead can be considered complete which does not include the attribute of Creator.

atoms formed any other connection, the *mésalliance* would prove infructuous and end in swift divorce. As good luck would have it, after numberless failures, they finally blundered into right relations; and behold a world!

Cicero's criticism on this theory — the comparison with the letters of the Iliad — is well known. The chief and fatal objection to it is its exorbitant postulate. Why not ask a finished universe, at once? One might as well grant the atoms in originally right relations as grant them in motion. For whence that motion? Motion is conceivable only as resulting from impulse, and impulse presupposes a force whose action it is. You cannot have motion without a power to originate motion. And that power must be self-determining, since by supposition there is nothing that could determine it; in other words, it must be a supreme Will. It is easier to suppose, with Spinoza, a self-existent universe, and so abandon the idea of creation, or an origin of things, than it is to suppose atoms in motion without a moving power. The theory of creation by chance must be rejected as less simple than no creation.

Creation by proxy was a Jewish device for saving the holiness of God from actual contact with matter. The strong repulsion of the Hebrew mind from Egyptian and Syrian Nature-worship had, in the period succeeding the Captivity, reached the point of entire separation from Nature. Starting with the notion of holiness in the sense of apartness, Jehovism had developed the idea of a God too holy for any thing. To impute creation, other than that of spirits like himself, to a Being so sublime, was to derogate from the awful Majesty. How could the high and holy One be supposed to occupy himself with fashioning the impure creatures of earth? If such creatures must be, it was absolutely necessary that some inferior agent should give them being. The God of Judaism dwelt apart in unapproachable holiness. You must not so much as speak his name. Hence the idea of a second, — a Creator-God, the Son or Wisdom or Word, — an idea which, in this aspect and application, is quite as much a Jewish as it is a Platonic conception.

Respecting this theory, it is enough to say that what is gained by it in one way is lost in another. If it saves the holiness of God, it does so at the expense of his personal interest in his creatures; which practically is the most essential element in the idea of Godhead, and without which God for us is an empty name. It gives us, for the Author of our being, a secondary agent, — a Creator who lacks finality, — and therefore can never quite satisfy the highest and freest aspirations of the soul.

The theory of creation by emanations, or æons,

has its root, or one of its roots, in the same idea of the absolute separation of Deity from Nature; and the other, in the correlate idea, which Judaism proper did not develop, — the essential pravity of matter. It was the doctrine of the Gnostic systems, which prevailed in the first three centuries of our era, and differs from creation by proxy in this: that creation by proxy, though accomplished by another, was willed by the Supreme; whereas, in the Gnostic theories, the Supreme had no part in the work, — did not even consent to it. The æons had it all their own way. Of these æons, there were several orders; according to Basilides, three hundred and sixty-five, — one for each day in the year, — all governed by "Abraxas," which means three hundred and sixty-five. The first two, a male and a female, were begotten by the will of the Father, — "Bythos" (the Abyss). These begat others; these, still others; and so on; each new generation, by its further remove from the Bythos, becoming less ethereal than its predecessor, but still inhabiting the "Pleroma," and sharing the divine essence. The outermost members of this hierarchy found themselves living on the confines of Matter, which some represent as coeternal with God; others, as the wreck of a fallen spiritual world. Perceiving its capabilities, they were tempted to lay hands on it, and make a world.

This huge indiscretion has been the source of unnumbered woes to the souls which the thievish æons, Prometheus-like, abstracted from the essence of the Supreme, and imprisoned in mortal bodies. It necessitates a long and painful process of redemption by which in time the captive souls shall be set free, and restored to the "Pleroma" from whence they sprang. Then God will exert himself, will dissolve the fabric of the material universe; Matter will be confined within its original bounds, and all will be as it was before the unlucky mistake of creation.

The theories vary, in some of their details, with the different schools of Gnosticism; but the fundamental principles are the same in all. Marcion supposes creation to be the work of a Demiurge, who holds a middle place between the Prince of Light and the Prince of Darkness, — between God and the Devil. He is the being whom the Jews, under the name of Jehovah, worshipped as supreme. That was their mistake. He is not the Supreme; he is only Demiurge. He is neither wholly good nor wholly bad: good, inasmuch as he rewards the good; but he also punishes the bad, which a perfectly good Being would not do.

On the whole, the farrago of theosophic foolery known as Gnosticism requires no comment from the modern critic. I have none to make.

Next come the two theories, of creation from pre-existing material, and creation out of nothing. The prevailing theory of the ancients, common to Hebrew and Greek, was that of creation from a given material. "The earth was without form and void," says the Elohist, when "the Spirit of God moved upon the face of the waters," and called into being, first, light; then the strong firmament separating the waters; then grass and trees; then sun, moon, and stars; then fishes and birds; then cattle; then man. "First of all," sings the Greek theogonist, "there was chaos; then the broad-breasted Earth; then Love; then Night and Erebus, and from their coition Æther and the Day. Then Earth created for herself the covering, Heaven." Ovid, some centuries later, knows no other beginning of things: —

> "Ante mare et tellus et quod tegit omnia cœlum,
> Unus erat toto naturæ vultus in orbe,
> Quem dixere chaos, rudis indigestaque moles."

"Moles," however, does not express precisely what the Greeks meant by the word "chaos." They understood by that term something less positive and solid, so far as we can judge from the etymology of the word. Chaos, from χάω(ειν), "to yawn, to cleave asunder." We have an English word which comes directly from the same root, — "chasm." Chaos, indeed, though not the mathematical "nothing" of the next theory, was a kind of nothing. It was substance without quality, — if such a thing can be conceived, — substance with no attribute but extension. It was the *μὴ ὄν* of Plato, which must not be confounded with *οὐκ ὄν* or *οὐδέν*. The French language expresses the difference by the two terms *néant* and *rien*. *Néant* is that which lacks all quality and life, whose nature we, even in English, express by the word "nothingness," but of which existence may nevertheless be predicated; whereas *rien* is pure privation, — absence not only of quality but of being. It is true, *néant* is sometimes used in the sense of *rien;* it comes from the Italian *niente*, which has that sense, and no other. But there *is* this distinction between comparative nothing and absolute nothing, the *μὴ ὄν* and the *οὐκ ὄν*. Schelling defines the former as that which is capable of all determinations, but devoid of all, — the pure sport of divine free-will. Chaos, then, in the old Greek sense, at least in the etymological sense, is, being emptied of all accidents, — emptiness. This, however, as it was not Ovid's, so it is not the common, understanding of the term; for the obvious reason that the vulgar mind can form no conception of being without accidents, and can see no distinction between undetermined being and no being. Accordingly, the latest modern form of the theory of creation from a pre-existing material invests that material with certain accidents, and supposes, if I rightly understand it, a heterogeneity of essence latent in homogeneity of mode. That latest form is the so-called nebular hypothesis, commonly referred to Laplace, but whose first suggestion, I believe, is due to Kant. The nebular hypothesis supposes the existing cosmos to be the product, under natural laws, of an aboriginal, gaseous mass, which took on a rotary motion, and continued to rotate around a centre of its own, until, the centrifugal force in the outermost portion exceeding the centripetal, it gave forth successively detached rings, which broke into fragments, and, still rotating, formed the various bodies of the planetary systems.

Of the truth or plausibility of this hypothesis it would be presumptuous in me to speak. As a statement of the immediate antecedents of the present cosmos, it seems to be generally accepted by physicists. But, considered as exhaustive cosmogony, it is obviously inadequate. Nor did Kant propound it in any such sense. Granted the existence of the vapor or gas-world as antecedent and material of the present creation, that material surely cannot be supposed to have existed from eternity, nor yet to have been created with a view to subsequent creations. Created out of what? Shall we say, Out of nothing? But we are speaking of the theory of creation from a pre-existing material. The hypothetical gas-world cannot be otherwise understood than as the result of a foregone creation, — the relic of a perished world, of which the present is but the *apokatastasis*, according to Origenic dreams, — the steam that went up from a universe in flames, and that will go up again when "the elements shall melt with fervent heat, and the earth that now is and the works that are therein shall be burned up." At any rate, it is wholly unintelligible as a finality in the investigation of the origin of things. It leaves unanswered the question suggested by so many other theories and argumentations, — Whence all this gas? The same objection applies to every form of the theory of creation from pre-existing material. Whence the material? If we say, Created outright, we abandon the theory. If we say, Given from eternity, we have a dualism which can never, I think, satisfy the philosophic mind; inasmuch as it militates with a fundamental principle of logic, — the principle of the "sufficient reason."

We come to the theory of creation out of nothing. I call it a theory, and yet it hardly deserves that name, if by theory we mean intellectual vision, with a veritable *theoroumenon* for its object. It has been and is still the prevailing doctrine of the Christian Church, stoutly maintained by Irenæus, who says, in his work against Heresies, that, whereas *men* can make nothing except from a given material, *God*, on the contrary, himself created the material of his creations, which had no previous existence: by St. Augustine, who, in his "Confessions," argues that God could not have made heaven and earth from his own essence, for then would they be equal with God; neither from a pre-existing material, for originally there was nothing but God; therefore he must have made them out of nothing: reaffirmed by Thomas Aquinas in the Middle Age, and insisted on by modern Orthodoxy. And yet it is not a Biblical doctrine, and derives no sanction from Scriptural authority. The only Biblical passage alleged in its support is an apocryphal one. In the second book of Maccabees, vii. 28, the mother of the seven martyrs says to her youngest, "I beseech thee, my son, look upon the heaven and the earth, and all that is therein, and consider that God made them of things that were not," — "*οὐκ ὄντων*," which the Vulgate renders "*ex nihilo*." The meaning of the passage is doubtful, and may be rendered, according to some, by *quum non essent*, "while as yet they were not." At all events, another apocryphal passage (Wisdom, xi. 17) tells us that the almighty hand made the world of formless matter, — "*ἐξ ἀμόρφου ὕλης*."[1]

[1] D. F. Strauss, Christliche Glaubenslehre, par. 46.

So both passages, being of equal authority, neutralize each other. Schelling, always reverent toward Orthodoxy, remarks that there must be something in a doctrine so universally accepted. "It is not to be unconditionally repudiated," he says; "only it must be explained." And he explains it to mean "*creatio absque omni præexistente potentia.*" Unquestionably, there is something in the doctrine. It was the Church's protest — and a very needful protest — against the Manichean and Gnostic dualism, which ascribed independent eternity to matter, and made it the source of all natural and moral evil. Further significance it has none. On the contrary, if creation is understood to be substantial, — if it means fabrication of matter as well as generation of forms, fabrication of a substance ontologically distinct from the substance of God, and whose only antecedent is the divine Will, — then the doctrine, fairly envisaged and analyzed, asserts something unintelligible and unimaginable; something which the tongue may profess, but which the mind refuses to appropriate. And, as to its being universally received, the fact is, that the deepest minds of the Church have either resolved it into something different, or emphatically denied it. John Scotus, the greatest theosopher of a thousand years, explains the "nothing" to be the ineffable, incomprehensible, and inaccessible brightness of the divine nature ; and Jacob Boehme, the unfathomable cobbler of Görlitz, says, "Many authors have written that heaven and earth were created out of nothing ; but to me it is strange that, among so many excellent men, not one has been found able to describe the true ground, seeing the same God has been from eternity what he is now. Where nothing is, there nothing becomes. . . . God had no other material from which he created the world than his own essence, no other than himself."

In none of the theories thus far discussed can I find a solution, which reason will accept, of the problem of creation. And still the idea of creation is one of those convictions which the human mind refuses to part with. Indeed, it is the necessary correlate and complement of the idea of God. According to Newton's great word in the "Principia," God is a relative term,—"*Deus est vox relativa.*" God is no more conceivable without creation as the objectivation of the infinite of that subject, than a universe is conceivable without God as the subject of that object. Angelus Silesius, a daring mystic of the seventeenth century, says, "I know that God cannot live a moment without me. If I perish, he must for want of me give up the ghost. I am as important to him as he to me. I help maintain his being as well as he mine."

> "That God so blessed is and lives without desire,
> He has from me as I from him acquire."

Is there, then, any theory of the origin of being which criticism will tolerate, not to say approve?

I am not so presumptuous as to think of offering any thing which claims to be a solution of the problem. I will but venture one or two suggestions concerning it.

In the first place, no theory of creation is admissible which does not exclude the relation of time. The idea of an historic genesis must be once for all abandoned. It is not an historic, but a metaphysical, origin of things which reason contemplates. For suppose a beginning in time, the question confronts us, Why at that particular moment, while eternity, *a parte ante*, awaited the beneficent act? If creation was good, why tarried that good? Whatever motive may be supposed to have actuated God in undertaking the work of creation at all, must have actuated him from all eternity, since God was ever the same. He could not have been influenced from without, while nothing existed but himself. Vainly does St. Augustine attempt to repel the pertinent question of the Manichees, "How came it, all of a sudden, to please your God to do what he had not done before through eternal time? And what did he before the good work of creation?"—"He made time," the Father answers.

If there was time before the creation of the world, God made that time, and that was his work, — an answer which evades, but does not solve, the question. Moreover, it belongs to the idea of God, as Hermogenes[1] argued long ago, that he is Lord, that he rules. "Deitas," says Newton, is "dominatio Dei, non in proprium corpus, sed in subditos." Deity is essentially dominion, and therefore requires subjects, and must have had them from all eternity. Those subjects, it is true, may have been spirits formed of his own essence. But then the question recurs, If a spiritual world sufficed before the creation of the material, why did it not always suffice, and what need of a material? An historic creation — a direct creation with a date, however remote — appears to me untenable, confuted moreover, as it is, by two axioms to be remembered in this connection: No force without stuff, and no stuff without force; and, The quantity of force in existence is always the same.

Another important element in the consideration of this question is the *necessary* character, the character of divine necessity, which belongs to the idea of creation, viewed in connection with the being of God. I mean to say, that creation is inconceivable as an act of divine free-choice, in the sense that the God who chose to create might as

[1] Quoted by Strauss, Christliche Glaubenslehre, par. 46.

well have chosen not to create, or might not have created had he so willed. For then might God have been other than he is, since the character of the being and the character of the will are inseparable. When we say that God might have done other than he has done, we say that he might have *been* other than he is, — a proposition which contradicts itself, since God by definition is *necessarily* God. Creation must be regarded as a necessary manifestation of the divine nature, — the inevitable going forth of himself, of the Creator, who only by going forth of himself becomes real to himself. "For," says the "Theologia Germanica," "God without creature has essential but not actual being." Moreover, if creation is not necessary, then it is fortuitous, — a chance creation, as Spinoza has aptly pointed out. "Necessary and fortuitous," he says, "are opposites; therefore, whoever asserts that God might have abstained from creating a world, evidently says, in effect, that the world was made by chance, as proceeding from a volition which might not have been." The idea of God involves creation. "God as spirit," says Hegel, "is essentially self-manifestation." This is his "idea." God before and without the creation of the world is pure abstraction. Without a world, God is not God.

Two difficulties which lie in the way of a rational

theory of the origin of things — the difficulty of imagining a beginning in time of the sensible world, and the difficulty of arbitrariness in the act of creation — being thus disposed of, there remains the difficulty arising from the supposition of a foreign substance distinct from God, and created by God in order therefrom to fashion the worlds which his fiat called into being. Creation of a foreign substance is creation out of nothing, — a view which we have seen to be based on no rational conception. The idea of a pre-existing material, coeternal with God, we have also seen to be inadmissible. Shall we say, then, that God himself is the substance of which the worlds are formed? This, in some sense, I am driven to admit; but not in the way of Spinozism. Spinoza invests Deity with the attribute of extension. Extension with him is not an operation, but a quality of God. This view obliterates all distinction between God and the sensible world, and gives us not merely Pantheism, — which, properly defined, is still Theism, — but Cosmotheism, Hylotheism. Spinoza is called by Novalis "a God-intoxicated man." His system has great fascinations, — it enlarges our sense of the divine Presence; but, after all, it takes from the idea of God its most essential element, that which religion will never consent to part with, — the attribute of lordship. Its logical defects are obvious; and Schelling's criticism is just, — that, whilst it invests God with the two qualities of thought and extension, it brings them into no relation. "Thought and extension are as much estranged from each other in the system of Spinoza as in that of Descartes. Thought, according to him, has no part in the modifications of the extended substance, although modification — that is, determination — is conceivable only as an act of thought. It is only on account of the actual existence of things that Spinoza posits modifications in his infinite Substance. The things are not products of thought; and, were there not things independent of his system, there could, from his principles, be none deduced."

I can see but two ways of escape from Spinozism on the one hand, and the ontological dualism of Descartes[1] on the other; to wit, the two theories last named in my catalogue, — creation out of spirit, and ideal creation.

Of the former of these, the Monadology of Leibnitz is an apt example. Leibnitz supposes the universe to consist of monads or entelechies; some of which are conscious, and some unconscious.

---

[1] The dualism of Descartes had its origin apparently in the supposed necessity of a second substance to serve as the ground of extension, which he conceived as a *state*. But extension may be conceived as a continuous act of spirit.

The conscious, or those which have apperceptions, are spiritual monads, or souls; the unconscious, or those which have only perceptions, are simply monads. They all exist by momentary fulguration from the central monad, which is God. The defect of this system is that it fails to account for the difference of conscious and unconscious in the different orders of monads, which, as momentary utterances from one and the same Being, should have equal worth.

Abandoning, then, the momentary fulguration of the monads, and substituting for it a momentary influx of the life by which they subsist and act, let us supplement the theory of Leibnitz with a thought of Boehme. Let us suppose that God in the beginning created a universe of spirits; that some of these spirits by self-will estranged themselves from the Fountain Spirit, until by utter defection they lost their self-possession, their conscious life. Suppose this, and we have the unconscious monads of Leibnitz. This theory, it is true, does not explain the defection of spirits. But defection is one of the liabilities of that free-will with which all spirits must be supposed to be endowed. And, certainly, it is a comfort to think that fallen spirits can be turned to so good a use as to furnish a *pièce de résistance* for their betters.

In discussing the origin of things, the existence

of things has of course been presumed: so much has been conceded to ancient universal prejudice. Bishop Berkeley, who seems of all philosophers to have most completely emancipated himself from this prejudice, and the fundamental position of whose ontology, in the "Principles of Human Knowledge," is "*Esse est percipi*," represents the ideal creation. For creation there may be, though things there are none. Strictly speaking, ideal creation is no cosmogony, but simply a theory of being, a *ratio essendi* of the sensible world, and as such worthy of all respect; not to be vanquished by the grins of coxcombs,[1] grin they never so knowingly. Creation, according to this view, is the immediate action of God on the mind of each percipient; the world, a continuous communication between the infinite Spirit and the finite spirits formed of his essence.

---

1 "And coxcombs vanquish Berkeley with a grin."—Pope.

VIII.

THE GOD OF RELIGION, OR THE HUMAN GOD.

WHEN we read in the Bible that God made man in his own image, we may see in that statement a reflex of the fact that man makes God in his. It is a necessity of his nature so to do. All that we converse with or think of takes its character from ourselves. The sensible world of our experience is a texture woven on the loom of our nerves; the ideal world is a fabric fashioned in the mould of our thought. We think as we are. And so man fashions his God in his own image, endows him with the attributes he has learned to respect in the wisest and best of human kind. He is right in so doing; for what better can any one imagine than the highest possible degree of the best known kind?

But how, on this principle, account for the fact of fetishism? Does man make his God in his own likeness when he worships a serpent or a stone? The answer is, that man in that stage of development in which alone such worship is possible has not yet become conscious of his own image; he has not yet seized the idea of his humanity; it has not yet occurred to him that man is greater than serpent or stone, — greater than the outside world of his surrounding. The outside world to him is ultimate and omnipotent; there is nothing behind it; he feels its overweight and pressure; there is a mystery in Nature which overawes him, and in whatever object that mystery happens to strike his imagination most forcibly, — serpent or tiger, or log or stone, — that object becomes a god for him. But when, with advancing intellectual development, visible objects no longer occupy that place in his imagination, no longer satisfy his want of a God; when driven to seek his God in the invisible, with nothing to guide him but his own thought, — then, I say, it becomes a necessity of his nature to fashion his God in his own image. Man is the highest that he knows. The highest he can imagine is but an enlargement and transfiguration of the human. His God must be man, — superhuman, indeed, as transcending, in power, wisdom, and goodness, all human experience, all actual humanity; but still essentially man.

The God of religion must be an intelligent and moral nature. No being destitute of these qualities can fill the place of God for us; and of these qualities we can form no conception, except as they are manifest in human subjects. We suppose them indefinitely, infinitely extended, and invest our God with their likeness. We cannot do otherwise. If we have a God, he must be in some sort the reflex of our own nature. Mr. Arnold objects to a "God who thinks and loves," as being but a "magnified, non-natural man."[1] I say this is precisely what the God of religion must be, if devotion is to have an intelligible object: man without human limitations; intelligence and love personified. Non-natural, because Nature is birth, and God is unborn.

Nevertheless, it must be confessed that a God in our own image is a kind of idol; and the worship of that image, without an accompanying consciousness of its inadequacy, may become idolatry. To find the just medium between vague abstraction — too vague for devotion — on the one hand, and idolatry on the other, is the problem of enlightened Theism. The question meets us at the threshold, Can we speak of God as person? And in what sense can we use that term? I answer, that, so far as religious uses are concerned, it is useless to talk of a God who is not in some sense person. Necessity, Fate, does not make a God; nor Power nor Intelligence alone; nor Mr. Arnold's "Eternal not ourselves that makes for righteous-

[1] "God and the Bible."

ness."[1] These may suggest the origin or express the moral order of the universe; but they do not constitute a God whom one can pray to, — a God whom one would care to worship, or would ever draw near to and seek to commune with. The God of our devotion, if devotion is any thing more than an empty farce, must be, in some sense, person. And in what sense?[2] I include in that idea intelligent Will, providential care, and a moral government of the universe. There may be other properties belonging to this idea; but these are essential. In this sense, then, the God of religion must be person. "Deus sine dominio, providentia, et causis finalibus," says Newton, "nihil aliud est quam fatum et natura."

But we know how difficult it is to disconnect

---

[1] "God and the Bible." Strange that a writer who criticises with so much acuteness should fail to perceive the hollowness of his own definition, which puts a vague abstraction in the place of a living Will.

[2] Words exercise a controlling influence on thought and belief. When turned from their original import, and fixed in some perverted use, they breed misconception and propagate ineradicable error. The word "person," which meant originally a mask, then the *rôle* of an actor on the stage, and which might be fitly employed to designate the manifestation of a Being in character and action, has come in its perversion to signify the conscious self, the human *ego*. That *ego* is not the deepest in man, but springs from an unknown ground. God, as the ground of all individuality, is superpersonal. He becomes personal to each believer through the medium of his own consciousness, as a thousand lenses may at the same moment concentrate, each in a separate focus, the rays of the sun.

the idea of person from that of form, from the individual human form. All the personality that we know any thing about is vested in human forms. A person, for us, means a human individual. The terms are synonymous. It is difficult not to invest Deity with a human form; but the moment we do so, we lapse into idolatry. The form becomes an idol. If it serves to represent Deity to us, it also necessarily misrepresents him. If it helps our conception, it also necessarily misconceives, — in fact, extrudes Deity from our thought, and installs another in his place. The very use of the masculine pronoun in this connection is misleading. It is unavoidable. We must say "He" and "His," if we speak of God at all; but what subtle illusions and idolatries lurk in those pronouns! How strong the tendency to conceive of God as not only distinct from creation in idea, but as spatially separated from creation, — as an individual in space! It is difficult, I say, to disconnect the idea of personality from that of the human form. And the human form is so dear to us, so essential to our affections! The imagination insists upon it. It seems scarcely possible to be much in love with any thing else, — with any thing that does not wear that form in our imagination. And this, I suppose, is the reason why Christians have made a God of Christ: they want an idol. I can fully appreciate the feeling which leads men to worship Christ as Deity. God, they say, the absolute Being, is to them a thin abstraction, too vague and vast and remote and inconceivable to serve them as an object of worship. They want for that purpose a God of their own make; a God who has appeared in human form; a God whom they can thoroughly apprehend with their idea. They believe in the infinite Father; but can better understand and more confidently approach and commune with the Son. This is the feeling of the great body of Christians everywhere. It is very natural, but nevertheless it is idolatry; it is the same feeling which, in ruder times, gave birth to graven images of wood and stone to represent God. Then it was a sculptured or pictured idol; now it is a mental one. It was natural that Christians should be led, by veneration for the founder of their religion, to worship him as God. But when I read in the Gospel that the Christ whom they worship was himself a worshipper,—was always looking to One who was higher than himself, that he prayed to One whom he called Father, revealing thereby the conscious limitation of his own finite nature,—I cannot but regard such worship as idolatry. Idolatry is every worship that stops short of the Supreme.

The God of our devotion must be person; but devotion does not require that we invest that person with a human form. It is a trick of the imagination, of the image-making faculty, that does this. If we give reins to the imagination, it is difficult not to confound person with form. But the understanding readily discriminates between the two. Take the analogy of the human individual. We call the human individual a person. But what constitutes personality is not the visible form, but the invisible soul which animates that form. What that soul is to the individual, that God is to the universe of things, — its central Soul, the supreme Personality, regent in all and present in all by diffused consciousness, as the human soul is present by diffused consciousness in every part of the human organism. The human organism is a world in little, of which the soul is its God. The organic Whole, the world in its entireness, is a body of which God is the soul, — not identical with the body in form, and not separated from it in space. This is the best conception I can form of Deity; conscious, nevertheless, how inadequate all human conceptions of Deity must be. In religion, it is a matter of less moment that the intellect should form a perfect conception, than that the heart should have perfect conviction. Happily, the eternal Mystery, which eludes the efforts of the most developed understanding that seeks to comprehend it, condescends to the crudest and most infantile mind that is satisfied with believing. "Thou hast hid these things from the wise and prudent, and revealed them unto babes," is as true of the being of God as it is of all his counsels.

Here, as in all things, the intellect has its rights; but the office of the intellect in relation to God is not to attempt to fathom the idea, but to clear it of what is false and unworthy, — to correct that idolatrous tendency which would make the infinite and inscrutable altogether such an one as ourselves. This tendency lurks in the characters we ascribe to him, when even in themselves and with proper limitations those characters are worthy and true, — are the best conceptions we can form of the Divine.

For example, we call God father, and we have the highest authority for so doing. The most touching and inspiring things that have been said of him by wise and holy men connect themselves with this epithet: "Like as a father pitieth his children, so the Lord pitieth them that fear him." What more endearing, encouraging, reconciling! "Our Father which art in heaven." How much of Godhead — of the beauty and loveableness of Godhead — that phrase conveys! God must be conceived as Father, in order that we may get the nearest access to him, and the best enjoyment of his idea. The love of God must be conceived as paternal, in order that we may conceive of God's loving at all. The idea of a rigid and unchangeable order of events, comprehending all our destinies and yielding now joy and now sorrow, according as our several spheres are adjusted to the general plan, does not satisfy us, — gives us really no God: it is too impersonal. We want to believe that the Being whose offspring we are has a care of his creatures, not only collectively but individually; perceives their necessities, feels them, ministers to them, making all things with set purpose work for their good. And this satisfaction we have when we think of God as father; this faith we express when, with a full understanding of its import, we employ that term. Still, it becomes us to remember that the term, after all, is a figure of speech, not a literal fact; and that the figure which likens the eternal Power to an earthly parent may be pushed beyond its just application. It is applicable only as expressing a Providence whose motive power is love. It is carried too far when it tempts us to impute to the Ruler of worlds the indulgent weakness of an earthly parent, who would spare his child all sorrow and suffering, and saturate him with perpetual felicities. The fatherhood of God consists with a great deal of misery and helplessness and want and distress; it consists with extreme suffering; it consists with fearful inequalities of fortune; with the existence of myriads who are born diseased and maimed and crippled, and drag their life through years of pain, without apparently one full draught of the joy of being. We call God father, but misery abounds; we believe him omnipotent, but misery continues. We think, Would an earthly father be willing to see his children suffer, and suffer hopelessly, who had power to help and relieve? And, when we look for explanation to the heavenly Father, he hides himself in thick darkness. And we have to modify and complement our idea of the fatherhood of God with other aspects and facts of the divine nature; and to learn that, though God is a father, it is a fatherhood which earthly relations fail to pattern, and which earthly experience fails to interpret.

Again, we call God moral governor and judge, and we are right in so doing. There is nothing more definitive in Deity than the moral jurisdiction which the Ruler of all exercises over moral natures. All religions recognize this moral government. Whatever else they may teach or fail to teach concerning God, they all inculcate the belief that he tries and judges men by their actions; recompensing good with good, and evil with evil. But here again it must be remembered that we are dealing with figures, and not with literal truths. The terms "moral governor" and "judge" are figures of speech derived from human relations, which fit the being and action of God in only one point, and are likely to mislead if taken as literal statements of divine operations. The point in which they fit is the fact, that, by the constitution of man and of things, well-doing is productive of well-being, and sin of suffering. This is all that is meant, or should be meant, by the moral government of God. The moment we exceed this, and transfer human methods to divine retributions, the terms "moral governor" and "judge" are found to be inapplicable. The judgments of men are an action on each particular case; those of God inhere in the case itself. Those of man are after the act; those of God are before the birth of the actor, from the foundation of the world. There is no trial and no judgment of evil-doers; their penalty is merely the relation of the seed to the fruit. Every act that a man performs as a moral agent is seed cast into the ground. When he acts a crime, he sows nightshade instead of corn, and his punishment is that he reaps poison instead of bread. The penalty is not always immediate and not always apparent, and human impatience is often disappointed in its expectation of visible retributions, and looks in vain for some stunning demonstration of divine vengeance. Here is an innocent man persecuted and trampled on by some unrighteous oppressor; here, one tortured and put to death for difference of opinion; here, again, a conspiracy of swindlers in office, banded together to defraud the government they are sworn to serve, and enrich themselves by enormous plunder. Will it please Omnipotence to give attention to these outrages, and send a swift thunder-bolt to smite the transgressors? Omnipotence attends; but as to the thunder-bolt the answer is, "Thou thoughtest I was altogether such an one as thyself," and must needs blaze forth in flaming fury at every enormity which my creatures perpetrate. "My ways are not as your ways." I make my sun to shine and my rain to fall alike on the evil and the good, and my thunder-bolts strike indifferently the just and the unjust. What need of thunder-bolts to smite the transgressor? The seed was planted when the deed was done, and no power in heaven or on earth can prevent the ripening of the penal fruit. The mills of God grind slowly, but they grind. Long-suffering turns the wheel, and patient Justice appoints the result, — tribulation and anguish to the evil-doer, and peace and contentment to the good.

These are illustrations of what is true and what is false in man's propensity to fashion God in his own image. The tendency is inevitable. Man must have a God in his own image, if he have one at all, or one that really answers to that name and need. The God of religion must be human. But this human God must be infinitely human, — man, without man's infirmities and bounds; personal, without individuality; the Father, without parental doting; the moral Ruler, without vindictiveness.

In religion, it is sentiment that furnishes the stuff; and the intellect, that, by modifying and eliminating, gives the form. All that is essential in our idea of God we get, not from the understanding, but from the heart; and all that is essential in it is secured to us by the heart's perpetual need. Philosophy may assail the conception, and science may disown the idea; but they furnish nothing that can fill its place. The pure in heart will still see God. The pure heart is a little child that knows its Father, and will hear of no substitute. In the morning of creation, it sought and found the unseen Friend, when "Enoch walked with God." From the "house of bondage," in after years, it sent up a sigh, and received for answer the great word, "I am." In the noontide of history, it paused to listen, and learned to say, "Our Father in heaven." And when time is old, when Science has fulfilled its career, and Speculation repeated its ever-recurring circle, and both have confessed their incompetence alike to grasp or refute; when prophecies fail, and tongues have ceased, and fancied knowledge of the Absolute vanished away, — the heart, the eternal child, with invincible faith, will still rejoice in Him "in whom we live and move and have our being."

IX.

DUALISM AND OPTIMISM.

FOUR differing views of the universe divide the belief of speculative minds.

I. The universe the sole product of a single, extramundane, intelligent Will. II. The universe the joint product and battle-ground of two opposing Powers. III. The universe the self-manifestation of an immanent, diffusive Soul. IV. The universe a self-subsisting, independent Reality. — Theism, Ditheism or Dualism, Pantheism, Atheism.

Theism is the view which lies nearest to us, as the common belief of the Christian world. But Theism, referring as it does all facts and events to a single supreme Power, encounters a difficulty in human experience which faith may adjust to its own satisfaction, but which philosophy is troubled to explain to the satisfaction of the understanding.

The difficulty is this: that while by supposition the Will that creates and ordains is one, the manifestations not only differ but conflict. The unity affirmed of the Cause is not apparent in the operation. The Power over all is conceived to be omnipotent, omni-beneficent, willing only the best; but the product is not, so far as we can see, that perfect world which ought to result from such a source. The Power is affirmed to be absolutely good, but the world abounds in evil. How from the one pure Source can contraries flow? How from the one Good can evil proceed? No question in theology, and none in philosophy, goes deeper than this. No problem has proved more perplexing.

The old Hebrew theology, as represented by the later Isaiah, was content to refer the evil with the good to the arbitrary power of Jehovah, whose simple will sufficed to justify the one as well as the other. "I am Jehovah, and there is none else. I form the light and create darkness; I make peace and create evil." It is not till after the Captivity that Judaism exhibits other views of the origin of evil.

Meanwhile, to the Aryan mind in its Persian development, the contemplation of a world where good and evil appear to contend for the mastery had suggested the existence of a principle of Evil, — a malignant being opposed to the good, sole cause of all mischief in the world of bodies and the world of souls. Two self-subsistent, independent forces, a power that creates and a power that destroys, a power that blesses and a power that harms, — this is the theory of the universe known in philosophy as Dualism, in religion as Parsism. Traces of it appear in the good and bad deities of the polytheistic religions; but its consummation, the sharp distinction of a good and an evil power, — the one to be sought, obeyed, worshipped, the other to be renounced and shunned, — is the prime and distinguishing feature of Parsism, the religion of ancient Persia, from which sprung the Manicheism, so threatening to Christianity in the fourth and fifth centuries, and of which a remnant still survives in the Parsis of India.

Parsism ranks with the oldest of existing religions, and, though greatly modified and perverted in its subsequent developments, still claims for its founder Zarathustra, — better known as Zoroaster, — one of the leaders of the human race, whose name at the distance of more than three thousand years, like that of Abraham, his Semitic compeer, represents a hero of faith. Like Abraham, Zarathustra repudiated the idol-worship of his time, and initiated a religion of the spirit. In the thirteenth century before Christ, according to Dunker, on a mountain consecrated to the ancient idolatrous worship of fire, the reformer appeared before an assembly of the nation convened for the celebration of an annual sacrifice, and called on king and people to renounce "the religion of lies," and embrace the truth of the spirit as he should declare it. Bunsen[1] compares the scene to that in which the prophet Elijah refuted the priests of Baal in the presence of the people of Israel. "Choose ye this day whom ye will serve," — Ahura-Mazda the wise Lord, or the false divinities of the lying priests of fire. "Two spirits there are," he says, "originally and fundamentally different, — a twin pair from the beginning, a good and an evil. They rule in thought, word, and deed; choose ye between them."

We have here the first historic enunciation of the principle of dualism, 1300 B. C., at the lowest computation; according to some authorities, especially Bunsen, many centuries earlier.[2]

But the principle itself, or the view of Nature in which it originated, is earlier still. It lay in the ideas and the corresponding worship which Zoroaster found established in Iran, and which it was his mission to reform. That elder religion consisted in the worship of fire and light. These types, while insisting on the worship of spirit, Zoroaster retained by way of compromise, as symbols of truth and good. Hence sprung the religion

---

[1] Gott in der Geschichte.

[2] Bunsen places Zoroaster, at the latest, 2500 B. C. See Gott in der Geschichte, Vol. II. p. 78.

of Parsism, one of the notable and representative religions of the world. In virtue of its ethical character, I reckon it among the revealed religions, although less entitled to that designation than the rest of its class, on account of its mixed origin, — not being like Jehovism or Mohammedism, the product of pure reflection, but admitting in conjunction with the inner light an element of naturalism. It has its root in a vivid sense of the primal antithesis of Nature, — the antithesis of light and darkness. No wonder that this eldest and sharpest of all antagonisms should assume in primitive thought a typical significance. The religion of Iran made it the symbol of moral good and evil. These opposites were represented by two antagonist powers, — Ahura-Mazda or Ormazd, the wise Lord, and Angra-Mainyus or Ahriman, the evil Spirit. Ormazd, the source of all good, dwells in perfect light. Ahriman, the source of all evil, resides in the deepest darkness. The visible world derives its character from the mutual relation and interaction of these two principles. Its origin, fortunes, and final consummation result from their antagonism. Spiegel, translator of the Avesta, has sketched the orthodox cosmology of Parsism, of which I here present the more salient features.

From the beginning the two powers were mutually abhorrent, though separated the one from the other by a boundless interval of vacant space. Ahriman became aware of the existence of his opposite; and, maddened by the sight of the strange apparition, rushed forward to destroy it. Ormazd, by virtue of his omniscience, had known of the existence of Ahriman, and saw in him an antagonist who must be overcome, but whose conquest would prove a difficult task; the two being equal in strength, and each supreme in his own domain. Now, it belongs to the nature of Ormazd to think before acting; to that of Ahriman to act before thinking. Consequently, Ormazd debated with himself the means of success in this impending warfare. He foresaw that a present attack might fail, but that victory was assured by postponing the conflict.

Meanwhile, he created beings adapted to his ends; and Ahriman on his part did the same: that is, he opposed to each of the creations of Ormazd a corresponding negative, — for Ahriman is incapable of independent creations. Three thousand years were consumed in these productions. At the end of that period, Ormazd persuaded Ahriman to enter into a compact by which it was agreed to defer their battle for nine thousand years. These, added to the three thousand which preceded, make up the twelve thousand of the world's duration. When the treaty was concluded, Ormazd uttered the prayer which Parsism hallows with the term "Honover." Then Ahriman, who, as usual, had acted before thinking, in agreeing to the treaty, perceived that he had been outwitted, and retreated, in his rage and terror, into the abyss of darkness, where he remained in a state of stupor for three thousand years. Ormazd improved the interval with new creations, in which he was assisted by certain spirits, — his former creatures. The earth with its belongings, previously called into being, but subsisting in heaven, was now let down into the vacant space which separates the kingdom of Ormazd from the realms of Ahriman. There it serves as an outpost and fortress to protect the world of light from the powers of darkness. When half the term assigned for the world's duration had elapsed, Ahriman, awaking from his long torpor at the instigation of his devs, began to bestir himself, and to make his preparations for the final conflict. Emerging from his darkness, he finds the earth placed between him and the hostile territory. He bores a hole through its bottom, and so reaches its surface. There he succeeds in seducing the first human pair, Meschia and Meschiane, from their allegiance to Ormazd, and thereby obtains a limited dominion over their posterity. All the imperfections and woes of life, all noxious creatures, all earthly evils and plagues, are his creation.

The earth, then, is the proper arena and battle-ground of these antagonistic principles. Inferior natures serve by compulsion their several authors; but man is free to choose which side he will embrace, which master he will serve. Neutral he cannot remain; he must declare himself for one or the other party, and abide the consequences of his decision. It is believed by the Parsis that Ahriman, originally the equal of Ormazd in power, has long since ceased to be so. He is constantly losing ground; so that when the nine thousand years of the compact are ended, and the final battle is fought, the good principle is sure to obtain an easy victory.

A different view of the origin of evil is entertained by a sect of the Parsis, called the Zervanites, as represented by the Arabian, Asch Schaharastani. According to him, a portion of the Persians believed in an aboriginal being, whom they named Zrvana Akerana (endless time). Zrvana offered a sacrifice in order to obtain a son; but a doubt arose in his mind whether a son would be given him. From this doubt sprang Ahriman: Ormazd was the fruit of the sacrifice. The father determined to confer the rule on the first-born. Ormazd, yet unborn, became aware of this intent, and imparted his knowledge to his unborn brother. Whereupon Ahriman broke through the maternal womb, and came first into the world. Nevertheless, Zrvana looked upon Ormazd as the rightful senior, and accorded to him the right of primogeniture. But not to do injustice to Ahriman, he gave him the dominion for nine thousand years, at the expiration of which the elder brother is to have the supremacy.

Of the whole cycle of twelve thousand years, which both systems accept as the allotted term of the world's duration, one-half had elapsed when evil appeared on the earth. The third quarter extends from the appearance of Ahriman to the birth of Zoroaster, and the reformation of the national religion. The servants of Ahriman, aware of the expected appearance of this prophet, exerted themselves to prevent his birth; and when that was found impossible, to destroy him when born. Rescued by a series of miracles, at the age of thirty he is brought into communion with Ormazd, and receives from him the revelation, which he is instructed to communicate to Vistaspa, King of Bactria, and to the rest of mankind. Accordingly, Zoroaster repairs to the court of Vistaspa, and, by miraculous demonstration of his mission, induces that monarch to accept the revelation of the Avesta. This revelation is conceived by the Parsis as a weapon which acts on evil spirits — the agents of Ahriman — when presented to them, as material weapons act on mortal bodies. It consists, in part, of practical rules of life for the conduct of believers, and partly of instructions concerning the life to come, — its rewards and punishments, — and concerning the issue of the conflict between Ormazd and Ahriman, and the end of the world.

As the final struggle approaches, Ahriman, conscious of imminent peril to his realm, exerts himself in convulsive efforts to recover the ground he has lost, and to harry his adversary. Hence, all the evils of the latter times, especially wars, oppressions, and persecutions of the faithful. To mitigate these sorrows, Ormazd sends every thousand years a new prophet, who brings from heaven some further dispensation of the Avesta, and intercalates in the midst of the evil years a temporary reign of justice and peace. The last of these expected prophets will be Soziosh, of the seed of Zoroaster, but born of a virgin; who, when he appears, will abolish the evils inflicted by Ahriman, and, with the assistance of seven — or, according to the Bundehesh, fifteen — of the most distinguished saints of all time, precursors of the final judgment, will establish a millennium of blessing. One sign of its approach will be a diminution of animal desire, to that extent that men will no longer care to eat. Then comes the resurrection of the dead, the accomplishment of which will occupy a period of fifty-seven years. After that the general conflagration, when "the elements shall melt with fervent heat, and the earth and the works that are therein shall be burned up." The whole race of men will pass through the flames, that all may be thoroughly purged of their sins. The righteous will experience no discomfort in the process; the godless, on the contrary, will suffer excruciating torments. But, purified by suffering, they, too, will survive the fiery trial, and come forth whole and happy; the universe will be freed from all evil. Ahriman is then defeated, hell destroyed, and Ormazd and his blessed family of spirits alone remain.

These are the main features of the Zoroastrian cosmology, with which the ethical system of the Parsis entirely corresponds. According to the life which the individual leads in this world will be his condition in the next. He whose thoughts and words, as well as deeds, are pure and true is accepted as a votary of Ormazd, and will be received into the fellowship of the spirits of light. Whoever was an adversary of Ormazd in this world will be surrendered to Ahriman, and have his abode in the deepest darkness in the world to come. On the third day after his death, the character and life of each individual are brought to judgment. The soul must repair to the bridge *Tschinvad*, where the ways that lead, the one to heaven the other to hell, diverge. There are seated the judges of the dead, who weigh all their deeds in a balance. If the good preponderate, the soul continues its journey over the bridge and arrives in Paradise, where it is welcomed by all the just and lives in joy and blessedness until the final judgment. If the good and evil deeds exactly balance each the other, the soul is sent to a place called Hamestegân, where neither reward nor punishment awaits it. But when the soul of the evil-doer, on the third day after death, arrives at the bridge Tschinvad and attempts to pass over, it seems so narrow and dangerous that the soul is seized with dizziness and tumbles into the abyss beneath, where it is received with taunts and scoffs by Ahriman and his devs, and tortured by them till the day of judgment. That the Parsi, if possible, may be saved from this doom, he is early instructed in the truths of his religion; and at the age of fifteen is invested with the *Kosti*, the sacred cord, in token of his formal reception into the communion of his faith. He then takes upon himself the responsibilities of life and the duties of religion. He is a member of the invisible Church of the faithful, whereby the good deeds of others, and especially of his ancestry, redound to his spiritual benefit.

Of ancient religions, Parsism is that in which moral good and evil are most sharply distinguished. In no other religion is the antagonism of a good and an evil principle so fundamental to its organism and so conspicuous in all its developments. In fact, whatever of a like antagonism appears in subsequent religions — especially in Judaism, Islamism, Christianity — has descended directly or indirectly from this Persian original. The Mosaic religion exhibits little or nothing of it previous to the return of the Jews from their Captivity, when they appear as a Persian colony in Palestine.

A striking illustration of the change which intercourse with Persia had wrought in the views of the Hebrew people may be found in the different accounts that are given in the Bible of the census ordered by David of the population of his realm. The earlier narrative in the second Book of Samuel ascribes the institution of this census to the prompting of Jehovah; the later, written after the Captivity, imputes it to the instigation of Satan.

Another proof of Persian influence is the fact that while the Old Testament has very little to say about the Devil (for the serpent in the Garden of Eden does not, as vulgarly supposed, represent the evil principle; and Satan in the Book of Job is not the Satan of the later theology, but one of the sons of God), — that while the Old Testament has very little to say about the Devil, the New Testament is full of him.

According to the doctrine of the Avesta, every man is a follower either of Ormazd or Ahriman. Neutrality is impossible: to one or the other party every soul, and indeed every creature, belongs. A line of unbending rigidity and unchangeable determination bisects the universe, disposing all that is genial and healthful and beautiful and lovable — good men and women, useful or harmless animals or plants — on one side, and arraying all bad people and noxious creatures, snakes and scorpions, and poisonous plants, on the other.

But man, and especially the Parsi, is vowed by his origin to fight the battle of Ormazd against his enemy. Hence, one of the good works of Parsism is to till and plant the earth with corn and wholesome fruit; and another is to hunt out and put to death all noxious and dangerous animals.

The religion is encumbered with a complex ritual; its purifications, its fasts and other formalities, impose a heavy burden on the worshipper. Still it is emphatically a *moral* religion; of all religions except the Christian the most moral. And the fundamental article of its ethical code is *truth*, the soul of all morality. Truth-telling and truth-acting is the duty, above all others, enjoined by the Avesta. Comparing this religion with other religions of antiquity, one is tempted to say that *truth* is a Persian invention. Accordingly, fidelity in contracts is one of the distinguishing virtues of the Parsi people, and has given them the high position they occupy in modern India, — where they have a flourishing settlement, and where the Parsi merchant holds, among all the nationalities represented in that land, the foremost rank in wealth and commercial repute.

I return to the principle of dualism embodied in the Persian faith. From the Zoroastrian religion it passed into Judaism, and thence into Christendom. The pseudo-Christian idea of the Devil is its lineal and legitimate fruit. I call it pseudo-Christian; for though Jesus employed the term, or, if you please, the conception, as a given article in the mental furniture of his time, he by no means accents it in a way to authorize its acceptance as a necessary constituent of the Christian creed. It is scarcely any longer regarded as such. Of Christian beliefs once universally received, and never so much as questioned, there is none which seems to have passed into such general discredit, none which is losing so fast its hold of the popular mind. The Devil is still a name to swear by, and still, as a figure of speech, represents a spiritual fact, but no longer stands for an ontological or statistical one. There is something very curious, and not easily explained, in this noiseless and imperceptible dropping out from the mind and creed of mankind of a once universal and rooted conviction. For nearly two thousand years the belief in Satan was as fixed as any belief whatsoever in the mind of Christendom. For more than a thousand, the doctrine of the Atonement was not, as modern Orthodoxy conceives it, a satisfaction of divine Justice, but was understood as a satisfaction of Satan, to whom the world was supposed to have become forfeit by sin. The early Church, among its regular officials, had always one whose business it was to fight the Devil in the person of any of his subordinates who might take possession of a human subject. In every church the exorcist was as much a stated functionary as the deacon or the priest. The idea of Satan was not one of those which the Protestant Reformation repudiated, as it did that of purgatory and the efficacy of the mass. Luther, the arch-reformer, insisted upon it, urged it as one of the fundamentals of the Christian system. The Devil was as real to him as the Pope, or Tetzel, or Dr. Eck. In his Commentary on the Epistle to the Galatians he says: "We are all subject to the Devil with our bodies and our estate. We are but guests in a world of which he is the prince and the god. The bread we eat, the water we drink, the garments we wear, the very air, and all by which we live in the flesh, is subject to his control."

From that time forward, until a comparatively recent date, Protestants — clergy and laity, with few exceptions — have assumed the existence of such a being with as little hesitation as they assumed the existence of God. They would as soon have questioned the latter as the former. Within this century ministers have been known to pray for his conversion, either hoping with Origen that such a consummation might be a part of the divine scheme, or holding with Burns, that, would he "tak' a thought and men'," he "aiblins might" "still hae a stake."

The belief in Satanic agency had a fearfully tragic side, in the contemplation of which one shudders at the awful and uncontrollable power of religious ideas over unenlightened human nature. The long delusion of witchcraft with the thence resulting persecutions, which desolated Christendom with ghastliest horrors and countless deaths, was the natural outcome of this belief. Those terrors which darkened and perplexed the life of former generations have passed away. Like spectres begotten of nightmare and the dark, with the dawn of a new intellectual day

> "The flocking shadows pale
> Troop to the infernal jail."

Satan, the head and sovereign of this spectral realm, is passing from the fear and faith of mankind, and a load whose agonizing pressure we but faintly conceive has been lifted from the mind.

The tragedy over, the farce succeeds. Where the fathers trembled, the children jest. Whom Luther declared to be the Lord of this earth is pursued with Lucianic derision as he goes the way of the Olympian gods, chased by inexorable science into the vast nowhere of the phantom world: no longer owned by enlightened theology; for purposes of fiction even, no longer available. The genius of Goethe has enucleated the true interior import of the theological Devil, — the spirit of negation. "Culture" — says Mephistopheles to the witch who finds him very different from her idea, — "culture that licks the world smooth has extended itself even to the Devil. The Northern phantom is now no more seen; in vain you look for horns, and tail, and claws." And when the witch breaks out, —

> "I shall lose my wits with joy, I fear,
> To see Squire Satan once more here," —

he answers, "Woman, I forbid that name!" Witch: "Why, what harm is in the word?" Mephistopheles: —

> "In the fable-book it was long since scored;
> But human kind therefrom have little gain;
> The *Evil One* is gone, but evil ones remain."

The real Devil, as figured in Mephistopheles, is "the spirit that denies," the opposing, unbelieving, bitter, mocking spirit, — the spirit whose idiom is sarcasm, whose life is a sneer. There is nothing more alien from Godhead, nothing more undivine, more antagonistic to all divineness, than such a spirit; whose natural symbol is the ape, and whose theological expression is "the sin against the Holy Ghost."

Satan has disappeared from the realm of accredited existences, but that which Satan stood for remains; and much as we rejoice to see, in the language of the Apocalypse, "the old Serpent which is called the Devil and Satan," "cast out," philosophy misses a convenient answer to the question, "Whence and why the evil that is in the world?" The idea of Satan was the eldest solution of that question. A very convenient solution it was; an easy way of disposing of every noxious and painful experience, of every calamity and mishap, and all moral evil as well, — to refer it, as Luther did, to the one arch-enemy of human kind. Men seemed to themselves to explain the existence of evil by personifying it.

Reject as we may the personification, the fact remains; what the world calls evil remains; and the questions, Whence? and Why? still haunt the philosophic mind. How reconcile the existence of evil with the being and rule of a wise and good God, almighty to effect what love proposes and wisdom plans?

There is but one answer to this question. What love proposes, and wisdom plans, must needs be good. This fundamental truth of practical reason is the only solution of the problem. In the view and intent of a Being of infinite wisdom and goodness there can be no evil. Such a Being sees, and knows, and does only good. What we call evil, therefore, the evil of our experience, when referred to its source, has precisely the same character with that which we call good. If God is good, and if all that is proceeds from him, there is no evil. Suffering, distress, privation, woes of every kind; but no evil. All is good in its origin and purpose, and must eventually approve itself as good in human experience.

This summary solution of the problem is not a

conclusion reached, or that ever could be reached, by reasoning, as theologians have commonly reasoned, from the world to its author. Had we no other knowledge of God, and no other way of arriving at the truth of his being than that which is given us in the contemplation of the world as it is, inferring from visible effects the invisible cause, I doubt if human wit would ever have reasoned out a Being all wise and good from the study of nature and life. Take the world as it is, with all its contradictions, woes, and wrongs; and without other light what sort of God would the contemplation of such a world present? Possibly, infinite Power; but not, I think, infinite Wisdom and Love. If we honestly reason from effect to cause, whatever is in the effect must be in the cause; whatever of imperfection and evil there is in the one must be in the other. There is no evading this obvious truth. The only way to vindicate the goodness of God, in view of the seeming ills of life, is to reason the other way, from the cause to the effect. We know, or believe that we know, the divine Cause. We have the idea of a perfect Being, an all-wise and utterly beneficent God. Starting with this, and reasoning from this to the facts of life, we conclude that all that is and befalls must be good,—good in its purpose, and good in its end.

To the question, then, How evil consists with

the goodness of God? I answer flatly, It does not consist with the goodness of God. One or the other of these conceptions must be abandoned. Either there is no God, such as we figure him, or there is no evil. Believing in a God on the strength of his idea in my mind, independently of the argument from Nature, I say there is no evil. Pain and suffering in abundance, but no evil. For only that is really and absolutely evil which is evil in its cause and effect, in its origin and end; evil in all its issues, evil for evermore. Nothing in God's universe answers to that condition.

Obviously, if we consider it, that which we call evil is as much a necessary part of the Divine order as that which we call good, or it would not be in the Divine order at all. And obviously, the Divine order by its very definition must tend to good. Without that tendency to good in human things, which even the Atheist admits, the world would long since have ended in ruin. And the tendency to good, for ever accumulating its blest results, implies perpetual growth in good, perpetual progress toward perfection. And endless progress toward perfection is surely a greater good than a perfect finite state.

But the stimulus to progress must come from conscious imperfection, want, and pain. Picture to yourself a world without a flaw, without a want, without a pang; a world in which no storm ever darkens the sky, no struggle ever taxes the will, and no discomfort ever ruffles the breast; a world in which no battle is ever fought, and consequently no victory ever won; in which there is nothing to be desired, and consequently nothing to hope, — imagine such a world, and what have you? A state of perfect blessedness? Nay, but a state of pleasureless torpor and measureless *ennui.* No dream, no fancy which the heart of man indulges, is so utterly baseless as that of unbroken and unqualified enjoyment, — a world without foes, and fightings, and pains. Suffering is the price we pay for enjoyment; disaster, the price of safety; difficulty and danger, the price of progress. It needed all the calamities that have ever befallen, to bring mankind thus far in the onward way of their destiny. It needs all the woes and sorrows of life to flavor its happiness. All the dark side of it is indispensable to constitute its bright side.

To say all in a word: it follows with logical necessity from the very idea of God, that the world of his making and ruling must be the best possible world.

Leibnitz was the first to take this ground of unflinching Optimism, the first to base his theodicy, or vindication of the goodness of God, on the doctrine that the actual world is the best possible world. He saw that the honor of God is involved in the absolute perfection of his creation, and that, if the world were not the best possible, the failure or neglect to make it the best possible would imply a defect in its author of ability or will, of power or goodness; that, consequently, its author would not be the perfect Being affirmed by, and essential to, Theism. And since the world as it is is the best possible world, it follows that the evil that is in it, and which forms an inseparable constituent part of it, is necessary to make it the best possible.

Moral evil as well as physical is included by Leibnitz in this view. The world is a whole so connected, compacted, and dovetailed in all its parts, that nothing in it could be altered without altering all the rest. Strike out from it any existing evil, and, though you get rid of one objectionable ingredient, the world being thereby changed in all its parts is no longer the best possible world. Strike out from it the life of any villain who did or is doing his mischievous work in it, and no longer is it the best possible world. As Judas, the "son of perdition," was a necessary agent in establishing the Christian dispensation, so every malefactor is a necessary agent in that system of blessing which, according to this philosophy, the existing order is supposed to be.

Lawrence Valla, a writer of the fifteenth century, in a "Dialogue on the Freedom of the Will and its Relation to Divine Prescience," supposes Sextus Tarquinius, of infamous memory, to consult the oracle of Apollo, and there to learn his fate, which was to be driven an impoverished exile from the enraged city. Tarquin complains of such a doom, and is advised of the crime by which he would deserve it. "No," he replies, "I will do no such thing." "How!" says the god, "do you make me to be a liar? I show you the future; I tell you that which must come to pass." "But am I not free?" the youth indignantly demands; "is it not in my power to obey the dictates of virtue?" "Know, my poor Sextus," Apollo rejoins, "the gods make every one such as he is. Jupiter has made the wolf voracious, the hare timid, the ass foolish, the lion brave. He has given you a wicked, incorrigible soul; you will act in conformity with your nature, and Jupiter will deal with you as your actions will deserve. He has sworn it by the Styx."

Here Valla had left the case of Tarquin, and here Leibnitz takes it up. He supplements the apologue with a sequel conceived in the spirit of his philosophy. Sextus quits Delphos and applies to Jupiter at Dodona. "Why have you condemned me, O God, to be wicked and to be miserable?

Change my lot, and change my heart, or acknowledge your injustice." Jupiter tells him that, if he will renounce Rome, the Parcæ shall spin him other destinies, — he shall be good and happy. If he goes to Rome he is lost. Sextus is unwilling to make this sacrifice, and quitting the temple abandons himself to his fate. But Theodorus, the priest of that temple, humbly entreats Jupiter to explain why he has not given Sextus a different will. Jupiter refers him to his daughter, Minerva, at Athens. Theodorus makes the journey, arrives in Athens, and sleeps in the temple of Minerva, where he has a dream which conveys to him the desired explanation. His vision takes him to the Palace of Destinies which contains, as the goddess tells him, the representations not only of all that is to happen, but of all that is possible. These possibilities Jupiter surveyed in the beginning, arranged as so many possible worlds, and, having selected the most desirable, gave it being ; and so made the actual world of our experience.

She then conducts him to an apartment containing the plan of one of these possible worlds. There he sees a possible Sextus, who, on quitting the temple of Jupiter, instead of going to Rome, goes to a city between two seas, which might be supposed to be Corinth ; purchases a small garden, in digging it finds a treasure of which he makes a good use, lives beloved and respected, and dies at an advanced age, mourned by all the city. Theodorus then passes into another apartment, representing a differently planned world and sees again a possible Sextus; who, on quitting the temple, goes to Thrace, where he marries the daughter of the king, and succeeds him on the throne. The apartments are arranged in the form of a pyramid; and when Theodorus reaches the apartment which forms the apex, he is transported with ecstasy at the sight of a world-plan which far surpasses all its predecessors in splendor and beauty. He is beside himself with joy: "*Il ne se sentoit pas de joie.*" Then the goddess informs him that the world which he beholds, and in which it appears that Sextus, rejecting the counsel of Jupiter, goes to Rome and commits the crime which causes his ruin, — that this world which seems to him so beautiful, of all possible worlds the best, is the very world in which he lives.

Optimism is the true solution of the problem of evil, a doctrine with which that of Theism must stand or fall. If this world is not the best possible world, then the God of Theism is not that world's creator: the best possible, not as a present finality, but as means and method of the perfect good. This is the only Optimism which reason can legitimate. The time will never come when evil shall wholly cease from the earth, when all wrong shall be expunged, suffering unknown, and

> "Fear and sin and grief expire,
> Cast out by perfect love."

Neither in this world nor in any future world is such a state possible. Evil there must always be. Old evils may be abolished, but new evils will spring. The health of humanity requires the existence of evil as incentive to effort and topic of action. Progress is better than all perfection. Finding is good, but seeking is better, if finding is to end with rest in the found. The kingdom of heaven must be always coming; but hope would expire were it fully come. And the saying remains for ever true, that "by hope we are saved."

X.

PANTHEISM.

PANTHEISM is a name of bad repute in theology, where it passes for something akin to Atheism, and a good deal more dangerous.

The justice of this reproach depends on the definition we give to the term, and on the correctness of that definition. The word, though designating views and opinions as old as any in philosophy, is comparatively modern. The first writer who is known to have used it is the English Deist Toland, who, near the beginning of the last century, 1705, published a work, entitled "Socinianism fairly stated; being an Example of Fair Dealing in Theological Controversies. To which is prefixed, Indifference in Disputes recommended by a Pantheist to an Orthodox Friend." Some years later, in 1720, he published a treatise, entitled "Pantheisticum, sive Formula Societatis Socraticæ." In this he defines his Pantheism as follows: "Vis et Energia Totius, Creatrix omnium et Moderatrix, ac ad optimum finem semper tendens, est Deus, quem

Mentem dicas si placet, et Animam Universi: unde Sodales Socratici proprio ut dixi vocabulo appellantur Pantheistæ, cum vis illa secundum eos non nisi sola ratione ab ipsomet Universo separetur." "The Force and Energy of the Whole, the Creator and Ruler of all things, always tending to the best end, is God, whom, if you please, you may call the Mind and Soul of the Universe. Hence the *Sodales Socratici* are called, as I said, by the appropriate term 'Pantheists,' inasmuch as, according to them, that force is distinguished by reason alone from the Universe itself."

God, the creative and ruling power of the universe, distinguished by reason alone from the universe itself: if this definition be accepted, we have in Pantheism a theory distinguished from Theism proper by the immanence in Nature of the Supreme Power, but not less widely distinguished from Atheism by the supposition of a Power to which the name of God is applied. The appellation of "atheist" is then only legitimate when freely assumed, — when the existence of God, or the agency of an intelligent Will in the conduct of the universe, is expressly denied. So long as the philosopher professes to believe in a God, in whatever sense, and gives that name to a Power over all, the belief in God must be allowed him, however his conception of Deity may differ from yours or mine, however it may seem to us to want what is most essential to Godhead. It is not misconception of the nature, but denial of the fact, of Godhead, that constitutes Atheism.

Toland, so far as we know, was the first to assume the name of Pantheist, but by no means the first to pantheize. Nor does his definition of Pantheism embrace all the varieties of view which might with equal propriety be so designated. The name is one of wide application. John Scotus, Giordano Bruno, Spinoza, Schelling, are all Pantheists, but with very considerable differences in their conception of God and the world. Atheism has no more sympathy with Pantheism than with Theism. The Atheist regards it as a shallow pretence, or a senseless abstraction. To Schopenhauer, the controversy between Theist and Pantheist suggests an imaginary dialogue, which might be supposed to take place in a theatre at Milan. One of the speakers imagines himself to be in the celebrated puppet-theatre of Girolamo, and admires the art with which the director has fashioned his puppets and guides their performance. The other says, "No! we are in the *teatro della scala;* the director and his associates are themselves the actors, and the poet also takes part in the play." "My principal objection to Pantheism," says this philosopher, "is that it settles nothing. Calling the world 'God' is not explaining it: it is only enriching language with a superfluous synonyme. Whether you say the world is God, or the world is the world, it amounts to the same thing. It is true that, if you start with the idea of God as something given, and then say, God is the world, that *is* a kind of explanation, although a mere verbal one, inasmuch as it refers an unknown to something known. But when you start with the idea of the world which is actually given, a given reality, and then say that the world is God, it is clear that nothing is explained thereby. At best, it is only a referring of the unknown to something still more unknown. . . . It would be much more correct to identify the world with the Devil, as the venerable author of the 'Theologia Germanica' has done. On page 93 of his immortal work (according to the restored text, Stuttgart, 1851), he says, 'Therefore the evil spirit and Nature are one; and, unless Nature is overcome, the evil Enemy is not overcome.'"

But Schopenhauer is wrong, whatever the "Theologia Germanica" may teach; wrong, if not wilfully unjust. No Pantheistic philosopher identifies God with the phenomenal world. "Jupiter est quodcunque vides, quocunque moveris," is a flight of poetic sentiment, not a philosophic statement. Even Toland, as we see, distinguishes God from the universe by the attribute of reason; and that distinction is infinite.

It is a vulgar impression, which Schopenhauer either ignorantly or wilfully indorses, that Pantheism is simply identification of God with the sensible world. Let us hear what Schelling, the greatest of recent Pantheists, says concerning this common error. I quote from the "System der gesammten Philosophie und der Naturphilosophie insbesondere" (p. 177): "You will say, then, that this system is Pantheism. Suppose it were Pantheism in your sense, what of it? Suppose that this system precisely, and no other, were the result of reason; ought I not, in spite of your terror at the word, to maintain it as the only true one? The most vulgar kind of polemic in philosophy is that which is waged by means of certain images of terror taken from the history of philosophy, and held up to every new system as so many Medusa-heads. But what is meant by your Pantheism? If I rightly conceive it, it is that the all-ness (allheit) of Deity is understood to mean that every thing, that is, the sum of *sensible* objects, is God. But this is not at all what we maintain. So far are we from saying that the sum of sensible objects is God, that, on the contrary, we contend that the very reason of their being objects of sense is their privation of Deity."

Giordano Bruno is unquestionably Pantheist; but Bruno distinctly acknowledges God as the

Author of Nature, which, he maintains, must have had a beginning and a cause. He calls Nature the mirror in which God is imaged.

Scotus Erigena, that wondrous intellect, the light of the ninth century, is commonly regarded as Pantheist; but the whole strain of the "De Divisione Naturæ" is an emphasizing of the distinction between the created and the uncreated. Nature in his division is four fold: (1) The Nature which creates and is not created; (2) Nature created and creating; (3) Nature created, which does not create; and, finally, (4) Nature uncreated and uncreating. The first of these — Nature which creates and is not created — he afterward identifies with the fourth; namely, Nature which is neither created nor creates. They are one and the same, viewed in different relations, according to the following remarkable statement, which I translate as illustrating Erigena's doctrine of the "Apokatastasis:" "When, therefore, we think of the divine Nature as the beginning and cause of all things (for itself is ἄναρχον and ἀναίτιον, that is, without beginning and without cause; since nothing precedes which can have to it the relation of beginning or cause, but itself, on the contrary, creates the nature of all things whose cause and beginning it is), we not improperly call it Nature creative and uncreated. For it creates, and suffers creation from no one.

But knowing this same divine Nature to be the end of all things, beyond which there is nothing, and in which all things eternally subsist and are altogether God, we rightly call it neither created nor creative: not created, indeed, because it is created by no one; neither creative, because it now ceases to create, all things being converted into its own eternal reasons (in which they will for ever remain), and ceasing to be designated by the appellation of 'creature.' For God will be all in all, and all creation will be shadowed into God (obumbrabitur), as the stars are hidden in the light of the rising sun. Do you not see, therefore, with what reason we may call one and the same divine Nature in view of a beginning uncreated, but creative, and, in view of the end, both uncreated and uncreative?"[1]

Even Spinoza emphasizes causality in God, and distinguishes between the infinite and the finite. God, he says, is the efficient cause, not only of the existence, but of the essence, of things. Eth. Part i. Prop. xxv.

I cite these four most eminent examples of pantheistic philosophy — Erigena, Bruno, Spinoza, and Schelling — as proofs that Pantheism does not, as Schopenhauer intimates, and as vulgar prejudice

---

[1] From the edition Monasterii Guestphalorum, 1838, Lib. III. p. 248.

supposes, confuse the distinction between God and the sensible world. It is not atheistic, but theistic, in its view of the visible creation. It agrees with the Theism which condemns it, in its putting of the world as secondary, as effect, and God as primary, as cause. It agrees with Theism in its confession of a supermundane God, — supermundane, but not extramundane. The popular Theism supposes a God existing outside of the universe which he has made. It supposes a Creator who once in time called a universe into being, and has been ever since a spectator and director of its ongoings, having no substantial connection with it, but only a providential and governmental one: providentially active, but substantially withdrawn; and not only withdrawn, but, as so many of the popular hymns represent it, removed to an inconceivable distance, —

> "Infinite lengths beyond the bounds
> Where stars revolve their little rounds."

The God of Pantheism is immanent, interfused, all-permeating, — copresent to all being, the ground of all appearance, the life of all life. This is the ontology of Pantheism; and, with this conception of Deity, the view of many whose Theism is unquestioned coincides. Newton, in his "Principia," says, "Omnipræsens est [Deus] non per virtutem solam, sed etiam per substantiam." Berkeley, whose position in the Anglican Church would seem to be a sufficient guarantee of his orthodoxy, is Pantheist in his ontology, though differing widely from Spinoza, — Pantheist in his denial of any other substratum of the visible phenomenal world than the immediate action of Deity. Père Malebranche, whose orthodoxy as a priest of the Church of Rome is equally unquestionable, is also Pantheist in this regard. It is but the combination of the two principles of Theism and Idealism. Every Theist who is an Idealist, is also a Pantheist to this extent. In fact, it is the Christian doctrine of omnipresence as affirmed by St. Paul: "In him we live, and move, and have our being;" "One God and Father of all, who is above and through all, and in you all." The alternative is Anthropomorphism in theology, and Materialism in philosophy.

But this is only one stage or one form of Pantheism. That which really and fundamentally distinguishes Pantheism, as represented by Spinoza, from Theism as usually understood, is not the doctrine of the one substance, but the doctrine of the one sole agent, — the denial of any other agency than that of the one God, as well in the spiritual as in the phenomenal world. In this there is something more than what is called in philosophy "determinism," or "necessitarianism," — a doctrine by no means peculiar to Pantheism. Spinoza not only denies freedom of will to man, but denies to man substantial existence, according to the Tenth Proposition of the Second Part of the Ethic. "Ad essentiam hominis non pertinet esse substantiæ, sive substantia formam hominis non constituit." "From which," in a corollary, "it follows," he says, "that the essence of man consists in certain modifications of the attributes of God." And in a corollary, under the Eleventh Proposition of the same Part, he infers the human mind to be "a part of the infinite intellect of God. So that, when we say the human mind perceives this or that, we say nothing else than that God, not in his infinity, but as explained by the nature of the human mind, or as constituting the essence of the human mind, has this or that idea." In other words, as appears more fully from what follows, there is in Spinoza's system no such entity as the human mind or soul. What we call such is only a thought of God.

Another characteristic of Pantheism as represented by Spinoza, and a point of marked distinction between it and Theism, is its non-recognition of that attribute of Deity which Theism expresses by the term "Lord." The God of Pantheism is in no sense Lord. Having no intelligent subjects,— the mind or soul not being in this philosophy a distinct entity, but only a mode of the divine thought, — the attribute of lordship cannot be ascribed to him. But that attribute is among the fundamentals of Theism. The two ideas of God and Lord, in the view of Theism, are inseparable. Godhead is lordship. In the words of Newton, — the words with which he closes his "Principia," — "Deus est vox relativa et ad servos refertur. Deitas est dominatio Dei, non in corpus proprium, sed in subditos."

It appears, then, that whilst, in its positive aspects, as recognizing the immanence of God in Nature, and affirming Him to be the real substratum and ground of the phenomenal world, Pantheism is not irreconcilable with Theism, — in fact, coincides with the Theism of theistic Idealists, — the negative difference between the two is very wide. In its denial, not only of proper agency, but of individual being, to man, and its consequent non-recognition of lordship in Deity, the Pantheism of Spinoza differs as widely from Theism on the one side as it does from Atheism on the other. A proof of this double discrepance is the curious fact of the diametrically opposite judgments of this philosophy pronounced by men of distinguished ability, according to their light. Bayle, a confessed and inveterate sceptic, — a man who acknowledged that his talent consisted in raising doubts, but whose sentence, unfortunately, determined the opinion entertained of Spinoza for a hundred years, — denounces him in very emphatic terms as an Atheist. On the contrary, the tender and devout Novalis, in whom no trait is more conspicuous than a living and profound faith, did not hesitate to characterize him as "God-inebriated,"[1] — a man drunk with the idea of God. The latter judgment, as it certainly is the fairest in its spirit and purpose, so it is also the most correct in fact. To designate as Atheist a man to whom God was all in all, is wilful absurdity. On the other hand, however, it must be confessed that a system which knows no being but God, ignores what is most distinctive in Godhead as conceived by Theism, — personal sovereignty and providential rule. For, "a God," says Newton, again, "without dominion, providence, and final causes, is nothing else than Fate and Nature."[2] This system misses, moreover, what is equally essential in Theism, — the attribute of holiness, and with it the related idea of a moral government exercised by God over rational moral natures.

Spinoza is the typical exponent of Pantheism. His system, given to the world two hundred years ago, remains to this day the most thorough and complete of all which bear that name. An immense influence the man has had with a certain

---

1 Mr. Froude, in his excellent essay on Spinoza, justly criticises this epithet as descriptive of a mystic, not of a logician.

2 "Deus sine dominio, providentia, et causis finalibus, nihil aliud est quam Fatum et Natura."

class of minds ; not conspicuous, but penetrating and profound, — an influence not in the way of commanding assent to his views, or of founding a school (his following in this sense has been small), but in that of giving direction and tone to philosophy, — an influence affecting the sentiments rather than the reason ; but, through the sentiments of minds in communion with his own, acting indirectly on the feelings and the faith of many to whom his system is unknown, and modifying the poetry, art, and religion of the time. Göthe confesses the power of this influence as he experienced it in early manhood. "I had received into myself, " he says, "the being and the way of thinking of an extraordinary man, — imperfectly, indeed, and as it were surreptitiously; but I was already experiencing therefrom the most momentous effects. This mind, which wrought so decidedly upon me, and which was to have so great an influence on my whole way of thinking, was Spinoza. After looking about in the world, to no purpose, for some means of fashioning my strange nature, I chanced at last on this man's 'Ethica.' Of what I may have read for myself out of that work, or of what I may have read into it, I can give no account. Enough : I found there a sedative to my passions. A large and free view of the sensible and moral world seemed to open itself before me. But what specially chained me to him was the boundless disinterestedness which shone forth from every proposition. That wondrous word, 'Who rightly loves God must not demand that God should love him in return,' with all the premises on which it rests, and all the conclusions that flow from it, entirely filled my thought. To be disinterested in all, and most disinterested in love and friendship, was my highest joy, my maxim, my practice; and so, that later petulant saying of mine, 'If I love thee, what is that to thee?' was spoken from my very heart. . . . The all-composing quietism of Spinoza contrasted my up-stirring endeavor; his mathematical method was the opposite of my poetical way of looking at and describing objects; and precisely that ruled mode of treatment, which was thought not suitable to moral subjects, made me his passionate disciple, his most ardent adorer."

Schleiermacher, in his "Discourses on Religion," renders this enthusiastic tribute: "Sacrifice reverently with me to the *Manes* of the holy outcast, Spinoza. Him penetrated the sublime world-spirit. The infinite was his beginning and his end; the universe, his only and eternal love. In holy innocence and deep humility, he mirrored himself in the eternal world. Full of religion he was, and full of a holy spirit; and therefore he stands alone and unapproached, — master in his art, but exalted above the profane guild; without disciples and without citizenship."

And who, on a nearer view, is the man whom two such witnesses, — Germany's greatest poet and greatest theologian, — not to speak of inferior spirits, concur in exalting? A Jew by race, by nearer ancestry a Portuguese, or, according to Auerbach, a Spaniard, with a mixture, on the mother's side, of Moorish blood, by nativity a Dutchman, — Baruch, afterward Benedict, son of Benjamin Spinoza, or Espinoza, was born in Amsterdam (where his father, with other Spanish and Portuguese merchants, had found refuge from Peninsular persecution of the Jews), on the 24th November, 1632. The boy received the best instruction which Jewish discipline — nowhere more thorough than in Amsterdam — could supply, and developed an early and marked proclivity to intellectual pursuits. Having mastered the Rabbinical lore of his day, well-grounded in the Law and the Talmud, and even, it is said, a proficient in the Kabbala, he carried his thirst for knowledge and his extraordinary power of acquisition into Gentile fields. He studied Latin under tutelage of the somewhat notorious Van den Ende, who was afterward put to death at Paris for complicity in the Rohan conspiracy.

With the aid of Latin, the sole language of science in that day, which he learned to write with great purity, he applied himself to Christian authors; studied theology and studied physics; made himself acquainted with the writings of Descartes, then supreme in philosophy, and through him was initiated in the world of ideal speculation. In the strength of this meat, he outgrew Judaism, or at least the traditional, ceremonial Judaism of the "Dispersion." But such a witness of the ancestral faith was not to be surrendered without a struggle by the Rabbins. They remonstrated with him, they flattered him, and finally resorted to bribes. An annual stipend of a thousand florins, according to Colerus, was offered him, if he would not altogether desert the synagogue. He spurned the lure, and went his way.

Finally, in 1657,[1] in the twenty-fifth year of his age, he was excommunicated, with the triple and extreme ban of Hebrew execration, devoting him to all imaginable ills; invoking the wrath of Jehovah and the curses of all good angels to light upon him and all his posterity; forbidding all men to have communication with him, or to show him mercy. An attempt was made to arraign him before the civil tribunal on the charge of blasphemy, but without success. Christian Dutchmen

[1] According to Auerbach's "Spinoza, Ein Denkerleben," p. 362.

would not lend themselves to the murderous spite of Portuguese Jews. His life was imperilled by the hatred of these zealots. Waylaid by night in a lonely street, the assassin's dagger pierced his coat, but missed his heart. He preserved the perforated garment by way of memorial.

Meanwhile his father had died; leaving him not without means, had he chosen to avail himself of them. This he declined doing. He made over his share of the paternal estate to his sisters, Miriam and Rebecca, reserving for himself only a bed ("si unicum lectum excipias"). Thanks to his Jewish training, and that wise provision of the Talmud which Christian laws and Christian systems of education would do well to imitate, — the provision which ordains that every youth, whether rich or poor, while receiving instruction in letters and science, shall also learn some manual art, — he had one resource. Any thing rather than dependence. He had learned to polish lenses; he would live by his craft. With this brave resolve, he hired a small attic, took thither his tools and his bed, and lived a true philosophic life, dividing his time between mechanical and intellectual toil. The profits of his craft were moderate; but his wants were equally so. A few stivers supplied the daily rations of a man who subsisted mainly on thought.

The machinations of his enemies, who still plotted against him, obliged him to quit Amsterdam. He removed his residence, first, to Auwerkerke; then to Rhynsburg, near Leiden; thence to Voorburg; and finally settled in the Hague, beneath the roof of his friend, Henry Van der Spyck, — a painter of note, of whom Spinoza learned the rules of that art, which he practised with some success.

Friends were not wanting of the highest rank and commanding influence, who were ready to patronize the martyr-scholar. Among them, Oldenburg, German ambassador to England, first under Cromwell, then under Charles II.; also, the great Condé; and that noble republican, John de Witt, grand pensioner of the States-General, who afterward fell a victim to the fury of the Orange party, and was murdered by a mob in 1672. Karl Ludwig, the elector palatine, offered him a chair in the University of Heidelberg, "Cum amplissima philosophandi libertate;" but he declined the position, preferring independence to the favor of princes. The wealthy Simon van Vries, one of his more intimate associates, sent him a donation of two thousand florins, which he returned; having no occasion, he said, for such subsidy, and fearing the disturbing influence of riches. That devoted friend would have made him his heir; but Spinoza entreated him not to pass by his own brother, to whom the inheritance of right belonged. The will was altered accordingly, but with the proviso that an annual pension should be paid to the philosopher out of the estate. The brother would have made it five hundred florins; Spinoza would accept three hundred, and no more.

Brief space was allowed him for the usufruct of this legacy. A pulmonary weakness, with which he had suffered from his twentieth year, though it could not restrain his indefatigable industry, abridged with a premature close his works and days. He died of phthisis, at the age of forty-four, on the 21st of February, 1677.

No philosopher has left a purer record; no scholar ever lived a more blameless life. All that is known of him, and especially the devotion of such friends, declares him one of the truest and bravest of the sons of men.

Of his works, beside the "Letters," and the "Exposition of the Philosophy of Descartes," there are four of pre-eminent importance, — the "Tractatus de Emendatione Intellectus," the "Tractatus Politici," the "Tractatus Theologico-politicus," and the "Ethica." The two last named have originated epochs in the history of human thought.

The "Tractatus Theologico-politicus" gave the impulse and direction to modern Biblical criticism; it presented or suggested views which German theologians have subsequently elaborated, applied, and set before the world, in the critical and exegetical results of their inquiries.

The "Ethica Ordine Geometrico Demonstrata," the most influential of all Spinoza's writings, is a postumous publication, and contains his philosophy proper, — those pantheistic ideas which, during the past century, have wrought with such marked effect on speculative minds. It is greatly to be regretted that the author chose for this work a form so forbidding in itself, and so ill-adapted to his theme. The method of geometry is applicable only to sensible objects, or topics that lie within the scope of exact science. When applied to topics of pure speculation, — to things which do not admit of exact demonstration, which are merely, and must always be, matters of opinion, — it challenges the counter-application of tests which speculative philosophy can never satisfy. Spinoza's system, judged by the test which he himself provokes, — considered as mathematical, or even as logical, demonstration of the views it propounds, — is a failure. Many of the fundamental positions, announced with such parade of mathematical certainty, are easily refuted, and have been refuted by critical analysis. Its primary and obvious error is the confusing of his own arbitrary positing of the one Substance (which is God) with the imagined self-evident proof of that Substance. In his third definition, he defines substance to be "that which is in itself, and is conceived by itself; that is, whose conception does not need the conception of any other thing by help of which it is found." And this definition he seems to regard as equivalent to a proof of the reality of that Substance. He proceeds to speak of it as a reality, and all at once, in the Seventh Proposition, affirms that "it belongs to the nature of Substance to exist." His demonstration of that proposition is, that Substance cannot be produced by another (according to the corollary of an antecedent proposition), and therefore must be the cause of itself, which (according to Definition First) means that its essence involves existence. This is all the evidence we have of the fact of the one Substance, on which Spinoza's whole system rests.

A remarkable instance of confusion of thought occurs in the Scholium to the Eleventh Proposition, which affirms the necessary existence of God. "Since the possibility of existence is a power ('quum posse existere potentia sit'), it follows that the more of reality belongs to the nature of any thing, the more of power it has from itself to exist; and that, therefore, the absolutely infinite Being, or God, has from himself an absolutely infinite power of existing, and must, therefore, absolutely exist."

He does not see that the possibility of existence, of which he speaks, is in himself, the subject, not in the object. It is simply his perception of the possibility that such a Being exists. Possibility is not a thing, but a thought, — the judgment of a thinking subject. It exists only as contemplated. If, therefore, the possibility of existence is referred to the Being in question, it must be a thought of that Being; and, to have that thought, he must already exist. Imagine a being contemplating the possibility of his own existence!

But the refutation of Spinoza's Propositions concerns only or mostly the form and demonstration of his philosophy: it does not essentially affect the underlying ideas, the grand intuitions, which make the essence of his system. These are true, and of infinite moment. All that is positive in his philosophy Theism may accept. What is wanting in it — the recognition of individual, self-determining spirits, and, correlate with them, of the proper lordship or moral government of God — Theism must supply.

Spinoza supposes a single and sole Substance comprising all that is, and of which all phenomena and all finite existences are modes and affections. Of this substance, all the known attributes are comprehended in the two determinations, — thought and extension. And this Substance is God. I give his own words: "Besides God, there can be no substance given or conceived."[1] "Whatsoever is, is in God; and, without God, nothing can be or be conceived."[2] "God is a thinking thing."[3] "God is an extended thing."[4] These are the extreme and most characteristic positions of his ontology. The last, the most characteristic of all, will seem to most Theists to be also the most questionable. But here, too, the question respects rather the form than the substance. What Spinoza really means is, that God is the cause of all extension. So, at least, I interpret him. The error — whether Spinoza's error or the reader's misunderstanding of his intent — the error lies in conceiving extension as passive, instead of active; as a state, instead of an act. Newton, as we have seen, says substantially the same thing.

It is clear that, if this Substance exists, it must exist necessarily. Spinoza does not prove its existence; but he felt this necessity, and points to it in his First Definition, — the opening sentence of the "Ethica:" "By self-cause, I understand that whose essence involves its existence." The phrase "self-

[1] "Præter Deum, nulla dari neque concipi potest substantia." Pars i. Prop. xiv.

[2] "Quicquid est in Deo est, et nihil sine Deo esse neque concipi potest." Ib. Prop. xv.

[3] "Deus est res cogitans." Pars ii. Prop. i.

[4] "Deus est res extensa." Ib. Prop. ii.

cause" is unfortunate, inasmuch as causality expresses a relation between an antecedent and a consequent, and cannot with propriety be predicated of that which had no beginning, and is out of the category of time. But Spinoza meant to indicate the fact of self-existence, which lies at the foundation of all philosophy. Self-existent is that which not only is uncaused, if existent, but which must exist, if any thing exists; which must exist in order that the idea of existence may be present to my thought; of whose existence, therefore, my idea is a proof. It is that which cannot be conceived as non-existent. Any particular thing may, with an effort of abstraction be conceived as non-existent, — a tree, a book, a planet, a solar system. But can you conceive of nothing existing, — of nothing having ever existed? Make the attempt! Take some quiet moment, and try to imagine — nothing. What will be the result? You will find yourself imagining two things, — space, and a thinking subject. You cannot get rid of these two. You have blown away the universe with your thought; but the thought remains. You cannot imagine it not to be. There is in your imagination some one who takes cognizance of the void, — a thinking subject. In other words, there is thought, — the first attribute of Spinoza's God. And there is the void, that is, space, which gives the idea of extension, — the second

U of M

attribute of Spinoza's God. Space itself is not extension: it is only the perceived possibility of extended existence; it is the first moment in the self-objectivation of the thinking subject. There is as yet no actual, but there is an ideal, extension of the self-existent. Since, therefore, in the absence of all other existence, a thinking subject and space are necessary conceptions, we have Spinoza's Substance, with its two attributes, — thought and extension.

A full exposition of the "Ethica" is not within the scope of this essay. A selection of some of its most characteristic positions may suffice to represent its spirit and purport.

"In the nature of things, there is given nothing contingent, but all things are determined from the necessity of the Divine Nature to a certain mode of existence and operation." Part i. Prop. xxix.

"The will cannot be termed a free, but only a necessary, cause." Prop. xxxii.

"Things could not have been produced by God in any other mode and order than that in which they have been produced." Prop. xxxiii.

"The power of God is his very essence." Prop. xxxiv.

"To those who ask why God did not create men in such a way that they should be governed by reason alone, I answer, Because there was in him

MOU

no lack of material for creating all things from the highest to the lowest grade of perfection. Or, more properly speaking, Because the laws of his nature were so ample that they sufficed to the production of all that could be conceived by an infinite intellect." Appendix.

"The ideas of the attributes of God, as of single things, have not for their efficient cause the things idea'd, or the things perceived, but God himself so far as he is a thinking thing." Part ii. Prop. v.

"The order and connection of ideas is the same as the order and connection of things." Prop. vii.

"He who has a true idea, knows at the same time that he has a true idea, and cannot doubt of the truth of the thing." Prop. xliii.

"Our mind does certain things, and suffers certain things. Namely, so far as it has adequate ideas, it does necessarily certain things; and, so far as it has inadequate ideas, it necessarily suffers certain things." Part iii. Prop. i.

"The mind cannot determine the body to think, nor the mind the body to move nor to rest, or to any thing else." Prop. ii. (The demonstration is that all thought, action, and rest are from God, according to his two attributes of thought and extension. The mind can only be determined by him as *res cogitans*, the body as *res extensa;* that is, like by like.)

"Experience as well as reason teaches that men

believe they are free, only because they are conscious of their actions, and ignorant of the causes by which they are determined." Scholium ad Prop. ii.

"Acts arise solely from adequate ideas; but passions depend solely on inadequate ideas." Prop. iii.

"Joy is the transition of man from a lesser to a greater perfection. Sadness is the transition of man from a greater to a lesser perfection." Affectuum Definitiones, ii. and iii.

"We know nothing, certainly, to be good or bad, except that which conduces to a true understanding, or that which hinders a true understanding." Part iv. Prop. xxvii.

"The highest good of the mind is the cognition of God, and the supreme virtue of the mind is to know God." Prop. xxvii.

"Nothing can be bad for us through that which it has in common with us; but, so far as it is bad for us, it is contrary to us." Prop. xxx.

"The good which any one who follows virtue desires for himself, he desires also for the rest of mankind; and that the more, the greater his knowledge of God." Prop. xxxvii.

"He who lives by the guidance of reason endeavors so far as possible to compensate the hatred, anger, and contempt of others toward him, with love or generosity on his part." Part iv. Prop. xlvi.

"Commiseration in him who lives by the guidance of reason is in itself bad and useless." Prop. l.

"Humility is not a virtue, or does not spring from reason." Prop. liii.

"Repentance is not a virtue, or does not spring from reason; but he who repents of his act is twice miserable, or twice impotent." Prop. liv.

"The greatest pride and the greatest abjectness are the greatest self-ignorance." Prop. lv.

"The greatest pride and the greatest abjectness indicate the greatest weakness of mind." Prop. lvi.

"The cognition of evil is an inadequate cognition." Prop. lxiv.

"Whence it follows that, if the mind had only adequate ideas, it would form no notion of evil." Coroll.

"The free man thinks of nothing less than of death: his wisdom consists not in the meditation of death, but of life." Prop. lxvii.

"If men were born free, they would form no conception of good or evil so long as they remained free." Prop. lxviii.

"Only free men are mutually most agreeable the one to the other." Prop. lxxi.

"The man who is led by reason is freer in the State, where he lives according to the common decree, than in solitude, where he obeys his own will alone." Prop. lxxiii.

"It is of the first utility in life to perfect as much as possible the intellect or reason. In this one thing consists man's highest felicity or beatitude, since beatitude is nothing else than that acquiescence of the mind which springs from the intuitive knowledge of God. But to perfect the intellect is nothing else than to understand God, and those attributes and acts of God which flow from the necessity of his nature. Wherefore, the chief end of man, the supreme desire by which he endeavors to regulate all others, is that by which he is led to an adequate conception of himself and of all that can come within the range of his intelligence." Appendix to Part iv. Cap. iv.

"Minds are not conquered by arms, but by love and generosity." Ib. Cap. xi.

"An affection which is passion ceases to be passion the moment we form a clear and distinct idea of it." Part v. Prop. iii.

"He who clearly and distinctly understands himself and his own affections, loves God; and the more, the more perfectly he understands them." Prop. xv.

"No one can hate God." Prop. xviii.

"He who loves God cannot endeavor that God should love him in return." Prop. xix.

"The mind cannot be absolutely destroyed with the body; but something remains of it which is eternal." Prop. xxiii.

"The more we understand single things, the more we understand God." Prop. xxiv.

"God loves himself with an intellectual love which is infinite." Prop. xxxv.

"The intellectual love of the mind toward God is a part of that infinite love with which God loves himself." Prop. xxxvi.

"From this we clearly understand in what our salvation, or blessedness, or liberty consists; namely, in constant and eternal love toward God, or in the love of God toward men." Schol.

"He whose body has the greatest number of aptitudes has most of that which is eternal in his mind." Prop. xxxix.

"The more any thing possesses of perfection, the more it acts and the less it suffers; and, on the other hand, the more active it is, the more perfect it is." Prop. xl.

"Not beatitude but virtue itself is the reward of virtue; we rejoice in it not because we restrain our lusts, but on the contrary, we are able to restrain our lusts because we rejoice in it." Prop. xlii.

The result of Spinoza's influence — an influence not to be measured by the number of his readers, which must always be small, but by the fructification of his idea in philosophy, religion, art, and generally in the thoughts and feelings of the thinking and cultured minds of our time, — the result of that influence may be summed up as emancipation from the Dualism and the Anthropomorphism of the old popular faith. Spinoza turned the Devil out of the universe, and has given us a God who is not an individual secluded and remote, — a regent enthroned above the skies, — but an all-present reality. In his attempt to establish this beneficent verity, he sacrifices, as we have seen, — and that is the vice of his system, — the proper personality of God. But this very extreme has contributed more effectually, perhaps, than a more theistic view would have done, to correct the opposite error. And this false extreme is not essential, I think, to the central and constitutive principle of the "Ethica." Unity of substance is not incompatible with the creation, by self-limitation, of individual existences having separate consciousnesses, and therefore distinct persons; whereby the personality of God is maintained in the one essential article of a conscious and moral relation to others.

The weakness of Spinozism, of Pantheism as expounded by him, consists in the relaxation of the moral sense, — the moral indifferentism resulting from a system which not only refers all action, good or evil, directly to God as the one immediate and only actor in all, but virtually denies all distinction between good and evil, by resolving, as we have seen, the notion of any such distinction into inadequate cognition.

Its strength is the quickened sense which, by its emancipation from Dualism and Anthropomorphism, it gives us of the all-pervading and immediate presence of God. The divine Omnipresence, once a cold, unmeaning dogma, it has made a fact of consciousness. This effect — to mention but one manifestation of it — is realized in the altered view and new enjoyment of Nature so conspicuously characteristic of the modern mind, and of which, among English poets, Wordsworth is the truest exponent. If Spinozism impairs the moral sublimity of the idea, it deepens our consciousness of the being of God. And the more profound our consciousness of God and the sense of his all-presence, the more intense our enjoyment of Nature. This explains the remarkable fact, that the love of Nature, in our sense of the term, — that joy in wild, sequestered nooks, that delight in the contemplation of mountain-slopes and the valleys they embosom, that "pleasure in the pathless woods," that "rapture on the lonely shore," — is wholly a modern sentiment. The ancients — at least, the Greeks and Romans — have recorded nothing, and probably experienced nothing, of the kind. They painted no landscapes, or none like ours with a background suggestive of mystery within and beyond. Mountains to them were merely an obstruction to their marches, a problem for the military engineer. Some of their writers must have seen the robe of glory which the setting sun flings over the shoulders of Mont Blanc; the charms of Como and Maggiore and the Rhine must have been familiar to their eyes: but of all this no word in their works, no sign that the meaning and beauty of the landscape had melted into their thought. It needs the sense of the one-pervading Presence to inspire that feeling in the soul. It is this that draws us to the heart of Nature, and presses the aspects of Nature on our hearts.

Pantheism and Theism are not contradictory, but complementary, the one of the other. Theism gives us the holy Person, the Providential care, the moral rule; Pantheism gives us the diffused Presence, the all-pervading Life, the Divine nearness in the outspread landscape. To Pantheism belongs the world of Nature; to Theism, the world of spirits.

XI.

THE TWO RELIGIONS.

WITHIN the compass of the Christian name — professing one origin, claiming one sanction — are two religions, which differ as widely, the one from the other, in principle and spirit, as Judaism differs from Christianity. The Pauline epithets, "carnal" and "spiritual," used to express the latter difference, are equally expressive of the former. But, as these are terms of blame and praise, I adopt in their stead the less offensive and equally significant phrases, *legal* and *liberal*. Judaism is represented in the New Testament as a religion of law. The ritual law, or law as a system, was repudiated by Christianity; but law as a religious principle survived the overthrow of the Jewish polity. It went over into the new dispensation; it reappears in Christian history, side by side with the principle of grace. And so we have a dual Christianity, — a legal and a liberal gospel, — the rigid and the fluid of Christian faith.

There are other classifications and other antitheses in religion, — ecclesiastical and personal, sentimental and dogmatic, sacramental and spiritual, — but none so comprehensive as this of legal and liberal, the religion of law and the religion of grace. There is none which bisects with so trenchant a stroke the Christian world.

Grace is a specialty of the Christian dispensation. This specialty legal Christianity excludes; and yet, by a curious perversion of speech, the "Orthodox" sects have been more free in the use of the word "grace" than liberal Christians. It is one of the technicalities of their phraseology, while the absence of the thing which that term denotes — the free forgiveness of sin to the penitent — is precisely the distinguishing trait in their systems. No two ideas can be more fundamentally opposite than that of grace is to the satisfaction of justice by suffering; and nothing in the history of sects is more extraordinary than the misapplication of the *word* "grace" to a system of theology which virtually repudiates the *thing*. In the judgment of liberal Christians, those systems which treat the death of Christ as a satisfaction of Divine justice, — whether in the sacrificial sense of expiation, or the more questionable "governmental" sense of a shift or compromise, — rule out of Christianity that which constitutes its distinctive feature, grace; and place it on a level with the old religions, in which law and sacrifice are the prominent elements. In these systems, the Christian's God, like the God of the Jews and the gods of the Gentiles, is a being to be propitiated by sacrifice; with this remarkable difference, that, while the Gentile and Jewish divinities, alienated from individuals and tribes by actual personal transgressions, and visiting ancestral crimes on the third and fourth generation, could be conciliated by the blood of bulls or rams, the Christian's God, averse from the whole human race by reason of aboriginal sin, can be placated only by the blood of a man. Liberal Christianity sees in this view a God less gracious than Hebrew Jehovah or Olympian Jove; and, instead of a dispensation of grace, the yoke of a new and sterner law.

The distinction of legal and liberal respects the philosophy of religion, rather than sectarian symbol or dogma. Every system of theology and every religious creed presupposes antecedent speculation, — some philosophic idea, some underlying theory of God and man, which, consciously or unconsciously, shapes the formula, and determines the doctrine. When we study the Homousian controversy of the fourth century, or the Monothelitic of the seventh, we see how each party starts from premises back of the point in dispute, and back of Christianity itself. Arius was a thinker of entirely different build from Athanasius, and would probably have dissented from him as emphatically, on every other subject involving a philosophical principle, as he did in his christology. Augustine differed as widely from Pelagius, and Maximus from Theodore. The Ebionitism which prevailed in the early Church was the natural product of the strong monarchian [1] proclivity of the Jewish mind. The Christo-theism which ultimately triumphed was nursed and matured, if it did not originate, in the bosom of Alexandrian speculation. And when we come to the mighty spirits of the twelfth and thirteenth centuries, — to Abelard and Anselm, and Hugo à St. Victoire; to Abbot Joachim and Raymond Lull and Thomas Aquinas and Roger Bacon, — we see them impelled to review the old dogmas in the new light of the great revival of the human mind, which began with the Crusades; we see how the reawakened intellect held creed and symbol in solution, and how theologians were obliged to reconsider and to seek a philosophic basis for the *placita* of the Church.

The "simple souls," who, according to Tertullian, compose, in every age, the great majority of believers,[2] experience no such necessity: they

[1] The monarchian heresies, properly so called, were of later date, and of Gentile growth; but the origin of one of them was unquestionably Jewish.

[2] "Simplices quique, ne dixerim imprudentes et idiotæ, quæ major semper credentium pars est."

swallow the symbol that is set before them, asking no questions for conscience' sake; they neither know nor care to know in what subsoil of philosophic speculation their dogma has its root; they suppose it delivered bodily by revelation from heaven. But revelation never dogmatizes: all dogma is grounded in antecedent philosophy. Every system of theology is the fruit of philosophic ideas applied to the facts of revelation. The two systems we are now considering presuppose very different classes of ideas as their antecedents and basis. Their oppugnance is quite as much a philosophical as a theological one. It respects the fundamental ideas which form the basis of all theology, and is best understood by comparing the views of God and spiritual topics proper to each kind.

In the view of the legalist, God is arbitrary power, — a despot whose will makes right. In the view of the liberal, God is moral ideal, power in which right precedes will, — a love which causes all things to work together for the good of all.

In the view of the legalist, man is naturally bad; sin his normal state. Depraved by an accident of history, he is incapable of good, except by a radical change in his nature. In the view of the liberal, man is naturally imperfect, liable to sin, but also capable of good. Sin is an abnormal action of his nature; rectitude, his normal state.

In the view of the legalist, revelation is a communication made by God to man from without; Christ is God in a human form. In the view of the liberal, revelation is the perfection of reason,—an intuition of the deeper soul,—God speaking from within; Christ is man in the likeness of God.

In the view of the legalist, salvation is escape from the punishment of sin; the death of Christ, placating the divine wrath, is a motive with God, inducing him to remit that punishment. In the view of the liberal, salvation is deliverance from the power of sin; and the life of Christ, consummated by his death, an aid to moral emancipation.

In the view of the legalist, Heaven is the local residence of the Lord and his redeemed, from which the vast majority of human souls are for ever excluded; Hell is the local and eternal abode of the remainder of the race. In the view of the liberal, Heaven is the method of moral ascension, also the totality of ascending spirits; Hell is moral declension, also the totality of descending spirits.

From this exposition, it appears of what opposite elements the two religions are composed, and how radical and irreconcilable the antagonism between them; how vain the attempt to symbolize these sharp antitheses, to atone the intellectual schism, or by any theological compromise to harmonize legal and liberal views in one dogmatic confession. The confession that shall reconcile this difference, and unite the sects it has sundered, must not be a dogmatic but a liturgical one. Such a confession and such a union I believe to be not impossible. What Christian heart does not rejoice in the thought? But every movement in this direction, every attempt to œcumenize Protestant Christendom in one association for liturgical or practical purposes, must start with a frank recognition, on both sides, of the logically and theologically unatonable discrepance between legal and liberal theories of religion, frank toleration of that discrepance, and such a yearning for practical atonement and reconciliation in Christ as shall place above all dogmatic interests and disputes the common Master and Lord, and that union of all men in him for which he prayed, "That they all may be one, as thou, Father, art in me, and I in thee, that they also may be one in us." Let no one think to forward that union by compromising doctrinal issues, by dogmatic adjustments, by attempts to symbolize theologically with other sects. All such attempts are like temporary bridges of ice, which connect in cold seasons two hostile shores, — hard and ungenial while they last, and soon dissolved. When, in times of suspended interest and theological torpor, sects unite by the crystallization of their differences, — when the very coldness between them becomes their bond,— it is easy to foresee the speedy dissolution of that bond in the new glow of returning interest, and the more direct light of the sun. There is one word which should never be heard in theology, — "compromise."

But under whatever organizations, whether ecclesiastically joined or disjunct, there will always be, as I believe, these two religions in the world. They are too abhorrent in their ground elements, too discrete in the last analysis, to be ever completely merged in one. They are exponents each of a quite distinct and peculiar order of mind; each expresses an indestructible spiritual type.

Legal and liberal! How many peculiarities, theoretic and dogmatic, — how many antagonist doctrines and creeds, theological formulas, sectarian issues, ecclesiastical disputes, — arrange and define themselves under these two heads! Christianity, whose strong, victorious current broke down so many barriers, and swept away so many distinctions, and floated and confounded, and finally swallowed, so many philosophies and faiths, — Christianity, the most powerful of intellectual and historic solvents, did not quite solve this obdurate dualism. It married these contrary elements, but did not fuse them. The Church was yet in its second decade when it fairly polarized into legal and liberal. The two types were visibly discriminated, formally organized, and locally and theoretically and practically divided. Jerusalem, the natural and ancestral home of legal religion, maintained that aspect of the gospel, as administered by the twelve apostles, with James the Just at their head. On the other hand, Antioch, capital of Syria, "the eldest daughter of Zion," birth-place of the Christian name, birth-place of Christianity itself as a world religion, dispensed through Paul, or, in his absence, through Hellenizing elders, the liberal faith.

The head and protoplast of liberal Christianity is Paul. But here I am bound to remark, that the classification given above of the doctrinal aspects of the two religions does not always, and in all particulars, coincide with legal and liberal in ecclesiastical position. The christology of Paul is less humanitarian, his redemptorial doctrine, notwithstanding his polemics against the law, has more of a legal complexion, than the views of the old Jerusalem Church, so far as we can judge from the scanty and uncertain notices which have reached us. In subsequent divisions of the ecclesiastical world, the Catholic party, while always legalizing in matters of Church polity, have often adopted more liberal views of questions purely theologic than the heretics with whom they contended. On the other hand, some of the sects — for example, the Montanists — have been legalists in doctrine and liberals in polity. Still, as a general rule, the theological position has, in this respect, coincided with the ecclesiastical.

The century waned; Jerusalem fell: with it the Jewish ritual, the Jewish polity. And with the subversion of Temple and state, Jewish Christianity declined; Hellenistic Christianity triumphed; the Pauline interest triumphed; the Antiochian school prevailed. With the exception of a feeble remnant of Ebionites and Nazaræans, the Jerusalem school and party were extinct. Monstrous to relate, a Gentile was chosen Bishop of Jerusalem. "In the fire-flames of the Holy City, God proclaimed the end of the Old Covenant; and the Roman, who for ends of his own threw a torch into the Temple, acted as the instrument of God in the interest of the Christian religion."[1] The century closed; Christianity became cosmopolite; and, notwithstanding heretical appearances here and there, the Christian Church was substantially one. But let another century pass, and the old contradiction bursts forth afresh. In the Latin and Greek churches of the third century, legal and liberal are reproduced with steep antagonism. When I speak of Latin Chris-

[1] Die Clementinen nebst den verwandten Schriften, und der Ebionitismus. Von Adolph Schliemann.

tianity as a theological influence, I am thinking of Africa, not of Rome. Rome was never an intellectual power in the world, though once and again the world's mistress. Ecclesiastical Rome was always more occupied with strengthening her own dominion than with illustrating Christian doctrine. Africa was the cradle, if not the birth-place, of Latin Christianity. On the northern coast of that continent, and especially in Carthage, — how planted, we know not, — there had sprung up a Church, which makes its first appearance in Christian history as a full-grown power and a mighty influence, in the time and person of Tertullian. The Greek Church dates from Paul. The Græco-Egyptian branch of it, its most intellectual and characteristic representative, — the Church at Alexandria, — had already illustrated the second century and itself with the writings of Clemens. Thus, Africa, by a strange destiny, had become the focus of the Christian world, the home of the two representative Churches of the post-apostolic time, — at once the palæstra and the mart of those spirits and ideas, the trace of which remains to this day. In Alexandria, *gnosis* contended with revelation ; in Carthage, independency struggled with ecclesiastical rule : but both of these Churches contrasted each other as exponents of speculative and dogmatic theology, of liberal and legal religion.

M. Charpentier, in a pleasant essay on the literary characteristics of the two Churches, speaks of the different training of the writers of each. The Greek Fathers had come into the Church from the schools; the Latin, from the bar. "Sortis par la plupart, les écrivains grecs, de l'école des sophistes, les écrivains latins, de l'enceinte du barreau, ils ont, les uns et les autres, retenu cette double origine."[1] We are inclined to think that their spiritual, as well as their literary, traits are referable in part to this previous discipline. The habit of the schools is free inquiry; the habit of the bar is sharp decision by precedent and authority. The one is discursive; the other, pragmatical: the one, liberal; the other, legal.

As a type of the Latin spirit, and a normal instance of legal Christianity, let us take Tertullian, first of the Latin Fathers. Tertullian was a heretic in ecclesiastical position; but when had ever Orthodoxy, in the popular sense of the word, a more perfect representative? We speak of Augustine as the Father of Calvinism; but the practical spirit of Calvinism is more fitly imaged in Tertullian. So assured and grim and pitiless! The Christian Church has had no abler writer and no greater bigot. How fiercely his intolerant zeal flashes out in his judgment of the polytheists!

[1] Études sur les Pères de l'Église. Par J. P. Charpentier.

How he burns and rages against them! How he revels in the thought of their sure damnation, and gloats over the picture of everlasting burnings! "Oh, how I shall admire, how laugh, how exult, when I behold so many proud monarchs, so many fancied gods, groaning in the lowest abyss of darkness! — so many magistrates, who persecuted the name of Christ, melting in fiercer flames than they kindled against the Christians!" What contempt he pours on ancient philosophy and philosophers! "What has the Academy to do with the Church, Christ with Plato, Jerusalem with Athens?" With what self-righteous disdain and conscious superiority he sneers even at Socrates, and ridicules his Dæmon, and all his pretended wisdom! Paul and John had not hesitated to acknowledge traces of moral truth and a divine spirit even in the Gentile world; but Tertullian flouts the notion of a possible wisdom or knowledge that was not derived from the Christian revelation. What could Socrates know of the soul? What right had he to think or talk about it? Christ had not yet come into the world;[1] consequently, no knowledge of spiritual things, no means of investigating, no possibility of apprehending them. All that the Gentile philoso-

[1] "Cui enim veritas comperta sine Deo? Cui Deus cognitus sine Christo? Cui Christus exploratus sine Spiritu Sancto? . . . Sane Socrates facilius diverso spiritu agebatur." — Tertull. *De Anima.*

phers could say on these subjects was of devilish origin, — "secundum Pythii dæmonis suffragium." Christianity was not only a revelation transcending philosophy, but a fierce cartel hurled at human wisdom. It was not enough to say that the gospel was the source of the highest knowledge and the fullest truth in relation to such matters. Tertullian's religion required him to believe that all previous theorizing, all the conclusions of the "natural man" on the subject, were adverse to the gospel; that this wisdom not only "descendeth not from above," but must needs be "earthly, sensual, devilish." His faith rejected with scorn the aid of reason. "Credo quia impossibile est." "The Christian religion," says Maurice,[1] in his admirable critique of this Father, "was good for nothing in his eyes, unless he could show that it set aside all that honest men had been thinking of and feeling before it was proclaimed. That was the proof that it came from God; that was the only comfortable evidence Tertullian could have that the inheritance which had been left him was safe against invaders."

This, in every period of the Church, has been the position of legal Christianity in respect to the claims of philosophy and the rights of the mind.

---

[1] Lectures on the Ecclesiastical History of the First and Second Centuries.

It loves to set revelation against humanity, instead of seeking to reconcile the two. So far from finding the word of God in human reason, and human reason in the word of God, it delights to sow enmity between them. It declares eternal feud to be their normal relation. Instead of adjusting itself with the natural faith and universal heart of man, it assumes in advance that human nature is an enemy, and must be crushed and trampled in the dust, in order to receive its impress. Compare with these flings of Tertullian the tone of discourse on such matters in modern writers of like faith. Thus, the author of the "Greyson Letters," quite in the spirit of the old African, assures his correspondent that Christianity goes desperately against the grain of human nature. "You cannot say that the Book has not given you every advantage ; for never was there one which more irritates the pride and prejudices of mankind, which presents greater obstacles to its reception, morally and intellectually ; so that it is amongst the most unaccountable things to me, not that it should be rejected by some, but that it should be accepted by any. . . . Said an old Deist, 'I do not perceive in myself any inclination to receive the New Testament.' There spake not Deism only, but HUMAN NATURE."

As Tertullian in the Latin Church is the type of legalism, so Origen in the Greek Church may be regarded as, next to St. Paul, the truest representative of liberal Christianity. In him as in few beside — perhaps we should say in none beside — were combined the scholar and the saint. Second to none in purity and singleness of heart, in self-denial, humility, devotion, in all Christian virtues, he added "to virtue knowledge," surpassing all others in intellectual activity and intellectual attainments, in the grasp of his thought, in the vastness of his erudition. Neander calls him the founder of sacred learning; that is, of the scientific study of the Bible and all related branches of knowledge. He introduced into Christian study a spirit of inquiry, and an element of intellectual freedom which ages of bigotry were unable wholly to eradicate thence. Unlike Tertullian, he believed in philosophy, and believed in reason. He believed in the necessary and perfect harmony of reason and revelation. Possessed with this conviction, his genius led him to spiritualize and allegorize whatever seemed contrary to reason in the letter of Scripture, and especially all that savors of anthropomorphism. Tertullian did not shun to ascribe corporeity to God. He must have an eye to watch man; a hand to protect him; an ear to hear him; a heart to love him. Origen, on the contrary, is careful to divest the idea of God of all material attributes: he conceives of Deity as pure spirit, infinitely transcending all human conception. He understands figuratively all those passages in the Bible which speak humanly of God. He cannot accept, in its literal sense, the Mosaic account of creation. A creation that had its beginning but a few thousand years ago is inconsistent with the nature of God, who must have created from all eternity. The existing universe must have been preceded by an infinite series of creations. He believes in the pre-existence of human souls. What is called native depravity is the taint contracted by transgression in some previous state. He believes in a plurality of intelligent and spiritual worlds, and regards the death of Christ as a sacrifice whose efficacy is not confined to this our earth, but includes the spheres in its complete grace, and carries atonement into all the heavens. His eschatology is as generous as his theory of redemption. He believes that all souls will be finally restored to God; Satan himself, as the Scottish bard hoped, will take thought and mend; the universe in all its abysses will be purged of evil, —

> "And Hell itself shall pass away,
> And leave her dolorous mansions to the peering day."

I do not propose Origen, no more than Tertullian, as authority or model; but only as type in his own kind, as the foremost instance of liberalism in religion. He represents the faults as well as the merits of that kind. In him the philosopher outruns the evangelist. The bold speculations in which he indulges, if not antagonistic to the teachings of the gospel, are foreign to the purport and simplicity of the gospel, which subordinates curious inquiry to moral truth, — the knowledge that puffeth up to the love that buildeth up.

Come down two centuries later, and the never-failing dualism reappears in the conflict of Augustinian and Pelagian anthropology. The Church, already divided on the nature of Christ, divides now on the nature of man, — on human free-will; on the agency which the individual has in his own salvation. Augustine, who never entirely outgrew his early Manichæan determinations, and whose theology was colored by his personal experience of sin, was deeply impressed with the might and extent of the empire of evil, which he conceived as reaching down to the very core of man's being. He could see in human nature only the arena of a contest between God and Satan. The human will is entirely passive in this conflict; it is not human nature that acts when one is converted and saved, but grace in the place of human nature, supplanting it, replacing it. The regenerate man is not a human original, but only a particular vessel into which God's grace is poured. Opposed to this is the liberal, Pelagian view, which recognizes human nature as itself an independent, sacred reality. Immensely important is this view, — far beyond its theological bearings, and beyond the comprehension of that time, — the first emphatic assertion, within the pale of the Christian Church, of the dignity of human nature. It is the basis of all civil and personal liberty. The Stoics had a glimpse of it; the gospel reveals it; the very term "Son of man" implies it; but this is its first distinct recognition as a Christian doctrine. Pelagius himself is not the best representative of this view, — himself less liberal on the whole, and with more of a legal cast in his doctrine, than Augustine, who as a thinker was immeasurably his superior. But this particular view of human nature (with him it was rather an instinct than a vision) soon found other and worthier exponents, as the liberal side of Christian anthropology contrasted with the legal positions of St. Augustine.

In the seventh century, the old antagonism breaks forth afresh in the Monothelite controversy of the Greek Church, repeating in substance the Nestorian and Monophysite disputes of the fifth and sixth. Maximus here represents the liberal, and Theodore the legal, side. In the ninth century, we have the question of the Double Predestination, — Gottschalk taking the legal view, and Scotus Erigena the liberal. And again, in the thirteenth, we have the practical antithesis of St. Dominic and St. Francis.

It is not my intent to pursue this parallel through all the epochs of ecclesiastical history. I will only remind the reader how the great Reformation, which at first combined and concentred the spirits and beliefs opposed to Romanism, soon disparted into two streams, into two religions, — iron-hearted Calvin leading and organizing Protestant legalism; Arminius, somewhat later, representing liberal Protestantism.

From their theological characteristics, if now we pass to their practical aspects, and survey the working of the two religions in organized communions, we are struck with the very decided superiority of legal over liberal Christianity as a method of church-life. It needs but a glance at ecclesiastical organizations to perceive what mighty advantage a church derives from legal views and a legalizing spirit. It is not too much to say, that a church is powerful and prosperous in precisely that degree in which it is possessed with such views and such a spirit. The Church of Rome, the most powerful spiritual organism the world has known, is a standing witness of the truth of this position. The Church of Rome owes all her strength to this cause. Whatever may have been her doctrinal decisions when defining her faith in relation to the heresies that sprung from her bosom, — whether narrower or larger than the views she eliminated, — the absolute authority of those decisions was always a fundamental point in her faith. Her intense ecclesiastical consciousness (infallibility) gave her decisions a binding force within the pale of her communion, in which the very essence of legalism consists. She broke with the Greek Church on a question of reform. Espousing herself the conservative side (which was also in this case the popular side), she gained new strength from the schism. The Greek Church, taking the side of reform, and thereby condemning her own practice, seeking orthodoxy at the expense of infallibility, failed to maintain her ground, and was finally worsted in the contest. A change of government restored idolatry to Constantinople, but not œcumenical *prestige*. With two successive empires for her allies, and historical antecedents in her favor, the "Orthodox" Church has never wielded the power of the "Catholic," with often an empire for her adversary. The Albigenses, — the most liberal and most powerful antagonists of papal rule in the thirteenth century, having virtual control of the fairest and most civilized portion of Europe, but without dogmatic authority or bond, and only agreeing in dissent from the Church, — were completely exterminated by the sword of De Montfort and the bloodhounds of Dominic. On the other hand, the Waldenses, who with equal hostility to Rome combined a more stringent faith, survived the most savage persecution, and continue to this day.

Need I point to Protestant Christendom, to our own most Protestant land, for illustrations? The superior strength of the self-styled "Evangelical" sects, as compared with the Liberal, stares us in the face. The Unitarians, with every advantage in the way of culture and of literary ability, have not only made, relatively to other sects, no appreciable progress, but have never organized with corporate effect, have never united in any uniform policy, have never cordially co-operated in any systematic attempt to extend their communion. Their theological views they have propagated by books and otherwise; their corporate influence they have not extended, have not even maintained. The management of the first University in the land had fallen providentially into their hands; they endowed it munificently, increased its professorial staff, and raised the standard of education, not only for that college, but through it, indirectly, for every college in the land. They might with all legal propriety have made it ancillary to their own ecclesiastical growth. They might, as other sects would have done in their place, have made it, what other colleges are, a sectarian institution. Far from this, they religiously refrained from any effort in that direction. I pass no judgment on this conduct; I only cite it as an instance of that lack of organic strength and ecclesiastical consciousness which seems to be inseparable from liberalism in religion. If corporate zeal were the test and measure of truth, Unitarianism would stand convicted and condemned by irrefragable fact. I often think, on the contrary, that zeal and truth are inversely related, — that the clearer men see, the less concerned they are to communicate their vision.

Whatever its theological merits, Liberal Christianity is not, ecclesiastically, a good working faith. It dwells too much in inquiry, is too "sicklied o'er with the pale cast of thought," to succeed in sectarian "enterprises of great pith and moment."

Nor is this its only defect. Not only does it fail in propagandism, not only does it lack the power to organize, — the corporate zeal which shows itself in vigorous and effective coaction, — but in every kind of religious demonstration, in all that is technically called religion, as distinct from moral and philanthropic action, it falls far short of the mark and standard of legal faith. The religious sentiment, properly so called, is less active, — or perhaps we should say less concrete and demonstrative, — in

Christians of liberal views, than in those of the legal communions. Popularly speaking, the former are less religious than the latter. It is useless to deny this; candor compels me to give to legal Christianity the preference in this particular. At what expense of other and equal good this advantage is maintained, is a point to be considered by all who would weigh the comparative merits of the two systems. It has been alleged by its adversaries that Unitarianism leads to irreligion. Whatever may be thought of the *animus* of that charge, it is not so utterly baseless as the prompt repudiation of it by the Unitarian consciousness might seem to imply. Viewed in one aspect, it is false, and even recklessly false; considered in another, it is not without some color of truth. It is false as a matter of fact, inasmuch as the larger proportion of unbelievers are notoriously the offspring of "Orthodoxy," and have come from the ranks of the legal sects. But, theoretically, it is true so far as this: Romanism being the positive extreme of the Christian world, and irreligion the negative, Unitarianism is further removed from the positive, consequently nearer the negative, than most of the Protestant systems. As Romanism has more of positive religion than Protestant Orthodoxy, so Orthodoxy has more of positive religion than Unitarianism. The charge is true in the same sense in which, from the Catholic point of view, Protestantism leads to infidelity. Or again, Unitarianism leads to irreligion in precisely that sense in which Orthodoxy leads to fanaticism, — which is no better than irreligion, and leads to hypocrisy, which is worse. It is a step in that direction ; but it does not follow that all the succeeding steps must be taken until the goal is reached. It is a question of comparative approximation. If one sect is nearer irreligion than another, that other is nearer to it than its antecedent, and so on. Heaven help us if we are never to move in any direction, because that direction may be followed to excess! In that case, Protestantism is the first misstep; and consistency would require the Protestant who recoils from a liberal faith, on the score of irreligion, to pursue the retrograde movement until he lands in the Church of Rome.

Religion is not a finality, but means to an end. The end is the perfect man. The two religions must be judged by the measure in which they contribute thereto. The first and principal function of all religion is to aid the development of the moral nature, to further moral purity and power. Only so far as it answers this end directly or indirectly, by quickening the conscience, by strengthening the social bond, or by fostering and stimulating beautiful art, — only so far as it makes men morally better, — is religion any real benefit to man. Sad to say, religion has not always wrought to this effect; and when it has not, it has been no blessing, but a curse. When the light that is in man is turned to darkness, that darkness is deeper and deadlier than mere brute night. When religion ceases to be regarded as means to an end, as an aid to moral and spiritual culture, a handle by which the soul lays hold of the eternal, — when it loses this function in men's apprehension, and becomes an end in itself, an exclusive and absorbing end, an end above truth and righteousness, — then it is apt to become a substitute for truth and righteousness, and then the light that is in man is turned to darkness and to death. What different growths of the spirit ostensibly spring from the same root! The belief in the invisible, which lies at the basis of all religions, — how diverse its action, how contrary its manifestations, according to the nature in which it is rooted and the nurture it receives! The same principle which made a Paul out of Saul and a saint out of Augustine, which ravished the soul of St. Francis and transfigured the life of Elizabeth, which lit up the eyes of Raphael's Marys and conjugated the notes of the *Miserere*, — that same principle macerated the bodies of the Encratites, and drove men to the tops of columns and into the bowels of the earth, and put a scourge into the hands of Piety, and planned the wiles of the Inquisition, and enacted the fiery Acts of Faith. "Doth a fountain send forth at the same place sweet waters and bitter," godlike charities and hellish crimes? Yes, human nature is such a fountain, and religion the prophet that unlocks its secret life. Human nature, the individual nature, is deeper than any system, and stronger than any faith. It reacts on religion in the same measure in which it is actuated by it. Religion is not responsible for all the aberrations it has seemed to sanction, or that rage in its name.

> "Though all things foul would wear the brows of grace,
> Yet grace must still look so."

At the same time, it is clear that different systems of religion, received by tradition from the visible Church, will act very differently on human nature; and, according to their proper complexion, will quicken or restrain, dissuade or reassure, the native proclivities of souls. On the whole, then, a religion may be judged by its moral fruits; or, since the causal relation of subject and accident in such matters is indemonstrable, let us say its moral accompaniments.

Tried by this test, and compared in this aspect, the two religions exhibit each their lights and their shades according to their kind. Neither will be found inglorious, and neither without spot. Great and holy characters and lives, noble men and noble women, have been reared under both. Each has had its heroes and confessors, and neither may claim precedence of the other in the heraldry of grace. Yet here also the two religions preserve their distinctive types. They differ in their moral traits, as in their intellectual. The characteristic virtue of the legal is scrupulous sobriety, that of the liberal, active beneficence; the one is more strict in its way of life, the other more intent on works of love; the one aspires to personal holiness, the other delights in public good; the one, contemning and renouncing the world, presses steadily on to the kingdom of God, the other would establish that kingdom in the world. The prayer of the one is, May we come into Thy kingdom! The prayer of the other is, May Thy kingdom come! Likewise the immoralities incident to either as a visible communion, the vices most often associated with them, are respectively and characteristically proper to each kind. The vices of the liberal are indolence, indifference, eudemonism, self-indulgence, fleshly lusts, and sensual excess. The vices of the legal are hypocrisy, falsehood, dishonesty in business, treachery, cruelty. I do not mean, of course, to say that either religion engenders these results; I am not speaking of necessary consequences, but of common accompaniments.

There is one diagnostic of the two religions, and that perhaps the most definitive of any, of which as yet I have not spoken, and can only now point to in passing, for want of room to do it justice. I mean the attitude they respectively assume in relation to public and private amusements. Legal religion is prevailingly ascetic; it regards the world as essentially godless, a Vanity Fair, a passing trial, a transient obstruction, with which the Christian has nothing to do but to make his pilgrim's progress through it, unbending and succinct, drawing close his robe of righteousness, that it take no defilement in the miry passage. It professes no sympathy with gayety and mirth, is cold to all pleasures but those which

> "Rise from things unseen,
> Beyond this world and time;"

and turns with special aversion from the dance and the play, if not as sinful in themselves, yet as perilously dwelling in the neighborhood of sin. If in any community it had full scope and unqualified sway, it would banish all this, spread sackcloth and ashes, and establish perpetual Lent. Liberal religion secularizes without reserve; it feels itself at home in the world, sanctions festive enjoyment, contends for public amusements, tolerates theatre and ball, with perhaps too little discrimination. If in any community it had full sway, there is reason to fear that society would miss the earnest shadow of the law, that the passions which thirst for enjoyment would never have done with their carnival, that "Joy and Feast" would encroach too far on the awfulness of life.

It has been my aim, in this brief sketch, to render strict justice to both of the religions which divide mankind, — to exhibit fairly their prominent traits, without disparagement and without exaggeration. It could never occur to me to pronounce definitively respecting their comparative value on the whole. As soon should I think of passing judgment respecting the comparative value of man and woman, or of body and spirit, or any two necessary correlates of being. Neither is best, and neither is sufficient in itself. Both are necessary, and both are partial, and both are permanent types. Each is the other's complement, and neither could be missed without loss to the world. Both will continue to exist in nearly the same proportions as now. I have no misgivings respecting the cause of Liberal Christianity, whatever may become of the churches that embody it. If these fail, other communions will arise in their place, or legal communions will enlarge themselves to receive this element. The gospel has this side, human nature has this side; and both will be sure to find expression. I have no misgivings about Orthodoxy.

I rejoice in Orthodoxy, and am deeply conscious how ill this factor could be missed from the sum of the forces that rule the world. Both religions will find their own. He who craves the largest liberty of thought and worship, and still affects the Christian name, and still acknowledges the mastership of Christ, will be naturally drawn to the liberal side. He who requires for his edification the strong embrace of a close communion, the pulsing life of a vigorous organism, the warm breath of the crowded conventicle, the frequent assembly, the large operation, the triumphant report, will seek a lodgement in some legal church. Happily, the Christian idea is wide enough for both.

XII.

THE MYTHICAL ELEMENT IN THE NEW TESTAMENT.

Φιλοσοφώτερον καὶ σπουδαιότερον ποίησις ἱστορίας ἐστιν.

ARISTOTLE.

WHEN Dr. Strauss, thirty-five years ago,[1] in his "Life of Jesus," advanced and applied to the narrative of the New Testament a theory of interpretation, in principle the same with that which a Christian Father of the third century had employed in his treatment of the Old, the theological world was profoundly shocked by what seemed to be the last impiety of criticism. A hundred champions rushed with drawn pen to the rescue of the old interpretation of the text. The truth of Christianity was supposed to be assailed; the belief in Christianity as divine revelation was felt to be imperilled by a theory which substituted mythical figment for historic fact. That no such harm was intended, or was likely to ensue from his labors, the author himself assures us in the preface to that extraordinary work. "The inner kernel of Christian faith," he declares, "is entirely independent of

[1] This was written in 1871.

all such criticism. Christ's supernatural birth, his miracles, his resurrection and ascension, remain eternal truths, however their reality as facts of history may be called in question."

In this declaration I find the motive of the following dissertation.

How far does the cause of Christianity depend on the facts, or alleged facts, of the Gospel narrative? Or, to state the question in other words, Is the truth of Christianity identical and conterminous with the literal truth of its record?

It is obvious at the start that a certain amount of historic truth must be assumed as implied in the very existence of any religion which dates from a personal founder whose thought it professes to embody, and whose name it bears. Christianity purports to be founded on the ministry of a Jewish teacher, entitled by his followers "the Christ." We have the testimony of a nearly contemporary Latin historian to the fact that an individual so named was the leader of a numerous body of religionists, and was put to death by command of Pontius Pilate, in the reign of Tiberius. But, without this confirmation, the very existence of the Christian Church compels us to accept as historic facts, the ministry of Jesus, the strong impression of his word and character, his purity of manners and moral greatness, his life of beneficent action, his martyr death, and his manifestation to his disciples after death, however that manifestation be conceived, whether as subjective experience or as objective reality. So much, beyond all reasonable question, must stand as history, vouched by documentary evidence, and by the existence, in the first century, of a Church universally diffused, which affirmed these facts as the ground of its being, and in the strength of them overcame the world.

But, observe, it is Christianity that assures the truth of these facts, and not the facts that prove Christianity. To base the truth of Christianity on the credibility, in every particular, of the Gospel record; to measure the claims of the religion by the strict historic verity of all the narrative of the New Testament, is to prejudice the Christian cause in the judgment of competent critics. It is to challenge the cavil and counter-demonstration of unbelief.

Christianity assures the truth of certain facts; but by no means of all the facts affirmed by the writers of the New Testament. Faith in Christianity as divine dispensation does not imply, and must not be held to the belief, as veritable history, of all that is recorded in the Gospel. Not the historic sense, but the spiritual import; not the facts, but the ideas of the Gospel, are the genuine topics of faith.

Christianity, like every other religion, has its mythology, — a mythology so intertwined with the veritable facts of its early history, so braided and welded with its first beginnings, that history and myth are not always distinguishable the one from the other. Every historic religion, that has won for itself a conspicuous place in the world's history, has evolved from a core of fact a nimbus of legendary matter which criticism cannot always separate, and which the popular faith does not seek to separate, from the solid parts of the system. And in one view the legends or myths which gather around the initial stage of any religion are as true as the vouched and substantial facts of its record: they are a product of the same spirit working, in the one case, in the acts and experiences; in the other, in the visions, the ideas, the literary activity of the faithful. It is one and the same motive that inspires both the writer and the doer.

When I speak of historic religions, I mean such as trace their origin to some historic personage, and bear the impress of his idea, in contradistinction to those which have sprung from unknown sources, the wild growths of Nature-worship as found in ancient Egypt, in the Indian and Scandinavian peninsulas, and in Greece.

No distinction in religion is so fundamental as that between the wild religions and those which have sprung from the word of a human sower going forth to sow; the religions of sense and those of reflection, the "natural" and the "revealed." The prime characteristic of the former is polytheism; that of the latter, monotheism. Mosaism, Mohammedism, Buddhism, — so far as it knows any God, — even Parsism, is monotheistic in so much as its dualism is resolvable into the final triumph and supremacy of the good. No founder of a religion ever taught a plurality of gods.

Another characteristic of the wild religions is their transitoriness. The Egyptian, the Greco-Roman, the Scandinavian, perished long ago. Bramanism, the last survivor of the ancient polytheisms, is fast melting beneath the advancing heats of Islam and the Brahmo Somaj. The "revealed" religions on the contrary are permanent. No religion of historic origin, so far as I know, has ever died out. Judaism, the eldest of them, still flourishes: never since the destruction of Jerusalem has it flourished with a greener leaf than now. Mohammedism is pushing its conquests faster than Christianity in the East; Parsism is still strong in Bengal; Buddhism in one or another form calls a third part of the population of the globe its own.

All religions have their mythologies, but with this distinction: polytheism is mythical in principle as well as form, in soul as well as body, and mythical throughout. Its whole being is myth. Whatever of scientific or historic truth may be hidden in any of its legends, such as the labors of Herakles, the fire-theft of Prometheus, or the rape of Europa, is matter of pure conjecture. In the "revealed" religions, on the contrary, the mythical is incidental, not principal, and always subordinate to doctrine or fact. Always the truth shines through the myth, explains it, justifies it.

Before proceeding any farther, I desire to explain what I mean by myth in this connection. I shall not attempt a philosophic definition, but content myself with this general determination. I call any story a myth which for good reasons is not to be taken historically, and yet is not a wilful fabrication with intent to deceive, but the natural growth of wonder and tradition, or a product of the Spirit uttering itself in a narrative form. The myth may be the result of exaggeration, the expansion of a veritable fact which gathers increments and a *posse comitatus* of additions as it travels from mouth to ear and ear to mouth in the carriage of verbal report; or it may be the reflection of a fact in the mind of a writer, who reproduces it in his writing with the color and proportions it has taken in his conception; or it may be the poetic embodiment of a mental experience; or it may be what Strauss calls "the deposit[1] of an idea," and another critic "an idea shaped into fact." I think we have examples of all these mythical formations in the New Testament; and I hold that the credit of the Gospel in things essential is nowise impaired, nor the claim of Christianity as divine revelation compromised, by a frank admission of this admixture of fancy with fact in its record. On the contrary, I deem it important, in view of the vulgar radicalism which confounds the Christian dispensation and its record, soul and body, in one judgment, to separate the literary question from the spiritual, and to free the cause of faith from the burden of the letter.

It has been assumed that the proof of divine revelation rests on precisely those portions of the record which are most offensive to unbelief. On this assumption the Christian apologists of a former generation grounded their plea. Prove that we have the testimony of eye-witnesses to the miracles recorded in the Gospels, and Christianity is shown to be a divine revelation. In the absence of such proof (the inference is) Christianity can no longer claim to be, in the words of Paul, "the power of God unto salvation." This is substantially Paley's argument. Planting himself on the premise that revelation is impossible without miracles, in which

---

[1] Niederschlag.

it is implied that miracles prove revelation, he labors to establish two propositions: 1. "That there is satisfactory evidence that many professing to be original witnesses of the Christian miracles passed their lives in dangers, labors, and sufferings, voluntarily undergone in attestation of the accounts which they delivered, and solely in consequence of their belief in those accounts; and that they also submitted from the same motives to new rules of conduct." 2. "That there is *not* satisfactory evidence that persons pretending to be original witnesses of any other similar miracles have acted in the same manner in attestation of the accounts which they delivered, and solely in consequence of their belief in the truth of those accounts." The argument is stated with the characteristic clearness of the author, and as well supported perhaps as Anglican church-erudition in those days would allow; but the case is not made out, and, if it were, the argument fails to satisfy the sceptical mind of to-day. To say nothing of its gross misconception of the nature of revelation, which it makes external instead of internal, a stunning of the senses instead of mental illumination, an appeal to prodigy and not its own sufficient witness, — waiving this objection, the argument fails when confronted with the fact that, in spite of the evidence which scholars and critics the most learned and acute of all time have arrayed in support of the genuineness of the Gospels, the number is nowise diminished, but rather increases, of intelligent minds that find themselves unable, on the faith of any book, however ancient, to receive as authentic a tale of wonders which contradict their experience of the limits of human ability and their faith in the continuity of Nature. For myself, I beg to say, in passing, I am not of this number. I do not feel the force of the objection against miracles drawn from this alleged constancy of Nature, which it seems to me reduces the course of human events to a dead mechanical sequence, makes no allowance for any reserved power in Nature or any incalculable forces of the Spirit, and virtually rules God, the present inworking God, out of the universe. I can believe in any miracle which does not actually and demonstrably contravene and nullify ascertained laws, however phenomenally foreign to Nature's ordinary course. But the possibility of miracles is one thing, the possibility of proving them another. With such views as these objectors entertain of the constancy of Nature, I confess that no testimony, not even the written affidavit of a dozen witnesses taken on the spot, supposing that we had it, would suffice to convince me of the truth of marvels occurring two thousand years ago, of the kind recounted in the Gospels. My Christian prepossessions might incline me to believe in them: the weight of evidence would not. No wise defender of the Christian cause, at the present day, will rest his plea on the issue to which Paley committed its claims. After all that Biblical critics and antiquarian research have raked from the dust of antiquity in proof of the genuineness and authenticity of the books of the New Testament, credibility still labors with the fact that the age in which these books were received and put in circulation was one in which the science of criticism as developed by the moderns — the science which scrutinizes statements, balances evidence for and against, and sifts the true from the false — did not exist; an age when a boundless credulity disposed men to believe in wonders as readily as in ordinary events, requiring no stronger proof in the case of the former than sufficed to establish the latter, namely, hearsay and vulgar report; an age when literary honesty was a virtue almost unknown, and when, consequently, literary forgeries were as common as genuine productions, and transcribers of sacred books did not scruple to alter the text in the interest of personal views and doctrinal prepossessions. The newly discovered Sinaitic Code, the earliest known manuscript of the New Testament, dates from the fourth century. Tischendorf the discoverer, a very orthodox critic, speaks without reserve of the license in the treatment of the text apparent in this manuscript, — a license, he says, especially characteristic of the first three centuries.

These considerations, though they do not discredit the essential facts of the Gospel history, — facts assured to us, as I have said, by the very existence of the Christian Church, — might seem to excuse the hesitation of the sceptic in accepting, on the faith of the record, incidental marvels of a kind very difficult of proof at best. I recall in this connection the remarkable saying of an English divine of the seventeenth century. "So great, in the early ages," says Bishop Fell, "was the license of fiction, and so prone the facility of believing, that the credibility of history has been gravely embarrassed thereby; and not only the secular world, but the Church of God, has reason to complain of its mythical periods." [1]

It is not in the interest of criticism, much less of a wilful iconoclasm, from which my whole nature revolts, but of Christian faith, that I advocate the supposition of a mythical element in the New Testament. I am well aware that in this advocacy I

---

[1] Tanta fuit primis seculis fingendi licentia, tam prona in credendo facilitas, ut rerum gestarum fides graviter exinde laboraverit, nec orbis tantum terrarum sed et Dei ecclesia de temporibus suis mythicis merito queratur.

shall lack the consent of many good people who identify the cause of religion with its accidents, and fancy that the sanctuary is in danger when a blind is raised to let in new light. I respect the piety that clings to idols which Truth has outgrown, as Paul at Athens respected the religion which worshipped ignorantly the unknown God. But Truth once seen will draw piety after it, and new sanctities will replace the old. No Protestant in these days feels himself bound to accept as history the ecclesiastical legends of the post-apostolic age. Some of them are quite as significant as some of those embodied in the canon; but no Protestant scruples to reject as spurious the story of the caldron of boiling oil into which St. John was thrown by order of the Emperor Domitian, and from which he escaped unharmed, or that of the lioness which licked the feet of Thekla in the circus of Antioch, or Peter's encounter with Christ in the suburbs of Rome. If we talk of evidence, I do not see but the miracles said to be performed by the relics of martyrs at Milan, attested by St. Augustine, and those of St. Cuthbert of Durham, attested by the venerable Bede, are as well substantiated as the opening of the prison doors and the liberation of the Apostles by an angel, attested by Luke. The Church of Rome makes no such distinction between the first and the following centuries: she indorses the miracles of all alike. But modern Protestantism draws a line of sharp separation between the apostolic and the post-apostolic ages. On the farther side the portents are all genuine historic facts: on the hither side they are all figments. While John the Evangelist, the last of the twelve, yet breathed, a miracle was still possible: his breath departed, it became an impossibility for evermore. And yet when Conyers Middleton first ran this line between the ages, and published his refutation of the claim of continued miraculous power in the Church, religious sensibility experienced a shock as great as that inflicted in our day by Strauss, and resented with equal indignation the affront to Christian faith. The author of the "Free Inquiry" published in 1748 was assailed by opponents, who "insinuate" he tells us "fears and jealousies of I know not what consequences dangerous to Christianity, ruinous to the faith of history, and introductive of universal scepticism." The larger work had been preceded by an "Introductory Discourse" put forth as a feeler of the public pulse; for "I began," he says, "to think it a duty which candor and prudence prescribed, not to alarm the public at once with an argument so strange and so little understood, nor to hazard an experiment so big with consequences till I had at first given out some sketch or general plan of what I was projecting."

The experiment which required such careful preparation was to ascertain how far the English public in the middle of the eighteenth century would bear to have it said that the miracles affirmed by Augustine and Chrysostom and Jerome, as occurring in their day, were not as worthy of credit as any of the wonders recorded in the New Testament. Up to that time, English Protestants as well as Romanists had given equal credence to both, and esteemed the former as essential to Christian faith as the latter. Men like Waterland and Dodwell and Archbishop Tillotson held that miracles continued in the Church until the close of the third century, and were even occasionally witnessed in the fourth. Whiston, the consistent Arian, maintained their continuance up to the establishment of the Athanasian doctrine in 381, and "that as soon as the Church became Athanasian, antichristian, and popish, they ceased immediately; and the Devil lent it his own cheating and fatal powers instead."

To me, I confess, the position of the Church of Rome in this matter seems less indefensible than that of Middleton and modern Protestantism. Either deny the possibility of miracles altogether to finite powers, or admit their possibility in the second century, and the third century, as well as the first, and in all centuries whenever a worthy occasion demands such agency. I can see no reason for separating, as Middleton does, the age of the Apostles from all succeeding. Had he drawn the line between the miracles of Christ and those ascribed to his followers, the principle of division would have been more intelligible, and more admissible on the ground of ecclesiastical orthodoxy.

But the question here is not of the possibility or probability of miracles, as such, in one age rather than another. It is a question simply of Biblical interpretation,—whether the literal sense of the record is in every case the true sense, whether history or fiction is the key to certain Scriptures. Those who insist on the verbal inspiration of the New Testament will be apt to likewise insist on the literal historic sense of every part of every narrative. And yet that mode of interpretation is by no means a necessary consequence or logical outcome of that theory. Origen believed in the verbal inspiration of the Old Testament, but Origen did not accept in their literal sense the Hebrew theophanies: he allegorized whatever seemed to him to degrade the idea of God. The Spirit can utter itself in fiction as well as fact, and in communicating with Oriental minds was quite as likely to do so. And surely, for those who reject the notion of verbal inspiration, the way is open, in perfect consistency with Christian faith, for such interpretation as reason may approve or the credit of the record be thought to require. The credit of the record will sometimes require an allegorical interpretation instead of a literal one.

It is a childish limitation which in reading stories can feel no interest in any thing but fact; and a childish misconception which supposes that where the form is narrative, historic fact must needs be the substance. Recount to a little child a fable of Pilpay or Æsop, and his questions betray his inability to apprehend it otherwise than as literal fact. He has no doubt of the truth of the story. "What did the lion say then?" he asks; and "what did the fox do next?" The maturer mind has also no doubt of the truth of the story, but sees that its truth is the moral it embodies. Of many of the Gospel stories the moral contained in them is the real truth. In the height of our late civil war there appeared in a popular journal a story entitled "A Man without a Country," related with such artistic verisimilitude, such minuteness of detail, such grave official references, that many who read it not once suspected the clever invention, and felt themselves somewhat aggrieved when apprised that fiction, not fact, had conveyed the moral intended by the genial author. But those who saw from the first through the veil of fiction the needful truth and the patriotic intent, were not less edified than if they had believed the characters real, and every incident vouched by contemporary record. The story of William Tell was once universally received as authentic history: it was written in the hearts of the people of Uri; and so religiously were all its incidents cherished, that when a book appeared discrediting the sacred tradition it was publicly burned by the hangman at Altorf. For five centuries the chapel on the shore of the Lake of the Four Cantons has commemorated a hero whose very existence is now questioned, of whom contemporary annals know nothing, of whose tyrant Gessler the well-kept records of the Canton exhibit no trace, whose apple placed as a mark for the father's arrow on the head of his child is proved to have done a foregone service in an elder Danish tale. The story resolves itself into an idea. That idea is all that concerns us; and that idea survives, inexpugnable to criticism, a truth for evermore. In the world of ideas there is still a William Tell who defied the tyrant at Altorf, and slew him at Küsnacht, and whose image will live while the mountains stand that gave it birth.

And so all that is memorable out of the past, all that tradition has preserved, the veritable facts of history as well as the myths of legendary lore, pass finally into ideas. Only as ideas they survive, only as ideas have they any abiding value. The anecdote recorded of Aristides — his writing his own name at the request of an ignorant citizen on the shell that should condemn him — embodies a noble idea which has floated down to us from the head-waters of Grecian history. Do we care to know the evidence on which it rests? If by critical investigation the fact were made doubtful, would that doubt at all impair the truth of the idea? The story of Damon and Pythias, reported by Valerius Maximus, for aught that we know, may be a myth: suppose it could be proved to be so, the truth that is in it would be none the less precious. We do not receive it on the faith of the historian, but on the faith of its own intrinsic beauty. There is scarcely a fact in the annals of mankind so vouched and ascertained as to be beyond the reach of historic doubt, if any delver in ancient documents, or curious sceptic, shall see fit to call it in question. But, however the fact may be questioned, the idea remains. We have lived to see apologies for Judas Iscariot, and the literary rehabilitation of Henry VIII. But Judas is none the less, in popular tradition, the typical traitor, the impersonation of devilish malice; and Henry VIII. is no less the remorseless tyrant whose will was his God. When Napoleon I. pronounced all history a fable agreed on, he reasoned better perhaps than he knew. The agreement is the thing essential; but that agreement is never complete, is never final. Every original writer of history finds something to qualify, and often something to reverse, in the judgment of his predecessors. How can it be otherwise, when even eye-witnesses disagree in their observation and report of the same transaction; when even in a matter so recent as the siege of Paris, or the conflagration of Chicago, the verification of facts is embarrassed by contradictory accounts? The best that history yields to philosophic thought is not facts, but ideas. These are all that remain at last when the tale is told,—all, at least, that the mind can appropriate, all that profits in historical studies, the intellectual harvest of the past. A fact means nothing until thought has transmuted it into itself: its value is simply the idea it subtends. Homer's heroes are as true in this sense as those of Plutarch. Ajax and Hector are as real to me as Cimon or Lysander; Don Quixote's battle with the windmills which Cervantes imagined is as real as the battle of Lepanto in which Cervantes fought; and Shakspeare's Hamlet is incomparably more real than the Prince of Denmark whom Saxo Grammaticus chronicles.

I do not underrate the importance of facts on their own historic plane. The historian, as annalist, is bound by the rules of his craft with conscientious investigation to ascertain, substantiate, and establish, if he can, the precise facts of the period he explores. I only contend that historic truth is not the only truth; that a fact, — if I may use that term in this connection for want of a better, — that a fact which is not historically true may yet be true on a higher plane than that of history; true to reason, to moral and religious sentiment and human need. The story of Christ's temptation is none the less true, but a great deal more so, when the narrative which embodies the interior psychological fact is conceived as myth, than when it is interpreted as veritable history. The truth that concerns us is that the Son of Man "was tempted in all points as we are;" not that he was taken by the Devil and set on a pinnacle of the Temple, and thence spirited away "into an exceeding high mountain."

We have now attained a point of view from which to estimate on the one hand the real import of what I have ventured to call the myths of the New Testament, and on the other hand to overrule the petulant radicalism which, not distinguishing truth of idea from truth of fact, contemns these legends, and perhaps contemns the Gospel, on their account. I have wished to show how unessential it is to the right enjoyment or profitable use of those portions of the record that we receive them as fact; to show that, if we seize and appropriate the idea, those narratives are quite as edifying from a mythical as from an historical point of view; in other words, that the Holy Spirit may and does instruct by fiction as well as fact. If I am asked to draw the line which separates fact from fiction, or to fix the criterion by which to discriminate the one from the other, I answer that I do not pretend to decide this point for myself, much less should I presume to attempt to settle it for others. I am not disposed to dogmatize on the subject. It is a matter in which each must judge for himself. I will only say that for myself I do not place the line of demarcation between miracle and the unmiraculous, for the reason that it seems to me, as I said before, unphilosophical to make our everyday experience of the limits of human power and the capabilities of Nature an absolute standard by which to measure the possible scope of the one or the other.

I content myself with a single illustration of what I regard as a mythical formation. My example is the story known as "The Annunciation." Luke alone, of all the evangelists, records the tale. The angel Gabriel is sent to a virgin named Mary, and surprises her with the tidings, "Thou shalt conceive in thy womb, and shalt bring forth a son, and shalt call his name Jesus. He shall be great, and shall be called the Son of the Highest. And the Lord God shall give unto him the throne of his father David. And he shall reign over the house of Jacob for ever, and of his kingdom there shall be no end." This beautiful legend, the most beautiful, I think, of all the legends connected with the birth of Christ, the favorite theme of Christian art, so lovingly handled by Fra Angelico, by Correggio, Raphael, Titian, Andrea del Sarto, and a host of others, is best understood as a Jewish-Christian conception, taking an historic form and "shaped into a fact." The legend represents the humility and faith of a pious maiden communing with the heavenly Presence, drawing to herself divine revelations of grace and promise, and thus sanctioning the hope so dear to every Jewish maiden, — that of becoming the mother of the Messiah. The sudden inspiration of that hope is the angel of the Annunciation.

A word more. How far is our idea of Christ affected by a mode of interpretation which supposes a mingling of mythical with historic elements in the Gospel record? That idea is based on the representations of the evangelists. Will not our confidence in those representations be impaired by this view of their contents? I see no cause to apprehend a result so distressing to Christian faith. The mythical interpretation of certain portions of the Gospel has no appreciable bearing on the character of Christ. The impartial reader of the record must see that the evangelists did not invent that character; they did not make the Jesus of their story; on the contrary, it was he that made them. It is a true saying that only a Christ could invent a Christ. The Christ of history is a true reflection of the image which Jesus of Nazareth imprinted on the mind of his contemporaries. In that image the spiritual greatness, the moral perfection, are not more conspicuous than the well-defined individuality which permeates the story, and which no genius could invent.

If the Christ of the Church, of Christian faith, is, as some will have it, an ideal being, it was Jesus of Nazareth who made the ideal. The ideal in him is simply the result of that disengagement from the earthly vestiture which death and distance work in all who live in history. By the very necessity of its function, history idealizes. The historic figure and the individual represented by it, though inseparably one in substance, are not so identical in outline that the one exactly covers the other, no more and no less. The individual is the bodily presence as it dwells in space; the historic figure is the image of himself which the individual stamps on his time, and, so far as his record reaches, on all succeeding time, — his import to human kind. That image is a veritable portrait, but not in the sense of a *fac-simile*. A material portrait, a portrait painted with hands, if the painter understands his art, is not a *fac-simile*: it presents the chronic idea or characteristic mode, not the temporary accidents, "the fallings off, the vanishings," of the person portrayed. In the hero-galleries of tradition, as in the visions of the Apocalypse, they are seen with white robes, and palms in their hands, and unwrinkled brows of grace, who in life were begrimed with the dust and furrowed with the cares of their time. St. Paul is there without his thorn in the flesh, Luther without his impatience, Washington without his fiery choler, Lincoln without his coarseness, Dante and Milton without their scorn. History strips off the indignities of earth when she dresses her heroes for immortality. And the transfigurations she gives us are nearer the truth than the limitations of ordinary life. The man is more truly himself in the epic strain of public action, with spirit braced and harness on, than in the subsidence and undress ot the closet. It is not the gossiping anecdotes, the spoils of the ungirt private life, so dear to antiquaries and literary scavengers, but the things which history hastens to record, that show the man. We must take the life at full-tide; we must view it in its freest determination, in its supreme moment, to know the deepest that is in him. And the deepest that is in him is the true man. That is his idea, his mission to the world, his historic significance. It is this that concerns us in all the great actors of history,—the historic person, not the individual. And the more the historic person absorbs the individual, the higher we rise in the scale of being until we reach the idea of God, from which all individuality is excluded, and only the Person remains, filling space and time with the ceaseless procession of his being.

We misread the Gospel and reverse the true and divine order, if we suppose the ideal Christ to be an essence distilled from the historical. On the contrary, the ideal Christ is the root and ground of the historical; and without the antecedent idea inspiring, commanding, the history would never have been.

It has not been my intention in any thing I have said to make light of the record. The record to me is a literary relic of inestimable value, aboriginal memorial of the dearest and divinest appearance in human form that ever beamed on earthly scenes. I sympathize with every attempt to clear up and verify its minutest details, with the labors of all critics and archæologists devoted to this end.

I rejoice in all topographical adjustments and illustrations; in all that local researches, following in the steps of "those blessed feet," have gleaned from the soil of Palestine. But all this is important only as it draws its inspiration from and leads my aspiration to the ideal Christ, "the same yesterday, to-day, and for ever." Dissociated from this idea, the acres of Palestine are as barren as any which the ebbing of a nation's life has left desolate.

XIII.

INCARNATION AND TRANSUBSTANTIATION.

HAD we no other record than that which the first three Gospels present of the sayings and doings of Jesus, the Christian religion would never have taken the form which it did in the teaching and creed of the Church. Whoever compares the fourth Gospel with the other three perceives a wide difference, not to say conflict, between the Jesus depicted by Matthew, Mark, and Luke, and the Christ portrayed by John. The difference appears in the acts recorded, and is still more conspicuous in the sayings ascribed to him. In their view of the Messiah, the first three evangelists—the so-called "synoptics"—are substantially one. Their record may be termed the Jews' Gospel; that of John the Greek.

The vexed question of authorship I shall not discuss. Whether written by John, the son of Zebedee, or by whomsoever written, it is very un-Jewish, and even anti-Jewish, in its spirit and aim.

The Jews' Gospel sees in Jesus simply the Jewish Messiah, the destined king of the Jewish people, having an hereditary claim to the national throne, — a claim which it seeks to establish by genealogies tracing his descent from David and Abraham. The Greek Gospel, on the contrary, cares nothing for the royal lineage and nothing for the Jewish throne. It has nothing to say of the human ancestry of Jesus, but leaps at once to his spiritual pedigree, in virtue of which he overtops Moses and out-dates Abraham. Its Christ is the Word made flesh. The Jews' Gospel presents its subject on the natural, national, human side; the Greek Gospel propounds a Christ who is superhuman and divine.

Here is a difference, which is very profound, between the first three Gospels and that of John; and one which involves a fundamental difference of race, — a difference which reaches down to the very roots of the human world. It takes us back to Shem and Japhet, the ancestors respectively, according to Biblical tradition, of two races whose mental characteristics and religious proclivities are widely distinct. "Semitic" and "Japhetic" represent two types of mind which differ generally in their intellectual manifestations, and more especially in their theology. They have given birth respectively to two distinct classes or lines of religions, whose beginnings are as old as history, and some of whose progeny remain to this day.

Judaism and Mohammedanism are the offspring of Shem; the Greek mythology, long since extinct, and Brahmanism and Buddhism, which still survive, are the progeny of Japhet.

Now, the chief characteristic of Semitic theology, as it seems to me, is not monotheism, as Renan and others have stated; for some of the Semitic nations — the Phœnicians, for example — have been polytheists; not the belief in one God, but the wide separation between God and man, the absence of any doctrine of incarnation. The Jewish mind, for example, knew no mediation between God and man but that of the prophet's word or the priest's atoning sacrifice. In the Jewish religion — and the same is true of the Mohammedan, its offspring — there is a gulf between God and man, not a consequence of sin, but inherent in the nature of Godhead, and which no atonement can do away. Jehovah is a being apart, uncommunicating, incommunicable. He sends his messengers abroad to make known and execute his will, but he himself inhabits the high and holy place, and never quits his local throne. His word goes forth, it comes to this or that individual; but never becomes man, never incarnates itself in a human person. The greatest of prophets is still but a prophet, nothing more. The Jewish Church never dreamed of deifying Moses, Islam never dreamed of deifying Mohammed, as the Christian Church has deified Christ. The fundamental principles of both religions forbid such deification. But when we turn to the religions of that other great division of the human race, the Japhetic, we encounter an entirely different conception of Godhead. Here deification and incarnation are familiar and ruling ideas. In the elder of the Hindoo religions we encounter a series of successive incarnations, of which the tenth and last is yet to come. In the younger faith of Buddhism we encounter a succession of deifications, — the Buddhist knowing no God but one who was first man, and, having become God, has again and again descended into humanity for the salvation of men. In the religion of the Greeks, the most cultivated nation of antiquity, we find gods and men conversing on easy and familiar terms, — Deity taking often a human form, mortals often raised to the rank of gods.

This fundamental difference of religious tendency in the two races, — the tendency, on the one hand, to separate God from man by an infinite distance not only of degree but of kind, and the tendency, on the other, to view them as distinguished only by degree, and as being in possible, close communion with each other, — this fundamental difference is reflected in the New Testament. The Jews' Gospel, comprising Matthew, Mark, and Luke, represents the former tendency; the fourth Gospel, bearing the name of John, represents the latter. And thus the difference, which even the superficial reader must notice between these two portions of the New Testament, has its origin in the deepest roots of human history. The fact to me is one of intense significance, proof, and illustration of the universality of adaptation, the reconciling spirit, the world-embracing scope, of the gospel of Christ. When Paul said that in Christ there is neither Jew nor Greek, he spoke with reference to the disregard of nationality and the equal acceptance with God, in the Christian view, of all the kindreds and tribes of men. But the saying is true in another and wider sense. In Christ — that is, in Christianity — there is neither Jew nor Greek, because both are merged in a third and new creation.[1] In other words, Christianity is a reconciliation and compromise between the Jewish and the Greek religion, between polytheism and monotheism, correcting the looseness of the one and moderating the stiffness of the other.

In accordance with this view, we have in the first three Gospels the Jewish conception of Christ

[1] "If any man be in Christ, he is a new creature."

as the national Messiah; no suggestion, no hint, of any doctrine of incarnation, no hint of what may be called the divine humanity, the union of God and man in Christ. The fourth Gospel, which, if written by a Jew, was written under Greek influences and for Greeks, abounds in hints to that effect. Of these, the most noticeable are the statement at the start that the Word which was in the beginning, and which was God, was made flesh in Jesus Christ; and the statement in the sixth chapter that the flesh of Christ is the life of the world, which, unless his disciples eat, they have no life in them. From these two statements the Christian Church in past ages developed two doctrines which are closely related the one with the other, and which constitute the two focal points in the Roman Catholic system of faith: first, the identity in substance of Christ with God, — in other words, the incarnation of God in Christ; second, the doctrine of the "real presence" of Christ in the bread of the Lord's Supper when consecrated by the priest, commonly known as the doctrine of transubstantiation. These are not doctrines of the New Testament, but the passages I have cited from the Gospel of John furnished the suggestions on which they are founded. It took three centuries to bring out the one, and seven centuries more to fix and complete the other. Most Protestant Christians, with some inconsistency, reject the latter while retaining the former; reject transubstantiation while retaining the doctrine of incarnation, that is, of the deity of Christ. With some inconsistency, I say, because they are closely related. The theological motive, the underlying principle, in both is the same. In both, the interior sense is the union of the human and divine, the principle that God is in real contact with human nature, and that only through that contact is man redeemed from the power of sin and death and made partaker of eternal life. Let us look at both doctrines in the light of this idea.

I. Incarnation, — God taking a human form in Christ. There is no trace of this doctrine in the first century. The Christians of the first century were strict monotheists, — Unitarians. They speculated very little, if at all, about the person of Christ. The facts of his history were too near to allow of such speculation. No mystic theory that might arise could compete with the recent impression which those facts had left in the mind. Here was the story of a man who had lived and died like other men, distinguished only by his moral elevation, his wonder-working power, and his martyr-death. Jewish converts still looked upon him, through the medium of their Messianic idea, as the national Messiah who would re-appear as earthly potentate and establish his throne in Jerusalem. Gentile Christians were content to see in him a teacher of saving truths, a deliverer from the errors of polytheism, from the bondage of superstition and sin, — the authoritative witness of the doctrine of one God and of the resurrection.

But when the historical Christ had receded into the distance of a by-gone age; when his image, as an actual person, had grown dim, and the tendencies of the Gentile mind, especially the tendency to deify illustrious and extraordinary men, had begun to react on the simplicity of the gospel, — Christian faith, no longer satisfied with bare historic fact, idealized the person of Christ, exalted him above earthly limitations into something superhuman and divine; and here and there went so far as to make him pure spirit, assuming the likeness of man but divested of all natural belongings, without flesh and blood, a divine apparition. Then came the doctrine of the Word, the personified Wisdom, in Jewish phrase "the first begotten Son of God," whom a portion of the Church, in accordance with the Gospel of John, supposed to have been united to the man Jesus, and to have constituted the true Christ. To these two influences, the deifying tendency and the doctrine of the Word, must be added a third. That third and most influential factor in the doctrine of the incarnation, as finally shaped by the Church, was the view entertained of man's redemption. The mission of the gospel was understood to be the redemption of human nature, and the reconciliation or reunion of man with God, in whose image he was formed. This redemption, it was maintained, could be accomplished only by actual communication and contact of God with man. This contact, it was therefore urged, must be supposed to have taken place in the person of Christ,—the divine and the human uniting in him. Accordingly, the Word incarnated in Jesus must be regarded as partaking of the nature or substance of Deity; not, as the Arians taught, a created being, however remote and antecedent to all other finite existence that creation might be conceived, but uncreated, without beginning of existence, born of God from eternity, and therefore one with God in substance,—"consubstantial." The Son consubstantial with the Father,—this was the doctrine of Athanasius, and the Council of Nicæa, where this point was decided.

The superficial mind is apt to regard these questions, which then agitated the Church and the world, as empty abstractions, senseless quibbles. But the union of God with man is no quibble; it is a truth of profound significance; and the Council of Nicæa which declared it is one of the most important assemblies that was ever convened on this earth: it dates a new era in the history of human thought. God in actual contact with man — God in man and man in God — is the underlying idea of the Athanasian dogma which asserts that the Son is consubstantial with the Father. Probably, Athanasius did not perceive the real drift and scope of his doctrine. It was only of the person of Christ that he affirmed substantial community with God. Christ united in his person two natures, the human and the divine; and, by this union of God with man in the person of Christ, human nature is redeemed and restored to health and God. This was the substance of his theology. He did not show, nor does it appear, how humanity in general is benefited by this exceptional participation of the divine nature. Of what avail to mankind at large that a single individual, of the countless millions who in all the ages of human history have walked the earth, was substantially united to God, if all the rest are substantially separated from him? Athanasius maintained, against some of his contemporaries, the real humanity of Christ. But if Christ was really man, he differed from other men only in degree. What he by nature possessed without measure, all men in a measure must also possess. This, Athanasius, from want of thoroughness, failed to perceive; or, from want of consistency, failed to admit. This was his doctrinal limitation and defect. The fault of the Trinitarian doctrine, so far as this point is concerned, is not what it teaches, but what it omits to teach. It is not the assertion of divinity in Christ, but the limitation of divine humanity to him, the implied exclusion of the rest of mankind from any part or lot in this matter. In the view of the Trinitarian doctrine, mankind at large are separated from Christ, not only in degree, but in kind; they have not that oneness with him which he himself accorded to them in his prayer, "That they all may be one; as Thou, Father, art in me and I in Thee, that they may be one in us." They have not that part in God which one of the New Testament writers affirms of Christians at least,— "Called to be partakers of the divine nature."

II. To remedy this defect, to assure to believers that participation of the Godhead, without which, it was maintained, there is no salvation, was the meaning and purpose of the doctrine of transubstantiation. According to this doctrine, the bread of the Christian ordinance of the Supper, when consecrated by the priest, is converted into the body of Christ, whereby they who partake of it are substantially, and, as it were, bodily, united to Christ and to God. Transubstantiation, as I said, is closely connected with, and a logical supplement to, incarnation.

Both of these doctrines, in the form in which they are held and maintained by the larger portions of the Church, are repudiated by rationalizing Christians, as opposed to reason and common sense. But in both of them there is an element of truth which, stripped of its doctrinal embodiment, is worth considering, and which most of us, I think, will heartily accept. To say that God incarnated himself in a single individual of all the multitude of the human family; that once, and once only, in all the ages of time he manifested himself in a human person, — is a proposition which cannot satisfy, if it does not shock, the unprejudiced mind. But expand the proposition; say that God is manifest (and that is the only logical sense in which we can speak of incarnation), — that God is manifest in every inspired teacher and prophet of truth and righteousness, in every holy, self-sacrificing life, in every martyr who, living or dying, devotes himself to any great and worthy cause, — manifest in all in whom love of truth or love of God and man is the ruling motive and principle of action; say, with Paul, that all "who are led by the Spirit of God are sons of God" in precisely the sense, if not in the degree, in which Jesus was the Son of God; that the real distinction and peculiar-ity of Christ was not an exceptional, but a sublimely typical, nature and life; not that he was the only God-man, but the type of the God-man, in all generations, — say this, and you assert what no unprejudiced thinker and no philosophic student of religion will deny. And this I believe to be the real interior truth of the Athanasian doctrine, albeit Athanasius himself may not have seized it in its fulness, as certainly he did not unfold it in his teaching.

So, likewise, the doctrine of transubstantiation, in its gross and literal sense the most monstrous that was ever propounded by any religion, has yet its true side. Strip it of the technicalities and sensuous imagery with which it has been associated by the Church of Rome, and it means that the consecrating action of faith transmutes the material into the spiritual; discerns a spiritual presence and finds spiritual nourishment in material things. It means the participation and assimilation of the spirit of Christ, symbolized by the eating of the bread which he called his body. Christ told his people, "Except ye eat of the flesh of the Son of Man ye have no life abiding in you." It was a daring figure which the Church understood in a coarse and literal way, and of which the doctrine in question was the practical interpretation. Let us understand by it the application of Christian truth to the present earthly life. Christianity requires the flesh of the Son of Man; that is, a visible world, in which the spirit of the Son of Man, a divine spirit, shall embody itself. And this idea, amid all the superstitions and monstrous perversions which gathered around it, is dimly shadowed forth in the Roman Church dogma of transubstantiation. Bread, which forms so important a part of this "flesh" or visible world, may be regarded as symbolizing the whole. The consecrated wafer, which Romish superstition conceives to be bread converted into Deity by the word of a priest, may be taken to represent the looked-for universal transformation of this human world by the communication of a higher and divine life.

Such meaning I discern in the doctrines discussed, and accept them in this sense. I believe in the ever-proceeding incarnation of the spirit of God in human life. I believe in the ever-proceeding transubstantiation of the world into the similitude of the divine idea. The Trinitarian doctrine was a crude attempt to formulate these truths, but instead of their exponent became their grave. Trinitarian theology has lost its hold of advancing Christian thought; but the thing it embodied, divine humanity, across all the mists of theology is struggling into light, is struggling into practical self-demonstration across all the atrocities and woes of time. Side by side with the horrors of carnage and the desolations of war, it bids the eternal charities bloom. It accompanies the march of devastating hosts with the sacred band of self-elected comforters, whose service no softness shuns and no danger dismays. It summons the civilized world to minister to the wants and woes of countries laid waste by famine or fire. It challenges science to show how ancient wrongs may be abated, and the life of man in society be made more beautiful and safe.

Thus, practical Christianity fulfils the truth that was hidden in the obsolete dogmas of the Church; and thus, where "the letter killeth, the spirit maketh alive."

XIV.

THE HUMAN SOUL.

ITS ORIGIN AND DESTINATION.

OUR being is deeper than we know; it undergrounds all conscious experience. This is true of all being, not excepting perhaps the Divine. Certainly, no finite consciousness reaches to the root from which it sprang. Scarcely in God can consciousness be coeval and co-ordinate with life. Divine consciousness may know, but does it bear, its own root?[1] All conscious being springs from a root unknown. Of all life the origin is lost to itself in blank unconsciousness. We reach back with our recollection and find no beginning of existence. Who of us knows any thing except by

---

[1] Schelling, the most profound of the Transcendentalists, in whose writings Mr. Stirling, would he know the true "Secret of Hegel," should look for the root of his subject, says: "God himself, in order to *be*, requires a ground [of existence]; only, that this ground is not outside of him, but in him. He has in himself a *nature*, which, although belonging to him is yet distinct from him." (Schelling's Werke, Erste Abth, 7ter Bd. p. 375.) Did Schelling borrow from Jacob Boehme, whose "First Principle" is unintelligent, although the Father of Intelligence, not God but the Source of God?

report of the first two years of earthly life? Who remembers the time when he first said "I," or thought "I"? We began to exist for others before we began to exist for ourselves. Our experience is not co-extensive with our being, our memory does not comprehend it. We bear not the root, but the root us.

What is that root? We call it soul. *Our* soul, we call it: properly speaking it is not ours, but we are its. It is not a part of us, but we are a part of it. It is not one article in an inventory of articles which together make up our individuality, but the root of that individuality. It is larger than we are and older than we are, — that is, than our conscious self. The conscious self does not begin until some time after the birth of the individual. It is not aboriginal, but a product, — as it were, the blossoming of an individuality. We may suppose countless souls which never bear this product, which never blossom into self. And the soul which does so blossom exists before that blossom unfolds.

How long before, it is impossible to say; whether the birth, for example, of a human individual is the soul's beginning to be; whether a new soul is furnished to each new body, or the body given to a pre-existing soul. It is a question on which theology throws no light, and which psychology but faintly illustrates. But so far as that faint illustration reaches, it favors the supposition of pre-existence. That supposition seems best to match the supposed continued existence of the soul hereafter. Whatever had a beginning in time, it should seem, must end in time. The eternal destination which faith ascribes to the soul presupposes an eternal origin. On the other hand, if the pre-existence of the soul were assured it would carry the assurance of immortality.

An obvious objection, and one often urged against this hypothesis, is the absence of any recollection of a previous life. If the soul existed before its union with this present organization, why does it never recall any circumstance, scene, or experience of its former state? There have been those who professed to remember a past existence; but without regarding those pretended reminiscences, or regarding them only as illusions, I answer that the previous existence may not have been a conscious existence. In that case there would have been no recorded experience, and consequently nothing to recall. But suppose a conscious existence antecedent to the present, the soul could not preserve the record of a former organization. The new organization with its new entries must necessarily efface the record of the old. For memory depends on continuity of association. When the thread of that continuity is broken, the knowledge of the past is gone. If, in a state of unconsciousness, one were taken entirely out of his present surroundings; if, falling asleep in one set of circumstances, like Christopher Sly in the play, he were to wake in another, were to wake to entirely new conditions; especially, if during that sleep his body were to undergo a change, — he would lose on waking all knowledge of his former life for want of a connecting link between it and the new. And this, according to the supposition, is precisely what has happened to the soul at birth. The birth into the present was the death of the old, — "a sleep and a forgetting." The soul went to sleep in one body, it woke in a new. The sleep is a gulf of oblivion between the two.

And a happy thing, if the soul pre-existed, it is for us that we remember nothing of its former life. The memory of a past existence would be a drag on the present, engrossing our attention much to the prejudice of this life's interests and claims. The backward-looking soul would dwell in the past instead of the present, and miss the best uses of life.

But though on the supposition of a former existence the soul would not be likely to preserve the record of that existence, it would nevertheless retain the effect. It would not, on assuming its present conditions, be as though it had never before been. Its past experiences would essentially modify it; it would take a character from its former state. If a moral and intelligent being, it would bring into the world of its present destination certain tendencies and dispositions, the growth of a previous life. And thus the moral law and the moral nature of the soul would assert themselves with retributions transcending the limits of a single existence, and reaching on from life to life of the pilgrim soul.

It is commonly conceded that there are native differences of character in men, — different propensities, tempers, not wholly explained by difference of circumstance or education. They show themselves where circumstance and education have been the same; they seem to be innate. These are sometimes ascribed to organization. But organization is not final. That, again, requires to be explained. According to my thinking, it is the soul that makes organization, not organization the soul. The supposition of a previous existence would best explain these differences as something carried over from life to life, — the harvest of seed that was sown in other states, and whose fruit remains, although the sowing is remembered no more.

This was the theory of the most learned and acute of the Christian Fathers,[1] and, though never

[1] Origen.

adopted or sanctioned by the Church, has been occasionally revived in later time. Of all the theories respecting the origin of the soul it seems to me the most plausible, and therefore the one most likely to throw light on the question of a life to come. It is easy to speculate about the hereafter, but most of the speculations on this topic have no fixed data, no authorized assumption on which to rest. They lack the first and most essential condition of a rational theory of future life, — to wit, a distinct conception of the nature of the soul, what it is that survives the event of death, what it is of which we predicate immortality. This should be the starting point in all our reasonings in this direction. Painting an imaginary heaven is an innocent enough entertainment of the fancy, but, as to any corresponding reality or probability, it is worth just as much as any other day-dream or castle in the air. A pleasant picture, nothing more.

What is it that survives the decease of this mortal? It is that from which this mortal life sprang, — its root, the soul. We are apt to fancy that we bear the root, not the root us. What we call "I" is not the origin, but a product of the soul, — a phase or mode of its present life. The soul was prior to the conscious self; it is the root or seed from which the conscious self has grown.

The future life, like the present, must spring from that root; and in endeavoring to construct a theory of that life the rational method is to follow the analogy of this. According to that analogy, the future life, like the present, will begin with infancy. The soul will wake from the sleep of death an infant child. A period of infantile unconsciousness will precede the development of conscious life. Gradually the new-born self will unfold and find and fill its appointed sphere.

Opposed to this view is the current opinion which supposes that souls are translated at once by death from a state of earthly imperfection to that region of spiritual life which is commonly understood by the term "heaven." A preposterous idea of human destiny! The purgatory of the Church of Rome is a less irrational conception of the future of the soul. The purgatory of the Church of Rome, indefensible as it is in the gross material form in which it has been held in time past, respects at least the moral conditions which, in every state, must shape the life of rational souls. The fact is that in Protestant communions, since the passing away of the old beliefs, the sentiments rather than the understanding have had the fashioning of the popular theories of the life to come. Very sentimental those theories are, and very regardless of the facts and probabilities of human nature. The fundamental error which pervades them is the notion of a state of unchangeable felicity, into which the soul is supposed to enter with full consciousness immediately after the body's death. The very word "heaven," in this view, is misleading. I hold to the analogies of the present life. I hold to what we know, or may rationally surmise, of the nature of the soul. Above all, I hold to the moral conditions which must govern the future as they governed the past of moral natures. Whatever of moral growth has been attained will tell on the future consciousness; and whatever of moral evil has been contracted will also tell. If the soul in this mortal, by will and endeavor, has laid hold of the divine, that divine when new bodied will put forth new and finer growths, and glorify itself with achievements which here perhaps were meditated but could not be realized. And if, on the other hand, through weakness or blindness or adverse fate, that better life has not been attained, its germ is still there, ineradicably there, and may under new conditions be brought to bloom. So long as the soul is a conscious rational force in the universe of things, the possibility will remain to it of the heavenly life. Somewhere or other in the boundless all, at some point or other of endless time, the good the soul seeks it will surely find. So long as it faithfully strives, its growth is sure, and if ever it can cease to strive, if ever it can cease to see and seek the good, then, as a conscious thing, it will cease to be.

Of the "spiritual," disembodied state, which by some is supposed to succeed this present, I can form no conception. A new and bodily organism I hold to be an essential part of the soul's destination. Whether the soul in that new organization will retain the memories which belong to this, is a question I am well content to leave as I find it, involved in impenetrable night. I cannot feel it to be essential to the question of immortality. I cannot feel that the fact of identity is involved in that of memory, that the soul which does not identify its being with a foregone existence is no longer the same. The soul is the same; but what it produces, the conscious life that springs from that root, is not the same. The former life has left traces which remain, which essentially modify the soul. Those traces, those modifications, are important; but that the acts and experiences which have wrought them should be recalled, that the soul should be able to recount to itself the story of its past existences, appears to me a matter of little moment. If the health and growth of the moral nature require those memories, they will be vouchsafed; and that is all we can venture to prophesy about it.

Another question immediately connected with

the memory of a former existence is one which affection persistently asks of all the oracles, — whether dear friends who were parted by death shall meet again. To this the answer is still the same: if the soul's well-being requires it, Heaven will grant it. If when the soul wakes to new existence it shall find in itself distinct impressions of a previous life, and among those impressions the image of any dear friend who has gone before, and shall long to recover the object of that affection, to bind again what death had severed; and if the friend so sought shall also experience a like reminiscence and reciprocal longings, — then I can suppose that the two, thus mutually drawn, shall find one another and renew their bond. I can suppose that love stronger than death may revoke the separation of death, and give like to like. Souls that belong to each other by all their affinities and all their yearnings, one would say, must sooner or later unite. And yet it is equally supposable, and I confess in my view more likely, that the coming together of the two so inclined shall be without recognition of identity and without recollection of foregone union. Who knows if the love which in this world draws with mutual and irresistible attraction two kindred and predestined hearts, be not an unconscious renewal of an old pre-natal bond?

But these are matters we may trustingly leave — where indeed, whether trustingly or not, we must leave them — with the infinite Love which embraces all our loves, and the infinite Wisdom which comprehends all our needs; assured that the Father of the house whose mansions are many, and the Father of spirits whose goal is one, will find the right place and connections and nurture for every soul he has caused to be; that in the eternities the thing desired will arrive at last; that seeking and finding are divinely evened. Let us rest in the thought that life must be richer than all our experience, nay, than our fondest dream.

THE END.

www.ingramcontent.com/pod-product-compliance
Lightning Source LLC
LaVergne TN
LVHW090548110826
845146LV00001B/70